Augustan
Historical Writing

*Histories of England
in the English
Enlightenment*

Laird Okie

UNIVERSITY
PRESS OF
AMERICA

Lanham • New York • London

Copyright © 1991 by

University Press of America®, Inc.

4720 Boston Way
Lanham, Maryland 20706

3 Henrietta Street
London WC2E 8LU England

Library of Congress Cataloging-in-Publication Data

Okie, Laird, 1950-
Augustan historical writing : histories of England
in the English enlightenment / Laird Okie.
p.   cm.
Includes bibliographical references and index.
1. Great Britain—Historiography—History—18th century.
2. Historiography—England—History—18th century.
3. Enlightenment—England.   4. Classicism—England.
I. Title.
DA1.038   1991
941'.0072—dc20   90–48419 CIP

ISBN 0–8191–8050–5 (alk. paper)

We read history not only for the light it throws on the past but also for the light it throws on the world of the writer. We cannot fully understand an age unless we understand how that age regarded the past, for every age makes its own past.

Christopher Dawson,
Gibbon

TABLE of CONTENTS

Preface

This book examines a period of historical writing that scholars have largely neglected. Historians of eighteenth-century Britain have moved beyond Namierism to investigate political parties and ideologies, but no sustained effort has heretofore been made to chart the evolution of English historiography in the first half of the eighteenth century or to explore the manner in which historical writing was affected by politics and ideology. I argue that Augustan England witnessed a major transformation in historical writing from the traditional humanist chronicle of the Renaissance to an essentially modern style of historical narrative. To study the histories of the era, moreover, is to explore the historical dimension of Augustan political debate.

This is a revised version of my 1982 doctoral dissertation for the Department of History at the University of Kansas. I am indebted to Ambrose Saricks, Richard Sheridan, John Kenyon, and the late Edward Ruhe for reading and commenting upon my manuscript. I am particularly grateful to Henry Snyder, who, as dissertation director, stimulated my interest in the subject and offered valuable advice. I am most appreciative of the hospitality and counsel extended by Prof. Richard Simmons of Birmingham University during a year's residence in England. Finally, I would like to acknowledge the assistance of Heather Williams, Ed Baldridge, and Cathy Jarrett.

Spelling, capitalization and punctuation have been modernized in all quotations.

Introduction

i

Studies of British historiography read like a roll call of famous names. Clarendon, Burnet, Bolingbroke, Hume, Robertson, Gibbon - these are the well-known historians whose works were published in the eighteenth century. Scholars have not neglected them. Less famous but also familiar to students of the period was the French refugee Paul de Rapin-Thoyras, whose *History of England* was the most popular and influential general history to appear prior to Hume.

Apart from the monographs and articles that discuss these authors, scholars have addressed two historiographical developments in the early eighteenth century. One of these was the rich efflorescence in antiquarian scholarship during the post-Revolution period, revolving around the debate between Royalist and Whiggish historians over the "ancient constitution." Through critical, sophisticated research, a new school of Royalist-Tory legal historians undermined the traditional Whiggish belief that the people's liberties were enshrined in an "ancient" or "fundamental" constitution.[1] Scholars have also illuminated the "debate on the English past" conducted by party polemicists in various newspapers during the 1730s. The name of Lord Bolingbroke stands out among the obscure and anonymous essayists who used English history as a weapon in the political war of words.[2]

The tendency of scholars to focus on a few big names has produced an incomplete and somewhat distorted picture of eighteenth-century historiography. Recently there has been a welcome renewal of interest in David Hume's *History of England*. Scholars like Duncan Forbes and Victor Wexler have shown convincingly why the *History* can no longer be dismissed as a rather superficial Tory tract.[3] By concentrating so much on one celebrated author, however, they inevitably ignore Hume's eighteenth-century predecessors, or, at best, discuss them incidentally as precursors of Britain's philosophical historian. The Augustan historians are seen as industrious toilers in the mine of history, significant only insofar as they supplied the raw materials with which Hume fashioned his classic work. This consensus is not borne out by a close reading of early eighteenth-century historical writing. Hume wrote the most polished and

1

readable history, but the central lineaments of Enlightenment historiography had already been established.

This study addresses a neglected period of British historiography.[4] It looks beyond the famous names to examine those early-eighteenth-century scholars - once well known, now long forgotten - who helped shape modern British historical writing. Although many varieties of history were published over these years, histories of England were by far the most common. They included ecclesiastical histories, historical biographies, and studies of particular reigns or events. My discussion will concentrate primarily, though not exclusively, on the general histories of England, the best-known genre. Most of these books begin with Roman Britain but they simply reiterate the antiquarian accounts of Henry Spelman, Robert Brady, Edward Coke, and others. The central issues raised in the debate on the ancient constitution had already been worked out when these histories were written, and as the topic has already been thoroughly investigated, I shall make only peripheral references to the medieval narratives. Historians, in any case, devoted more space to Tudor-Stuart England. As will become apparent, historians generally viewed Henry VII's establishment of the Tudor dynasty as a pivotal event in the country's history, inaugurating a new epoch. The Reformation provoked much historical argument, but it was the seventeenth "century of revolution" that elicited the most discussion. The upheavals of the Stuart era engendered continuous historical debate in Hanoverian England, and the extensive discussion of the seventeenth century in this study reflects contemporary interest in the period.

This work also traces the myriad connections that existed between historical writing and party politics in the early eighteenth century. It examines how the changing political climate influenced historical writing and, at the same time, explores the historical dimension of the Augustan political debate, as revealed in the histories of England. Specifically, it testifies to the ascendancy of a Whiggish historical ideology and offers little support to those scholars - most notably J. C. D. Clark - who argue that Tory attitudes were dominant.[5]

The Augustan age coincided with the early Enlightenment, and Whiggism, insofar as it embraced secularism and rationalism, contributed to the growth of Enlightenment historical writing. The final objective of this monograph is to illuminate the historical dimension of the English

Enlightenment. Although the philosophes of the Enlightenment glorified England as the birthplace of Newtonian science and Lockean philosophy, historians have been reluctant to treat England as part of the Enlightenment. This is because most English intellectuals, unlike the French philosophes, were not anti-Christian, and because there was no ancien regime - no divine-right monarchy and inquisitorial church - to be assailed. Nevertheless, the very structure of English society and politics allowed room for Enlightenment values - personal freedom, religious tolerance, economic individualism - to find expression.[6] Historians now argue that rapid economic growth and social change made eighteenth-century England the first "consumer society."[7] Knowledge was popularized and more English people than ever before pursued material abundance, personal happiness, and "modernity." In the words of J. H. Plumb, "the ever expanding world of knowledge and of things led, or helped to lead, to the acceptance of modernity - of the replacement of the providence-dominated world of early and medieval Europe by the world of expanding knowledge and science, of discoverable nature and rational explanation."[8]

Recently, the early Enlightenment in England has come into clearer focus. Margaret Jacob has defined a "Newtonian Enlightenment," denoting more than simply Newtonian science: it meant a rationalistic Christianity in which the state and society were regulated by divine providence, and it championed reason, toleration, and the beneficent power of science.[9] Voltaire substituted a deistical god for Newton's Christian one, but otherwise Voltaire and most of the philosophes championed the ideals of the Newtonian Enlightenment. In Augustan England Newtonianism was disseminated in sermons and lectures by Whig ideologists like Samuel Clarke and William Whiston. Tory publicists assailed the Newtonians as godless libertines. Also opposed to this moderate, establishment Enlightenment was the radical Enlightenment, propagated by pantheistic republicans like John Toland and Anthony Collins. Jacob has unraveled an international network, centered primarily in the Hague and London, of anti-Newtonian freemasons and freethinkers, who circulated their ideas in clandestine journals and manuscripts.[10] The ideas of this radical fraternity indirectly molded the thought of Diderot and Holbach. Jacob's work highlights the fact that the English Enlightenment was diversified and politicized. Although none of the historians discussed below can be labeled as Newtonians or republicans, they do represent various ideological perspectives, from Jacobite Toryism on the right to liberal Whiggism on the left.

Historians have not hesitated to include England's neighbor to the north among the ranks of Enlightened states. Two exemplars of the "Scottish Enlightenment," David Hume and William Robertson, wrote celebrated histories. Hume's *History of England* and Robertson's *Emperor Charles V* share with Voltaire's *Siecle de Louis XIV* and Gibbon's *Decline and Fall of the Roman Empire* the distinguishing characteristics of Enlightenment historical writing. Whereas traditional Christian-humanist historiography chronicled the political and military exploits of great men, the philosophe-historians broadened the scope of historical inquiry to encompass social history (manners and customs), cultural history (art and literature), and economic history. Members of the Scottish Enlightenment - Lord Kames, John Millar, Adam Ferguson, Adam Smith - sketched distinct economic stages of history from primitive, pre-agricultural societies to contemporary, commercial civilization. The philosophes were not dispassionate scholars. They mocked the follies of past benighted epochs and celebrated the gradual rise of reason and learning from medieval barbarism and superstition. If they lacked the scholarly standards of modern historiography, they did, nevertheless, make an effort to treat documents critically and to generalize on the basis of historical evidence. Stylistically, the philosophes disparaged the plodding, voluminous annals of the past and strove to fashion readable, explanatory narratives.

But it was, above all else, the "secularization of historical cause" that defined Enlightenment historical writing.[11] The philosophes were not all deists but they all rejected divine action in history.[12] Traditional humanist history was written, in part, to illuminate the workings of divine providence. Enlightenment historians dismissed all invocations of the deity - all attempts to show the hand of God behind great events - as super-historical exercises in theology. Although an anti-clerical bias runs through the "new history," on balance the secularization of historical inquiry made for better history. "God's disappearance," writes Peter Gay, "left a vacuum that the secular intelligence was called upon to fill."[13] Rather than invoke providence to explain change, historians focused on the mundane realities - social, economic, political, cultural - of what actually happened. By disjoining history from theology they began to practice history as a social science.

The early eighteenth century witnessed the transition to Enlightenment history in England and thus marked a watershed in the evolution of

British historiography. Coincident with the shift toward a more modern style of historical writing was the rise of the general, narrative history as the standard form of historical exposition. A bibliographical scholar pointed this out more than a century and a half ago, characterizing the early 1700s as:[14]

> the period when the general histories were written in a methodical order - when the stream of events flowed on uninterruptedly; and when the reader might commence with the invasion of Julius Caesar, and conclude with the elevation of the House of Hanover. The previous histories contained detached memoirs or lives, or annals. They supplied materials for the picture, rather than exhibited the picture itself.

It was during the Augustan era that historical compilations and collections were gradually replaced by full narratives, composed by one author. Indeed, the many scholars who wrote about specific historical topics or events without framing their analysis in a narrative structure were regarded as antiquarians rather than historians.

Voltaire applauded David Hume for writing the first "judicial" English history, thus removing the stain of partisanship that had traditionally marred histories of England.[15] It was a common complaint in the late seventeenth-early eighteenth century that historical writing was trammeled by the rage of party. Many historians were party publicists who engaged in history as a glorified form of pamphleteering. Others were not propagandists as such but wrote histories that conformed to the political views of their patrons. Even in those cases when historians wrote independently without political backing - or wrote only for booksellers - they still displayed an unmistakably partisan slant.

The nature of Augustan historical writing cannot be fully comprehended without considering the political context in which it was produced. Between the Revolution of 1688 and the Hanoverian Succession, and especially during the reign of Queen Anne (1702-1714), British politics revolved around the conflict between Whigs and Tories. The Revolution of 1688 overturned the Tory doctrines of divine right kingship and hereditary succession. A minority of Tories became Jacobites, supporters of the exiled Stuart claimant, but even the loyal majority clung to the ideal of a patriarchal, divinely sanctioned monarchy. The Whigs, by contrast,

affirmed the right of resistance and stood for a limited monarchy balanced
among king, Lords, and commons.   Another issue of contention was
religion.   The Tories regarded the toleration of Protestant Dissent as a
threat to Church and state, while the Whigs viewed the Dissenters as
political allies.

There is considerable disagreement among historians about the shape
of politics after the Hanoverian Accession in 1714.   The case has recently
been made that the Tory party flourished in early Hanoverian England.[16]
Most historians, however, continue to believe - and it is the position taken
here - that the Tory party shrank drastically, and that the pervading
conflict between Whigs and Tories gave way to a less polarized dichotomy
between Court and Country within an overarching Whiggish consensus.[17]
The Country opposition, consisting of dissident Whigs and Tories,
employed an "old Whig vocabulary."[18]   Country spokesmen accused the
Court administrations of subverting the balanced constitution through
placemen in Parliament, standing armies, and financial machinations -
measures defended by the ministerial Whigs as necessary to protect liberty
and property.

Although the Tories continued to lament the Church's loss of power
and prestige, religious strife faded under the first two Georges.   Whig
ideology, as it evolved in the age of Walpole, was secular.   The Church
was regarded as a junior partner of the state.   Eighteenth-century
Whiggism contained a strong dose of anti-clericalism and some radical
Country Whigs were outspoken deists.[19]   Reason was favored over revelation, latitudinarianism over High Church intolerance.

Whiggism, insofar as it embraced secularism and rationalism,
contributed to the growth of Enlightenment historical writing.   Of course
Whig history per se was no less tendentious than Tory history.   Nevertheless, as party conflict gradually eased after 1715, historians made more of
an effort to write objectively, to point out and correct the partisan
excesses of their predecessors.

When one surveys the half century of historical writing from the
reign of Queen Anne to the 1750s, three phases are discernable,
corresponding to changes in the political climate.   Whig and Tory divided
the nation in Anne's reign, and the histories of the period mirror this
dichotomy.   The Tories, for example, published Clarendon's *History of the*

Rebellion as part of a propaganda offensive against the Whigs. Religion figured prominently in the political debate between 1702 and 1714 and religious themes echoed in the histories. Not only did churchmen take leading roles in the political and propaganda battles of the reign, but the best known historians were clerics. Moreover, historians in the first two decades of the eighteenth century - Whig and Tory - shared a conservative religiosity that identifies them as representatives of the late Renaissance humanist tradition.

The Whig rule of Robert Walpole (1721-1742) coincided, historiographically, with the ascendancy of Paul de Rapin-Thoyras, whose moderately Whiggish *History of England* (1726-31) was at once the most celebrated and most criticized history prior to Hume. Rapin's work exhibited a level of scholarship, a secular analysis, and a degree of objectivity that distinguished it from previous histories. Rapin set the standard for historical writing in the 1720s and '30s, but even in the inferior productions of his rivals we see a more secular and politically liberal approach to history than in the past. It will be argued that this reflected the increasingly liberal and secular intellectual currents of Hanoverian Whiggery.

The last phase of historical writing extends approximately from the fall of Walpole to the appearance of Hume's *History* (1754-62). While a major continuation of Rapin's *History* was produced at this time, three histories were undertaken, almost simultaneously, to refute Rapin. These works were sponsored, at least initially, by disparate political factions in the 1740s, while the Pelhams consolidated their hold on power. The two ablest historians of the 1740s, James Ralph and William Guthrie, learned their craft as essayists for Country Whig newspapers. The histories of Ralph and Guthrie, like that of David Hume, exemplify the Enlightenment style. They display a thoroughgoing secularism, an appreciation of social and economic change, a modicum of partisan polemics, a narrative fluency, and - in the cases of Ralph and Guthrie - a critical approach to their sources.

i i

In his *System of Universal History* (1714) the antiquarian scholar Thomas Hearne listed the benefits of reading history.[20] It encourages us to emulate past heroes, arouses affection for our ancestors and our country, offers diversion, instructs professional men, provides shining examples of virtuous conduct, and reveals how God manifests himself in the affairs of man.

Hearne's list indicates that Augustan ideas about history owed much to the Renaissance humanist tradition. History served as both a moral and a practical guide to live. In the private citizen and - more importantly - the public statesman, history should inculcate morality and virtue. A work of history should also function as a practical guide for statecraft. Francis Bacon, following Machiavelli, was among the first Englishmen to stress this utilitarian aspect. Politicians and gentlemen aspiring to enter politics stood to learn a great deal from the triumphs and blunders of past statesmen.

Belief in the moral purposes of history was not confined to churchmen, who naturally stressed the importance of Christian virtue. Like their philosophe counterparts on the continent, Hume and Gibbon affirmed the moral and didactic value of history. Since the instructive uses of history were considered to be of special value to statesmen - and simply because histories were read by the upper, traditionally literate classes - history in late Stuart-early Hanoverian England was the story of an elite. Court annals, trumpet and drum accounts of heroic battles, lengthy character portraits showing the virtues and vices of great men - these were the stock-in-trade of most historical literature. Except for freethinkers like Hume and Gibbon, virtue meant Christian virtue. Humanist historians in England embraced a theological conception of man and history. In particular, history was studied to disclose the workings of providence.

Because of history's lofty ethical and instructive purpose, it was a commonplace in Augustan England to praise it as the highest form of literature. Writers as diverse as John Locke and Thomas Hobbes, William Temple and the Earl of Chesterfield shared this view.[21] It is striking how many of the literary titans of the age dabbled in history, although their endeavors were frequently never completed or published. Daniel Defoe, Jonathan Swift, Henry Fielding, Samuel Johnson, Tobias Smollet, Oliver Goldsmith, and Edmund Burke all wrote on English history. Swift wrote abstracts for a general history of England.[22] Fielding, at one time a friend and colleague of the historian James Ralph, was an avid reader of English history and imbued his fiction with profound historical insight. Smollet and Goldsmith wrote popularizations of English history - enormously successful and remunerative ventures. In the early 1740s Samuel Johnson apparently wrote a substantial portion of a projected history of England, now lost. Despite his occasional witty sallies against historians, Johnson once drew up a list of books he would recommend, and one third of these were histories.[23]

Books of history were written by literati, clerics, antiquarians, journalists, and political propagandists, but rarely by full-time professional historians. History in the eighteenth century had not yet become a specialized academic discipline. Chairs of history had been established at Oxford and Cambridge, but the professors did little historical research and produced few works of history. Not until the mid-nineteenth century could historians benefit from university appointments and extensive opportunities for archival research, from the Public Record Office and state-sponsored publications of historical documents, or even from public libraries. England lagged behind the Continental states, especially France, in its support of historical scholarship. The British Museum was not opened until 1759 and there was no British equivalent to the Academie des Inscriptions, established by Louis XIV to promote historical study and to preserve historical remains. Neither did England possess the archival resources or clerical scholarship of the Catholic Church.[24]

Englishmen extolled history but lamented the paucity of good English histories. This complaint rose in part from literati who found the standard chronicles plodding and uninspired. Many histories were merely collections of documents, threaded together with a fragmentary commentary. Tobias Smollet was one who bemoaned the "dry, tedious, fatiguing collections of public acts and statutes" that passed for history rather than "a well connected detail of historical events."[25] Another genre consisted of chronologies or annals, almanac-like lists of facts that lacked even any connecting commentary. Narrative histories were largely compilations - scissors-and-paste conflations or paraphrasings drawn from other histories and printed documents, from newsletters, newspapers, and pamphlets.

Many of these works were massive, unwieldy folio volumes and did not sell well. Smaller, more readable books reached a wide audience. John Lockman's popular *New History of England by Question and Answer, Extracted from the most celebrated English historians* (1729) was designed "for the entertainment of our youth of both sexes" and for all adults unfamiliar with English history. The so-called historical and geographical grammars also sold well. The grammars contained a narrative of English history sandwiched between much geographical and miscellaneous information.[26]

Chronologies and compilations were typical of late Renaissance historiography in England and can be traced back to the medieval chronicle. Scholars often did not distinguish between the raw material of history - the primary sources and corpus of factual data - and the finished product. The Augustan preoccupation with appearing impartial played a role here: one way to look impartial was to infix polemical points within a mass of detail and extracts from documents.

The detailed narrative form of historical composition inhibited the development or elaboration of a distinct philosophy of history. Instead, it attached great weight to the chain of circumstances in history, to a view of history as an almost accidental series of events. Implicit in this conception was the notion that great events often followed from minor causes. Scholars have noted this theme in Clarendon's *History of the Rebellion*.[27]

Clarendon wrote within the traditional Christian humanist framework of history. Even the "philosophical" historians of the Enlightenment owed a considerable debt to the humanists, particularly to the historians of the Italian Renaissance. Francesco Guicciardini was sometimes cited as a model historian in the prefaces of early eighteenth-century English histories. In the works of Guicciardini and Leonardo Bruni we find many of the ingredients that went to make up Enlightenment historiography: an emphasis on the moral and instructive value of history, a critical, scholarly approach to the documents, a propensity for secular, naturalistic explanations of causation, and an appreciation of change in history.[28]

The differences between the two styles, however, are equally striking. They are a measure of the difference between the Renaissance and the Enlightenment. Guicciardini, the greatest of Renaissance historians, dwelled on secular causes, yet at the same time peppered his *History of Italy* with supernatural tales, omens, and portents. The Italian humanists did not write providential history but retained a secularized variant of providence in the form of "fortuna." When Guicciardini is at a loss to explain particular events - such as the Florentine defeat at Poggibonsi in 1479, Alviano's military losses, or the civil strife that erupted in Italy in 1517 - he resorts to such vagaries as the "malice of fortune" and the "unhappiness of fate."[29] The philosophe-historians of the Enlightenment, by contrast, provided strictly naturalistic, mundane explanations.

The most clear-cut difference between the humanist historians of the fifteenth and sixteenth centuries and the Enlightenment historians of the eighteenth, lay in the narrowly political orientation of the former. Guicciardini, Bruni, and Machiavelli evinced no appreciation of social and economic factors in history. They fixed their gaze on the actions of princes and generals. Individual great men were the agents of change.[30]

Finally, although the humanists were the first historians to employ textual criticism, they also imitated their classical forbears by fabricating orations and occasionally transcribing their sources verbatim without acknowledgment.[31] The philosophe-historians regarded any such stylistic liberties as unscholarly and unhistorical.

Notes

[1]See John G. A. Pocock, *The Ancient Constitution and the Feudal Law: A Study of English Historical Thought in the Seventeenth Century* (Cambridge, 1957); David C. Douglas, *English Scholars, 1660-1730*, 2nd ed. (London, 1951).

[2]See Isaac Kramnick, "Augustan Politics and English Historiography, The Debate on the English Past, 1730-35," *History and Theory*, (1967), 33-56; *Bolingbroke and His Circle: The Politics of Nostalgia in the Age of Walpole* (Cambridge, Mass., 1968), 124-136.

[3]See Duncan Forbes, *Hume's Philosophical Politics* (Cambridge, 1975); Victor Wexler, *David Hume and the History of England* (Philadelphia, 1979).

[4]Other periods of English history-writing, including the seventeenth and late eighteenth centuries, are not so neglected. F. Smith-Fussner, *The Historical Revolution: English Historical Writing and Thought, 1580-1640* (London, 1962); Joseph Levine, *Humanism and History: Origins of Modern*

English Historiography (Ithaca, 1987); Royce MacGillivray, *Restoration Historians and the English Civil War* (The Hague, 1974); Thomas P. Peardon, *The Transition in English Historical Writing, 1760-1830* (New York, 1933).

[5]See J. C. D. Clark, *English Society, 1688-1832* (Cambridge, 1985). Much has been written in recent years about the eighteenth-century political tradition of civic humanism. But this is not a central theme in Augustan historical writing and is only peripherally addressed in this study. On civic humanism see J. G. A. Pocock, *The Machiavellian Moment* (Princeton, 1975); *Virtue, Commerce, and Industry* (Cambridge, 1985).

[6]See Roy Porter and Mikulas Teich, eds., *The Enlightenment in National Context* (Cambridge, 1981), 1-18.

[7]See Neil McKendrick, John Brewer, J. H. Plumb, eds., *The Birth of a Consumer Society: The Commercialization of Eighteenth Century England* (Bloomington, 1982).

[8]J. H. Plumb, "The Acceptance of Modernity," in McKendrick, Brewer, and Plumb, 333.

[9]See Margaret Jacob, *The Newtonians and the English Revolution* (Ithaca, 1976).

[10]Jacob, *The Radical Enlightenment: Pantheists, Freemasons, and Republicans* (London, 1981).

[11]Peter Gay, *The Enlightenment: An Interpretation*, 2 vols. (New York, 1969), II, 391.

[12]Gay, II, 368-396.

[13]Gay, II, 390.

[14]T. F. Dibdin, *The Library Companion* (London, 1824), 212.

[15]Quoted in Ernest Campbell Mossner, *The Life of David Hume*, 2nd ed. (Oxford, 1980), 318.

[16]See Linda Colley, *In Defiance of Oligarchy* (Cambridge, 1982).

[17]The traditional view is set forth in John Cannon, ed., *The Whig Ascendancy: Colloquies on Hanoverian England* (London, 1981).

[18]John G. A. Pocock, "Radical Criticisms of the Whig Order in the Age between Revolutions" in Margaret Jacob and James Jacob, eds., *The Origins of Anglo-American Radicalism* (London, 1984), 41.

[19]H. T. Dickinson, "Whiggism in the Eighteenth Century," in Cannon, 41.

[20]See James William Johnson, *The Formation of English Neo-Classical Thought* (Princeton, 1967), 35.

[21]Johnson, 33.

[22]John Nichols, *Literary Anecdotes of the Eighteenth Century*, 9 vols. (London, 1812), II, 578-579.

[23]Godfrey Davies, "Doctor Johnson on History," *Huntington Library Quarterly*, XII (1948-49), 13.

[24]The deficiencies in professional support for historical scholarship are succinctly described in Roy Porter, *Gibbon* (New York, 1988), 33-37.

[25]*Critical Review*, II, May 1757, 449-458.

[26][John Lockman], *A New History of England by Question and Answer, extracted from the most celebrated English Historians, particularly Rapin de Thoyras, for the Entertainment of our Youth of both Sexes* (London, 1725); William Guthrie's *New Geographical, Historical, and Commercial Grammar* (1770) went through at least thirty editions and revisions; Thomas Salmon's *New Geographical and Historical Grammar* (1749) went through its thirteenth edition in 1785.

[27]See H. R. Trevor-Roper, "Clarendon and the Great Rebellion," in *Men and Events* (New York, 1976), 244-249.

[28]See Erich Cochrane, *Historians and Historiography in the Italian Renaissance* (Chicago, 1981), 3-6, 15, 303, 493; John R. Hale,

"Introduction," in Francesco Guicciardini, *History of Italy and History of Florence*, ed. John R. Hale (New York, 1965).

[29]Hale, xxxii-xxxv; Mark Phillips, *Francesco Guiciardini: The Historians Craft* (Toronto, 1977), 136.

[30]Cochrane, 299-300.

[31]Cochrane, 4, 304.

Part One

Tory and Whig History in the Age of Anne

Chapter I

Tory and Whig, Clarendon and Burnet

Queen Anne's reign witnessed the publication of Clarendon's *History of the Rebellion* (1702-04) and the composition of Gilbert Burnet's *History of His Own Time* (1724-34), the two most famous histories prior to Hume. If they seem more like memoirs today, Burnet's contemporaries made no neat distinction between historical memoirs and history proper. Clarendon and Burnet have not been neglected by scholars, and they will not be discussed in depth here, beyond considering their place in the development of early eighteenth-century historiography. The appearance of Clarendon's *History* in 1702-04 was particularly significant because it stimulated historiographical debate, as writers took up their pens to denounce or defend "the noble historian."

Among these post-Revolution histories, a new genre was beginning to emerge - the narrative, general history of England. Instead of simply collating documents, listing facts chronologically, or specializing in a specific event or reign, historical writers began synthesizing the printed historical documents and tracts into an extended narrative form. In the broad context of literary history, both the historical narrative and the novel evolved from the epic during the Augustan period.[1]

Nevertheless, history in late Stuart England stood firmly within the Christian humanist tradition. Historians piled fact on fact and stuck to political, moral, and religious themes. Although historians brought up secular "second causes" of events, worldly explanations were regarded as poor substitutes for the unfathomable workings of providence.

As has been noted, it was conventional in the late seventeenth-early eighteenth century to lament the absence of a good general history of England. Certainly by the opening of the new century a wealth of printed source materials existed, ready to be tapped by an aspirant for the palm of English historiographer. The late seventeenth century had seen a profusion of documentary collections, annals, lives, and memoirs. These included John Rushworth's eight folio volumes of *Historical Collections* (1659-1701) and the collections of John Nalson, printed in the 1680s. Several anonymous collections of state tracts and statutes were printed, in addition to the various memoirs and memorials of Bulstrode Whitelock, Philip Warwick, William Temple, James Welwood, Denzil Holles, and Stephen Fox. Commentaries and collections pertaining to the history of Parliament by William Hughes, John Selden, William Petyt, and Robert Atkyns were published in the late seventeenth century. Moreover, the lapsing of the Licensing Act in 1695 and the Revolution Settlement facilitated the publication of newspapers and newsletters, the prototypes of which had existed, tenuously, through most of the seventeenth century. To this list should be added the *Annals* of John Strype and the massive *Foedera* of Thomas Rymer, a collection of treaties and diplomatic conventions. Both these works began appearing in Anne's reign. Finally, mention should be made of the growing interest in works of contemporary history during this period. The annals of Abel Boyer and David Jones - compiled as *The History of the Reign of Queen Anne Digested into Annals* and *The Complete History of Europe*, respectively - recorded parliamentary debates and affairs of state in great detail. They proved to be valuable sources for generations of historians.

There was no public access to manuscript collections in the early eighteenth century, although scholars occasionally gained access to the private Cotton Library, the State Paper Office, and the Tower of London archives - the latter two being the only official repositories of government documents. And it was during the reign of Queen Anne that Robert Harley began amassing his huge library, richly endowed with printed books and manuscripts.

In no period of British history was literature more closely connected with politicians and the "rage of party" than in the age of Anne. The nature of historical writing in the first two decades of the eighteenth century cannot be understood without appreciating the charged political climate in which they were written. Staunch defenders of Anglican primacy, the Tories rejected Whiggish latitudinarianism and toleration of Protestant Dissent. Less interventionist than the Whigs, they opposed protracted land campaigns in the War of the Spanish Succession (1701-1714). The Whigs, by contrast, consistently supported continental engage- ments against France. Although the Tories had helped topple James II, thereby traducing their own doctrines of divine right kingship and passive obedience, they did not completely abandon their pre-Revolutionary prin- ciples. A section of the Tories were Jacobites, but even the non-Jacobite majority continued to hold a deep-seated reverence for what they saw as a divinely ordained Church and throne. They were more inclined than the Whigs to defend the powers and privileges of the crown.

A clash of economic interests also divided Whig from Tory. The Tory gentry, middling and lesser squires, resented the high land tax levied to meet war costs. Much of this revenue went to pay interest on the mushrooming national debt. The Tory party denounced government creditors as mercenary financiers, self-seeking nouveaux riche Whigs who threatened the landed order and the state over which it presided. J. R. Jones identifies the Tory mentality in Anne's reign: "The Tories saw themselves as the sole authentic representatives of the landowning classes, free-holders as well as gentry, and as upholders of national and social unity and harmony."[2] From the Whig perspective, the typical Tory was an ignorant and indolent backwoodsman, ill prepared to deal with the great affairs of state.

Although the Whigs maintained the right of resistance and pointed to arbitrary power in the form of popery as the greatest danger to Church and state, the Whig party in late Stuart England was neither radical nor liberal.[3] The Revolution of 1688 and the expiration of the Licensing Act (1695) cleared the decks for all manner of political theorizing. A group of "Old Whigs," John Locke among them, celebrated the people's natural rights, including the right to overthrow tyrannical governments. Whig radicals wanted the Revolution to inaugurate an age of reform in which the constitution would be made more representative and libertarian. Many of the radicals, moreover, were religious freethinkers or outright deists. Locke's heterodox *Reasonableness of Christianity* (1695) was quickly followed up by John Toland's deistical *Christianity Not Mysterious* (1696).

The establishment Whigs had little in common with their Old Whig cousins. While the radicals invoked ahistorical and abstract natural rights doctrine, the mainstream Whigs grounded their defense of liberty and property in historical appeals to the ancient constitution. They justified the Revolution of 1688 as an act of divine providence. This theory was especially favored by the clergy of both parties. Margaret Jacob has addressed the critical role of providence in the theology of the Church:[4]

> On the existence of a divine plan in history rested the entire fabric of latitudinarian natural religion . . . . Just as the providence of God had played a crucial role in latitudinarian thinking during the

Restoration, the same providence provided a necessary and suitable explanation for the Revolution. Churchmen avoided any justification of the Revolution that rested on contract theory. To their minds the theories of Locke and other contractualists disregarded the necessity of God's active participation in the affairs of man.

During the reign of Anne, churchmen - especially bishops - were leading propagandists for both the Whig and Tory parties. The Whig clergy were as vehement as the Tories in branding the radicals as revolutionaries and atheists, a threat to the divinely sanctioned social order. The essential conservatism of mainstream Whiggery and Toryism, and of their clerical exponents, is reflected in the historical writing of the period.

Conflicting views over the relationship between Church and state served to stimulate historical writing. During the Convocation Controversy (1697-1717) High Church Tories argued with Whig latitudinarians over whether convocation was, historically, independent of Parliament. Learned treatises poured from the presses as divines burrowed through documents to find precedents for their respective positions.

The Convocation debate revolved around medieval precedents, but the "ancient constitution" dispute was by no means the only source of historical argument. As Pat Rogers points out, "four great events had impinged deeply on the national consciousness" at the start of the eighteenth century: the Civil War, the Great Plague, the Fire of London, and the Glorious Revolution.[5] Political controversy swirled around each of these episodes. The reaction to the last event has already been mentioned. Even the plague and the fire were not immune from political interpretation. It was commonplace to explain these disasters as either God's punishment for bad policies by the government or, in the case of the fire, to accuse the ancestors of one's political opponents of starting it.

As for the Great Rebellion, to the Tories it was the great calamity of modern history, portending what could happen to Church and throne if religious dissidents were tolerated, if Parliament became too obstreperous, and if popular tumults were not promptly suppressed; Whigs and Dissenters were secret revolutionaries and regicides, carrying on the subversive tradition of their Puritan-Parliamentarian forbears. While the Whigs did not endorse the Great Rebellion, they laid most of the blame on the Stuart regime. As they saw it, the Tories and High Church party bore the legacy of Stuart tyranny and popery.

The political and ideological divisions we have been considering found expression in Clarendon's *History* and in other histories dating from this period. Although written decades earlier, *The History of the Rebellion* was published as a propaganda broadside against the Whigs during the Tory reaction of Anne's reign. Toryism had its philosophical roots in the Royalist political ideas enunciated in Clarendon's work.

Clarendon's *History* appeared soon after his granddaughter, a woman of Tory sympathies, assumed the throne. Published in the Tory stronghold of Oxford, its preface by the Earl of Rochester - Clarendon's son - was actually a bombastic Tory manifesto. Coupled with the revival of the cult of the "Royal Martyr" after 1702, the release of Clarendon's *History* was designed to lend historical and ideological credibility to the Tory-High Church offensive.[6] Without doubt, *The History of the Rebellion* set forth the essentials of the Royalist-Tory creed in magisterial fashion. It extolled the sacred character of Church and king; it depicted Puritans and other religious dissidents as regicides and revolutionaries; insofar as he spoke in terms of class Clarendon favored the landed men - the aristocracy and gentry; finally, the *History* constituted the definitive apologia for what Rochester called the "old royalist party," synonymous, according to Rochester, with the Tory-High Church Party.

The History of the Rebellion met with great success. Revenues from its sales were large enough for the book's publishers to build the Clarendon Building at Oxford. One reason the Tories could take great satisfaction in this successful vindication of their principles was that Clarendon's lofty reputation as a statesman was not confined to the Tories. He was generally respected by the political establishment as a voice of pious and sober moderation in the counsels of both Charles I and Charles II. Hence, Clarendon - the man and historian - received qualified praise from those staunch but conservative Whig pamphleteers and historians, Bishops Gilbert Burnet and White Kennett. As late as the historiographical debate in the press during the 1720s and '30s, the "noble historian" was cited frequently and favorably by both Walpole's essayists and opposition writers. Clarendon's essential moderation manifested itself in his strictures against Charles I's bad policies and counselors, in his respect for the caliber of his Parliamentarian opponents, particularly

Cromwell, and in his affirmation of the balanced constitution and rights of Parliament.

C. H. Firth pointed out seventy years ago that Clarendon wrote the history of a religious revolution with the religious conflict left out.[7] Like most seventeenth-century chronicles of the Civil War, there is no analysis of Puritanism and very little discussion of the divisions over Church practice and doctrine. But also like most contemporary accounts, religion is discussed in terms of divine providence. Clarendon was meditating on the workings of providence in history. He considered the Civil War to be divine punishment for the sins of the nation: for excess, luxury, factiousness. When detailing the particular circumstances and pattern of events that resulted in civil war, Clarendon was merely paying heed to those "second causes" through which providence acted. The hand of God is especially evident in Clarendon's account of the Restoration. Quite suddenly, miraculously, God intervened through his agent General Monck to bring back Charles II. As the leading authority on Clarendon's thought observes, for Clarendon, "meaning could be attached to the movement of events if it was studied in a profoundly religious spirit" which could "trace therein the action of providence."[8]

Clarendon's providential conception of history identifies him as a representative of the late Renaissance, pre-Enlightenment tradition of historiography. For all the *History*'s breadth and detail, memorable characters, and shrewd off-hand observations, the historical methodology deployed was not significantly different from that of many other seventeenth-century memoirs and histories. Clarendon relied more on experience and memory than on documents. He offered occasional perceptions about class alignments during the Civil War, but the *History* contains no substantial discussion of socioeconomic or cultural developments. The chain of political circumstances is minutely detailed, expressed in lofty, oratorical prose. The Royalist case as related by Clarendon differs little in substance from other such accounts such as Philip Warwick's *Memoirs* published only a few years previously.[9]

If *The History of the Rebellion* set forth the moderate, Royalist/Tory version of the mid-century revolution, Gilbert Burnet's *History of His Own Time* expressed its Whig counterpart for the Revolution of 1688. In exile under James II, Burnet returned with William III and was later rewarded the wealthy bishopric of Salisbury. His *History of the Reformation in*

England, written before the Revolution, was the first historical narrative to be published in England based on extensive documentation.[10] Burnet's main concern in this ecclesiastical history was not to unravel the mundane realities of politics and power in the Reformation. Rather, it was to celebrate the providential triumph of reformed Christianity. In his account of the Reformation, Burnet repeatedly explains how the "secret direction of an overruling providence" miraculously extirpated popery and ushered in the right and true Church of England.[11]

Burnet began writing *History of His Own Time* in 1683. Inspired by Clarendon's example, he continued writing and rewriting it until 1711. Burnet, like Clarendon, designed his history not for the current political war of words, but to vindicate himself and his ideals to posterity. When he finished the *History,* four years before his death in 1715, he bequeathed the manuscript to his son for posthumous publication. When Burnet's work finally reached the press in 1724 it met with considerable success. Twelve hundred ninety-five people subscribed to it, way above the mean for subscription books of around 250-500.[12] Volume II eventually appeared in 1734 and did even better, eliciting no less than 2,049 names. The prestige accorded Burnet's *History* is suggested by the number of peers who subscribed - 140 for volume II. The king and queen and other members of the royal family also subscribed.

History of His Own Time was widely read and talked about. The arch-Tory Thomas Hearne bemoaned the fact that "nothing is now hardly read but Burnet's romance or libel . . . . Tis read by men, women, and children. Indeed, it is the common table book for ladies as well as gentlemen, especially such as our friends to the Revolution scheme."[13] Nearly all the Augustan literary lights commented upon it, including Swift, Defoe, and Pope. Despite the popularity of Burnet's *History* - or perhaps because of it - several book-length rejoinders quickly appeared, bitter polemics that testify to the vitality of Tory ideologues a decade after the Hanoverian accession.[14]

Burnet avowed that his *History* was meant primarily to teach those precepts that would best serve England's governors, not to entertain readers with a lively pageant of events.[15] Clearly, latitudinarian Protestantism and moderate Whiggery were the ideals that Burnet held dear. The book's theme was to show how these ideals triumphed through God's beneficence in the Revolution but had to be continuously defended during the reigns of William and Anne against the onslaughts of papists, Tories, and "atheists." In good Whig fashion, Burnet upheld the right of resistance, parliamentary monarchy, and, above all, religious freedom - except for fringe freethinking groups like the Unitarians. He rejected elective monarchy, Lockean contract theory, electoral reform, and other rallying cries of radical Whiggery.

For all his glowing tributes to the wondrous, providential nature of the Revolution, an oddly somber strain can be discerned when Burnet discusses William's reign. Burnet shared the conservative Whig - and Tory - concern about the rise of vice, irreligion, and popular discontents after the Revolution. The nation teetered on the edge of "democracy"; luxury and vanity prevailed over virtue, the private interest over the public good.[16]

We see in Burnet the conservatism of establishment Whiggery. Burnet's Whig credentials, however, were impeccable and the *History* is a Whig tract. Burnet backs the Whig ministers under William and Anne and censures the Tories. The highlight of the book is Burnet's distinguished conclusion, in which he reformulates his chief concerns and purposes. A kind of instructor's manual for future kings, Burnet moralizes about the nature of government with special emphasis on the interaction of Church and state. While pronouncing divine right kingship dead, Burnet upholds the efficacy of God-like dignity and splendor. Princes should be "exalted for the good of their fellow creatures, in order to raise them to the truest sublimity, to become as like divinity as a mortal creature is capable of being."[17] Burnet's concept of kingship differed sharply from the secularized constructs of radical Whigs like Locke or Algernon Sydney. As Lawrence Stone has observed, "a modified version of divine right continued to rival Lockean Whiggery at least until 1702."[18] In his providential conception of William's kingship and in his spiritualized image of the crown, Burnet exemplifies the conservative establishment, religious vein of Whiggery.

Burnet, like Clarendon, says little about social and economic developments. He depicts the "rabble" as irredeemably brutish and volatile. True to his Whig colors, he portrays the gentry as ignorant, idle, and tyrannical. But "as for the men of business, they are, generally speaking, the best body in the nation, generous, sober, and charitable."[19]

Although Burnet examined at least some histories and collections, including Rushworth, Whitlocke, and Clarendon, oral testimony and his own direct experience played a far greater role in shaping his narrative than did documentary evidence. The *History* is famous for its anecdotal, even gossipy style. Reliance upon firsthand knowledge was one of several approaches to history methods that Burnet and Clarendon had in common. *The History of the Rebellion* and the *History of His Own Time* stand in the traditional, pre-Enlightenment style of historiography. Both works share a theocentric, providential view of history. Writing in large part to vindicate a particular political and religious cause, the authors pay scant attention to social, economic, or cultural history. Despite their obvious political differences, Clarendon and Burnet adhered to the same moderate Anglicanism. They represented the tradition of Hooker and the Cambridge Platonists, linking the destiny of England with the fortunes of the English Church.

Notes

[1]Leo Braudy, *Narrative Form in History and Fiction* (Princeton, 1970).

[2]J. R. Jones, *Country and Court: England, 1658-1715* (Cambridge, Mass., 1978), 321.

[3]See H. T. Dickinson, *Liberty and Property: Political Ideology in Eighteenth Century Britain* (New York, 1977), 57-91; J. P. Kenyon, *Revolution Principles* (Cambridge, 1977); Margaret Jacob, *The Newtonians and the English Revolution* (Ithaca, 1976).

[4]Jacob, 94.

[5]Pat Rogers, *Grub Street: Studies in a Subculture* (London, 1972), 94.

[6]G. V. Bennett, *White Kennett, Bishop of Peterborough*, 1660-1728 (London, 1957), 86-88.

[7]C. H. Firth, *Essays Historical and Literary* (Oxford, 1938), 119.

[8]B. H. G. Wormald, *Clarendon: Politics, History, and Religion* (Cambridge, 1951), 324.

[9]Royce Macgillivray's conclusion seems apposite. Clarendon was "a conventional and even platitudinous thinker" who, for all his erudition and insight, "had not much more originality than we normally expect or find in a retired statesman who writes his memoirs in his new found leisure." See Royce Macgillivray, *Restoration Historians and the English Civil War* (The Hague, 1974), 224.

[10]T. E. S. Clarke and H. C. Foxcroft, *A Life of Gilbert Burnet* (Cambridge, 1907), xx.

[11]Gilbert Burnet, *The History of the Reformation of the Church of England*, 7 vols. (Oxford, 1829) new edition, I, 70-71.

[12]The subscriptions are discussed in Pat Rogers, *The Eighteenth Century* (London, 1978), 48-51.

[13]Quoted in Macgillivray, 193.

[14]At least eight ripostes to Burnet were published. The best known are John Cockburn, *A Specimen of some free and Impartial Remarks on Public Affairs and Particular Persons, occasioned by Dr. Burnet's History of his Own Times* (London, 1724); Bevil Higgons, *Historical and Critical Remarks on Bishop Burnet's History of his own Time* (London, 1725); Thomas Salmon, *An Impartial Examination of Bishop Burnet's History of His Own Time* (London, 1724).

[15]Gilbert Burnet, *History of His Own Time* (London, 1857) new edition, 904.

[16]See especially *ibid.*, 669.

[17]*Ibid.*, 921.

[18]Lawrence Stone, "The Results of the English Revolutions," in *Three British Revolutions: 1641, 1688, 1776*, ed. J. G. A. Pocock (Princeton, 1980), 69.

[19]Burnet, *History of His Own Time*, 911-917.

Chapter II

White Kennett and Laurence Echard

i

One of Bishop Burnet's clients and colleagues within the Church was White Kennett, author of *A Complete History of England*, vol. III (1706). Burnet and Kennett were two of the most effective clerical publicists for Whig politicians and policies in the reign of Anne. Burnet admired and patronized Kennett, appointing him as prebend in the cathedral city of Salisbury.[1] When Kennett was working on *A Complete History*, Burnet gave him access to the manuscript of his as yet unpublished *History of His Own Time* from which Kennett borrowed.[2]

Kennett marshalled his pen to combat the High Church Tory onslaught in Anne's reign. His biographer has described Kennett's outlook at this time:[3]

> The High Church revival of Queen Anne's reign seemed to him to savour much more of seventeenth century political theory than of the reformed religion of the Established Church, and he was extremely apprehensive of the fact that the logic of high-flying divine right doctrine pointed to the Roman Catholic Stuarts rather than to Anne or the Lutheran House of Hanover.

Kennett, who eventually was nominated Bishop of Peterborough in 1718, first made a name for himself during the Convocation controversy by defending the Whiggish Upper House against the High Church-Tory revolt spearheaded by Francis Atterbury. Two of Kennett's ecclesiastical histories, the *Ecclesiastical Synods* and *Occasional Letter*, both from 1701, were direct products of the debate between Whig and Tory divines over the constitutional relationship between Convocation, Commons, and king.

Even before the Convocation crisis, Kennett had already made a significant contribution to medieval scholarship. In the decade after the Revolution, he was a member of that Royalist-Tory school of antiquarian scholars, led by Robert Brady and located at Oxford University, that was systematically exploding Whig myths about the "ancient constitution."

27

Although Kennett gradually moved to the political "left" in response to the High Church resurgence and Jacobite threat, he maintained a scholarly but distinctly Tory view of the origins of Parliament and impact of the Norman Conquest.

To simply catalogue *A Complete History* as an extended piece of propaganda detracts from Kennett's scholarly achievement. Nevertheless, it constituted an historical counterblast to the Tory offensive, of which Rochester was the political head and Atterbury the clerical. Rochester claimed, when publishing Clarendon's *History*, that it supported the cult of the royal martyr. On January 31, 1704, shortly after the Tories had published *The History of the Rebellion* and on the fast day designated for mourning the martyrdom of Charles I, Kennett attacked the Royalist-Tory version of the English Civil War in his sermon, *An Enquiry into the Causes of the English Civil War*, which was quickly recast in pamphlet form. Kennett blamed the Stuart's French alliance and toleration of popery for producing the conflict.

A Complete History of England elaborated upon Kennett's sermon. It was written, partly, to refute the Tory version of the English Revolution and Restoration. More precisely, it was meant to give a new rendering of Clarendon's *History*, drawing attention to those points that supported Kennett's conservative Whiggery and demonstrating that the "noble historian" could not be appropriated by any one party. Kennett wrote the third volume of a three-volume history, the first two volumes consisting of old chronicles. The idea of forming a continuous history of England by collating past histories into a single work had been floated originally by William Temple in 1695. *A Complete History* was the eventual result. Kennett, who contracted with booksellers in 1701, was to receive 150 pounds and cover the reigns of Charles I through James II. To forestall partisan attacks, Kennett's volumes were published anonymously.

A Complete History was among the most ambitious and expensive publishing ventures up to that time, a fact testifying to the popularity, or at least the prestige, attached to histories of England.[4] Thirteen booksellers joined together to bring it out. Proposals listing the publishers were sent throughout the provinces so that booksellers would drum up subscriptions from their customers. Seven hundred twenty-five people subscribed to receive the history, even though it was not issued serially in numbers. It went through four reprints and a new edition in 1719.

Kennett wrote what G. V. Bennett calls a "tirade against 'popery' and its inevitable result, 'arbitrary power'."[5] Even more than Burnet, Kennett centered his discussion on the mortal battle between Catholicism and Protestantism, darkness and light. He followed Clarendon very closely down to the Restoration, quoting from him extensively and making virtually no direct criticisms. *A Complete History*'s explanation of the Civil War differs from Clarendon in emphasizing Stuart laxity toward Catholics and Catholic powers, due mainly to the nefarious influence of Henrietta Maria. Kennett is marginally more critical than was Clarendon of Charles I's misgovernment during the eleven years of personal rule.[6]

Kennett liked to employ religious terminology. In Charles I's reign, for example, the supporters of forced loans were papists while, he writes, the opponents were stigmatized as Puritans.[7] However, although Kennett dwells on the popish threat to Church and state, it is the political implications of popery, not doctrinal or ecclesiastical concerns, that worry him. "The doctrinal controversy would have created no great difference," he writes about the Laudian Church, "if there had not been a political division in it."[8] Popery, signifying arbitrary government and French slavery, tainted the Caroline court and administration.

The opposition to Charles I consisted of upright defenders of liberty and property along with self-seeking opportunists.[9] Kennett blames both crown and Parliament for the slide into revolution and civil war. His description of Cromwell and the Interregnum echoes Clarendon. Ruthless and hypocritical, Cromwell nonetheless displayed skilled statesmanship, particularly in the field of foreign policy.[10]

Only with the Restoration does Kennett assume a consistently Whiggish tone. He presents Charles II as a crypto-papist and dupe of Louis XIV who wasted his revenues on court extravagance and high living.[11] Kennett endorses the Exclusion Bill and accepts the Popish Plot as authentic - positions to which no Tory would subscribe. James II strove to make "the Churchmen sacrifice their Dissenting brethren, and so to unite and advance the cause of popery."[12] All those loyal to the Church banded together to resist the popish threat. The Revolution was based not on "Revolution principles" but on "Church of England principles."[13] Hence, Kennett implicitly separates himself from the ·more secular views of Whig politicians like John Somers and the Earl of Sunderland to whom Revolution principles were an article of faith.

Kennett gives an adoring portrait of William III.[14]   He waxes enthusiastic about the Whig financial institutions - the Bank, the New East India Company - but warns against unscrupulous stock jobbers. Kennett, like Burnet, deplored the plague of immorality, corruption, and freethinking that seemed to break out after the Revolution. He was one of those Low Church publicists whose fear of popery was matched by fear of radicalism and vice.[15] Consequently, he actively supported the Society for the Propagation of Christian Knowledge and the Society for the Reformation of Manners.

Kennett placed less emphasis on the workings of providence than did either Clarendon or Burnet, but he shared their providential conception of history.[16]   It was divine providence that dissuaded Cromwell from crowning himself king; providence that restored Charles II in a Protestant kingdom; providence that James II's daughters grew up as Protestants and that James II and his son forfeited their hopes of retaining the throne by steadfastly proclaiming their allegiance to Catholicism; providence that the Huguenots were well treated after they emigrated to England; and it was the "breathings of providence" that sailed William III's invading force to a safe landfall in Devonshire.

In *A Complete History* Kennett elucidates a religious, conservative Whig view of English history. A staunch churchman, he saw popery as the gravest threat to England. He perceived the hand of God shaping the course of events and had little to say about social and economic developments. Kennett's themes were embedded in copious documentation. His history consists largely of state documents and extensive extracts - memoirs, histories, collections, newspapers, newsletters, trials - threaded together with Kennett's matter-of-fact narrative. The scholarly value of the work lies in the wealth of documentation and the relative impartiality of Kennett's narrative interpolations.

The Tories had no doubt about Kennett's political motives. The Jacobite historian Thomas Hearne branded it "full of Whiggism, trifling, Grub-Street matter and base reflections."[17] By far the most substantial critique came from Roger North, whose *Examen* was published posthumously in 1740 but was probably written circa 1709-14. Over 700 folio pages in length, *The Examen: or an Enquiry into the Credit and Veracity of a pretended Complete History* focused exclusively on the reign of Charles II and was intended to rescue the king from Kennett's slanderous attacks. North (1653-1734) was a king's counsel and attorney general under Charles. A lifelong Tory, North refused to take the oaths to William and Mary and resigned from his successful law practice. In 1690 he bought an estate near Norwich and lived the rest of his life in rural seclusion, turning out books on all manner of subjects, most notably biography and autobiography.[18]

Although *The Examen* was one of North's works that appeared after his death, the tone and substance suggest that it was, at least originally, intended as a timely refutation of Kennett, not simply as a record for posterity. North dedicated *The Examen* to Thomas Hanmer, the Tory leader in the House of Commons during Anne's reign, from whom he presumably received a financial reward. North proclaimed that his objective was to repudiate Kennett's error-ridden history and, as one who lived through the period, to set down what really took place, free of partiality.[19] In reality, *The Examen* exemplifies North's extreme High Toryism. Just as Kennett directed his broadsides against the Catholics, so North waged war against Dissenters and Low Churchmen. For North - a believer in divine right kingship and passive obedience - all Low Churchmen were Dissenters, all Dissenters were revolutionaries, and all revolutionaries were regicides.

North's hero was Charles II, his villain the Earl of Shaftesbury. Shaftesbury and his Country Party colleagues conspired to topple the government by inciting "mob" violence.[20] Throughout his narrative North is haunted by the spectre of popular tumults, particularly in the City. Although he professes his belief in mixed monarchy, North submits that if he had to choose between an "absolute potentate" and the "perpetual fear" of popular government, in which "all power is from the people," he would have no difficulty plumping for the former.[21] True to his anti-Lockean outlook, North held a low opinion of human nature: people "are more touched by fear than all other passions or affections, being inclined to argue evil rather than good . . . ."[22] Religion is the great antidote to popular passions, "given to men to supply the defects of their capacity of judging, . . . for it makes the poor and simple happier in observances of duty, than politicians are with all their craft."[23] And true to his Tory affiliation, North makes the point repeatedly that "manufacturers, traders and the rabble" supported the Whigs while their betters, the gentry, backed the King.[24]

North, correctly identifying Kennett as a historical apologist for the Whigs, produced an impassioned, massive, and well-written rebuttal. Paradoxically, however, North and Kennett shared many of the same conservative, authoritarian premises about English history and politics. Neither accepted Lockean-liberal principles. Both believed deeply in a divinely constituted social and political order in which the Church functioned as a guardian of the state against "the common people" and radical politico-religious ideas.

It is not surprising that Kennett, with his religious and conservative outlook, admired Clarendon and wrote a Whiggish elaboration upon *The History of the Rebellion*: Kennett belonged to the same Christian humanist tradition. A compilation of documents and commentary, *A Complete History* does not depart from the conventions of historical writing that prevailed in the English Renaissance and whose roots go back to the medieval chronicles. Kennett possessed a static conception of history, betraying no awareness of historical anachronism. For Kennett, English history was the story of how the English people managed to stave off popery and absolutism. He supplied no analytic description of how English institutions evolved. Except for the fact that the Glorious Revolution secured England from the popish threat, the state of the realm Kennett described in the 1690s was basically the same as it was in the 1620s. Although *A Complete History* was, in its time, a notable publishing event and a well-known historical work, it was soon matched and in some ways superseded by Laurence Echard's *History of England*.

i i

In 1707, a year after *A Complete History* appeared, the first volume of Laurence Echard's three-volume *History of England* (1707-1718) was published. Echard's history was widely recognized as the first full narrative history of England. Earlier works were either annals or mere chronologies, or they studied particular events or reigns. The general history of England - the genre of Rapin, Hume, Hallam, Lingard, and J. R. Green - really began with Laurence Echard in the age of Anne.

Born in 1671, Echard was educated at home by his father before being admitted to Christ College Cambridge in 1688.[25] He received a B.A. in 1692, an M.A. in 1695, and had already had three books published by the time he was nineteen. Ordained as priest in 1696, Echard was a rector at Louth, Lincolnshire, until 1722, at which time George I presented him to the rectory of Kendelsham in Suffolk. He held several livings in plurality and was made Archdeacon of Stowe in 1712. From 1697 until his death in 1730, Echard was chaplain to Bishop William Wake and prebendary of Lincoln Cathedral in Louth. Despite his preferments Echard was never well rewarded. The expenses incurred in producing his histories meant that he was frequently in financial trouble.

Although Echard was a practicing cleric, he employed most of his time compiling his lengthy histories and geographies. Probably his most popular work was *The Gazetteer or Newsman's Interpreter* (1695), a geographical dictionary. Its seventh edition was much expanded, and the fifteenth edition was translated into French, Italian, and Spanish. *The Gazetteer or Newsman's Interpreter* answered the growing demand for books of geographical, topographical, and general information. Echard gauged the work for a wide audience, noting that this *The Gazetteer or Newsman's Interpreter* was a "pocket volume, partly designed for all such as frequent coffee-houses, and other places for news."[26]

Another successful work was his *Roman History* (1695-1698), which by 1699 had gone through four editions. In the eighteenth century it was probably the most popular royalist (pro-Augustan) history of Rome and was, like all his histories, mainly a conflation of earlier printed books. Echard, as William Aiken observed, had "a passion for digesting, abridging, compiling, and regurgitating."[27] His interest in ancient history led Echard to translate Terence's *Comedies*, praised by Robert Graves as the finest English translation of that work.[28]

There has been some confusion about the political slant of *The History of England*, no doubt stemming from the fact that Echard was patronized by an illustrious Whig bishop and that contemporaries were not unanimous in their judgments of Echard. Most commentators and fellow historians, however, identified Echard as a Tory historian.[29] Moreover Echard was assisted by Tory politicians. It was James Butler, the Second Duke of Ormonde - a redoubtable Tory - who set Echard to work on *The*

History in the first place and, according to Echard, gave "life and being" to the first volume.[30] Daniel Finch the Earl of Nottingham, a Tory leader in Anne's reign, helped Echard write portions of the manuscript.[31]

   In his general *History of England* to 1688 and in a supplementary volume covering the Revolution, Echard elucidates a moderate but distinctly Tory version of English history. His bias shows in his portrayal of the early Stuarts - largely a paraphrase of Clarendon - in his hostility to the Exclusionists in the 1670s, in his lionization of Danby as hero of the Glorious Revolution, and in his conclusion that James II forfeited the throne because his flight constituted desertion, not because he broke the original contract or was deposed by Parliament. Echard was a Hanoverian Tory but was not an active combatant in the political war of words in the manner of Kennett. He was clearly willing to cultivate friends in high places of either party and even serve Whig eminences. Echard said that he wrote his *History* at the urging of "several considerable persons." They pointed out to Echard the usefulness of English history for the "nobility, gentry, and great numbers of others," and lamented the fact that "an Englishman who was desirous to know his own country's story was obliged to read over a library rather than a single history." Echard noted that he sought out "men of all ranks and parties" in London and the universities to consult, and to help him locate rare books and manuscripts.[32]

   If we include Echard's postscript volume, *The History of the Revolution and the Establishment of England in the year 1688* (1725), Echard's bulky history amounts to about three thousand folio pages. He intended to continue his narrative at least through King William's reign but never got beyond the Revolution of 1688. The third and final edition of his general history (1720) contained an appendix in which Echard responded to his critics.

   Stylistically, Echard marks an improvement over Burnet, Kennett, and - it could be argued - Clarendon. His prose is more animated and vivid, less stately and sonorous than previous historians. Substantively, Echard relies upon many of the same printed sources as Kennett, but his research is shallower, his critical acumen duller. Unlike Clarendon, Burnet, and Kennett, Echard emphasizes that he wanted his history to entertain readers as well as instruct them.[33]

The principal theme of Echard's history is to illustrate and glorify the workings of providence in history. Indeed, there is probably no eighteenth-century English history that stresses divine intervention in human affairs as much as Echard's. It is the crucial contrivance he falls back upon repeatedly in order to explain historical change. Echard said that the great weight he placed upon providence provoked more criticism of his history than anything else. In his *Appendix* Echard refused to budge an inch, defining history as "a subject where we discover so many noble instances of divine providence."[34]

Five events stand out in the *History* as especially portentous - the reigns of Henry VII and James I, the Great Rebellion, the Restoration, and above all, the Revolution of 1688. Naturally, providence had a hand in all these. The last two we owe exclusively to God's beneficence. As for the other three, when one looks beyond appeals to heaven, more worldly explanations come into play, including social and economic considerations. Following Francis Bacon and James Harrington, Echard describes how Henry VII pursued policies that elevated "the middle sort" and diminished "the exorbitant power of the nobility."[35] By alienating the barons' lands and promoting husbandry, Henry raised the House of Commons to a position of power and prestige it had not theretofore enjoyed. This picture of the first Tudor humbling his overmighty subjects and promoting the commons recurred throughout the eighteenth century and has, in fact, only recently been superseded.

Echard gives an idealized account of Henry VIII and the Reformation, which, he writes, sprang from the king's pangs of conscience and "the wisdom of providence."[36] Although the Reformation was a providential blessing, Echard sees its religious idealism tarnished almost from the start by the plutocratic interests of many nobles and gentry, intent on plundering Church property. Thomas Cromwell persuaded Henry to sell the monastic lands cheaply to aristocrats and gentry in order to secure their support for the Reformation and for the crown. Corruption and continuous religious strife, culminating in Mary's reimposition of Catholicism, were "divine judgments due to the sins of the people."[37] Echard conformed to the conventional wisdom of his time by exaggerating the brilliance and popularity of Elizabeth in contrast to the ineptitude and infamy of her successor.[38] He presents her as the greatest and most loved monarch in history. Most of his account is taken up with foreign and military affairs, celebrating the triumphant, divinely inspired preservation of Protestantism in the face of popish tyranny.

Echard, like most Augustan historians, traces the roots of the English Civil War back to the reign of James I and characterizes the first Stuart as a worse king than his unfortunate son.[39] The main charge leveled against James is that he overspent on an enormous scale. Although Echard admires the peace and prosperity enjoyed under James, the king nonetheless bequeathed to his successor "an unnecessary war, an exhausted treasury, and a crown of thorns."[40] Consequently, by the time Charles I assumed the throne the nation was wracked with discontents and divided between Court and Country. The new king confronted a weakened nobility and a recalcitrant populace.

Following Clarendon closely, Echard sees the Great Rebellion as divine punishment for the sins of the nation: for excess, wantonness, and irreligion.[41] Echard, however, suggests a socioeconomic dimension to the Civil War that is absent from Clarendon. Recalling James Harrington's analysis of the Civil War, he relates the conflict to changes in the balance of property, suggesting that the loss of crown lands had undermined the monarch's traditional powers. The Parliamentarians, believing "that all empire is founded on property," strove to establish a limited monarchy in which the king could no longer rule without Parliament. However, the Harringtonian strain in Echard remains elliptical and rather incoherent, secondary to the providential explanation.[42]

Like most seventeenth- and eighteenth-century historians, Echard has virtually nothing to say about the religious and organizational nature of Puritanism. The Puritans were simply the power hungry, those greedy for Church property, "neglected and unemployed by the court," and wicked troublemakers generally.[43] He does vaguely suggest the emergence of lower class participation in the Revolution. Plagiarizing Clarendon, Echard notes that by 1640 "a more inferior sort of the common people came into power."[44] During the Protectorate Cromwell and his generals "lorded it over all the nobility and gentry of the nation."[45]

Echard's critical portrait of Cromwell echoes Clarendon. It was the "vengeance of heaven" that Cromwell died when he did and that General Monk served as "God's instrument" in effecting the Restoration.[46] Echard describes Charles II in terms somewhat less critical than Kennett, as too pro-Catholic and pro-French.[47] He even offers qualified praise of the Country Party opposition to Charles. However, he castigates the Dissenters and supports the Clarendon code.[48]

Echard condemns James II wholeheartedly and hails William III as the savior of the nation, an instrument of divine providence. For Echard the Revolution constituted the outstanding example of divine intercession in the affairs of man, to the point where mere terrestrial explanations of what occurred dwindle almost into insignificance. Echard depicts James II as a Catholicizing absolutist intent on throttling his kingdom and handing it over to Rome. The resistance to James is presented as a national movement, and no mention is made of the Whig or Tory parties. Echard lavishes praise on the Earl of Danby, a Tory, and is silent on Whig heroes like Somers and Sunderland. Moreover, Echard adheres to the Tory rationale of the Revolution: James II forfeited the throne by "deserting" the country through his flight.[49]

Without God's intervention in the Revolution, the collective efforts of all concerned would have come to naught: "The arm of God seemed more visible and manifest than all the powers of mankind."[50] Echard's invocations of preternatural power extend beyond providence to include superstition and magic. In 1639, for example, on the eve of the Scottish War, Echard reports that a bird defecated on a statue of the king. The excrement changed into three drops of blood. This, of course, was a bad omen. Echard goes so far as to include Colonel Lindsay's fanciful story about having witnessed a conversation between Cromwell and the Devil on the eve of the Battle of Worcester. One of the notable developments in Charles II's reign, according to Echard, was the remarkable vocation of Valentine Greatstrokes, who cured people of diverse ailments merely by stroking them.[51]

William Aiken described Echard's history as "a mosaic of original, printed, and manuscript materials embedded in a matrix of the author's own prose and arranged in that manner to form the patterns of a consecutive narrative."[52] Although Echard made use of unnamed manuscripts, the great bulk of his research was based on printed sources. He drew upon most of the standard collections and chronicles but overlooked several important works, including Rushworth's collections (dealing with the Civil War period) and Rymer's *Foedera*, printed prior to Echard's second edition. Insofar as Echard possessed a sense of style and was less prone to transcribe long documentary extracts, *The History of England* marked an advance in narrative form. Echard's work, however, did not signal a breakthrough in historical method. He mastered the art of paraphrase, weaving his sources together uncritically, with little or no change in wording from the original text. Only occasionally did he cite his source. Echard proclaimed unabashedly that he copied extensively from Clarendon, his most important single source.

Echard's penchant for paraphrasing and plagiarizing his sources was one objection made to his history by Edmund Calamy III in his *Letter to Mr. Archdeacon Echard upon Occasion of his History of England* (1718). Calamy's book-length critique was the first and most formidable rejoinder to Echard's history, and Echard himself complained about its deleterious effect on his reputation.[53] A prominent Dissenting clergyman, Calamy had chronicled the persecution of his Dissenting brethren after the Restoration and written one of the first biographies of Cromwell. Calamy never used the terms Whig and Tory but criticized Echard for writing against revolution principles.[54] Calamy said that he had looked forward to reading *The History of England* because he, too, wanted to see the workings of providence detailed in a general history. Furthermore, Calamy shared Echard's view that "it has long been complained that we wanted an history that should with an even thread continue the account of ages passed down to our own." Calamy could summon no words of praise for Echard's work. He upbraided Echard for being too lenient toward Charles II and James II, for denigrating the Dissenters, and for taking a complacent attitude toward the papists.

Calamy's admonitions were positively genteel compared to the scathing aspersions and biting witticisms of John Oldmixon. A whig polemicist and historian, Oldmixon blasted Echard in *The Critical History of England* (1724), a running critique of "monkish writers" like Echard and Clarendon. Oldmixon assailed Echard for maligning Puritans and Dissenters, for defending popery, for claiming that *Eikon Basilikon* was genuinely written by Charles I, for rejecting the warming pan story (which held that the birth of James III was supposititious), and for favoring all the Stuart kings.[55] Oldmixon also inveighed against Echard's superstition, his "stories of apparitions, magic, healings, and the like." For instance, he ridiculed the account of Cromwell's conversation with the Devil, calling it a "miserable tale which would not bear telling to children and servants around a Christmas fire."

Echard's *History* deserves mention in any survey of English historiography inasmuch as it was the first substantial work to unfold the history of England in a full, continuous narrative. Certainly, however, it was not an innovative work, either in methodology or in the philosophy that informed Echard's interpretation. On the contrary, it exemplifies the prevailing late Renaissance tradition of historiography: the propensity to compile rather than explain, the narrow political perspective, the surfeit of trivia, and above all, the reliance on preternatural power to disclose the meaning and course of history.

* * * *

Echard's Tory bias distinguished him from his Whig rivals, Kennett and Burnet, but the historians we have been considering all possessed a similar methodology and philosophy of history. All fall within the conservative compass of establishment political attitudes in post-Revolutionary England. John Locke, a comparatively radical theorist, is scarcely mentioned in these works. The Whiggish histories of Burnet and Kennett do not propound liberal ideas such as the natural rights of man, elective monarchy, and the ultimate sovereignty of the people. Because a variation of divine right lingered on in the early eighteenth century in the form of providence, historians could gloss over the controversial legal and ideological wrangles surrounding the Glorious Revolution. They could acclaim the Revolution wholeheartedly because it seemed so manifestly the work of divine providence.

Burnet, Kennett, and Echard were impeccably orthodox clerics, solidly rooted to revelation, Biblical authority, the Holy Trinity, miracles, and providence. Their conservative Christianity found expression in their historical writing. The new philosophy had not yet called the old religious historiography into doubt. In Anne's reign the status of the Church was a central political issue. Debate over the relationship between Church and state were based on appeals to history and encouraged historical writing. The political capacity of the Church was uppermost in the minds of these historians: not because the Church operated as a department of government, but because the Church functioned to uphold liberty and property, order and authority in the state. Popery, by contrast, represented arbitrary power and foreign domination. Strictly religious issues - matters of Church form, practice, and doctrine - were not presented as questions of great urgency. Rather, religious labels like Puritan and papist signified certain political and even social categories.

A new style of history began to emerge in the age of Anne - the narrative general history. In most respects, however, historians resembled their seventeenth-century forebears more than their eighteenth-century "philosophical" descendants. Echard has more in common with Clarendon, or for that matter Bishop Bossuet in France, than he does with Bolingbroke or Hume. Historians in this period had little sense of historical evolution: there is no appreciation in their works of such long-term developments as the rise of Puritanism, political parties, or the power of Parliament, and little discussion of social and economic change. Seventeenth-century historians were more interested in cataloging facts, conflating documents, scoring political points, and disclosing the workings of providence.

Notes

[1] G. V. Bennett, *White Kennett, Bishop of Peterborough* (London, 1957), 89. Unless otherwise indicated the biographical remarks that follow are drawn from Bennett, 12-22, 85-106, 158-177.

[2] Richard Ollard, *The Image of the King* (London, 1979), 178.

[3] Bennett, 85.

[4] See David Harrison Stevens, *Party Politics and English Journalism, 1702-1742* (Menasha, Wisconsin, 1916), 2-4.

[5] Bennett, 169.

[6] For Kennett's account of Charles I's reign see especially White Kennett, *A Complete History of England*, 2nd ed. (London, 1719), III, 30-32, 57-63, 139-143.

[7] *Ibid.*, 30.

[8]*Ibid.*, 10.

[9]*Ibid.*, 93.

[10]*Ibid.*, 209-216.

[11]On Charles II see especially *ibid.*, 370, 417-419.

[12]*Ibid.*, 440.

[13]*Ibid.*, 518.

[14]See especially *ibid.*, 722, 747-750.

[15]See Margaret Jacob, *The Newtonians and the English Revolution* (Ithaca, 1976), 25-26, 92-94.

[16]For Kennett's invocations of providence see Kennett, 204, 238, 321, 498, 528.

[17]Quoted in Bennett, 97.

[18]For information on North see Lois G. Schwoerer, "The Chronology of Roger North's Major Works," *History of Ideas Newsletter*, Oct. 1957, III, 73-78; R. W. Kelton Cremer, "Roger North," *Essays and Studies, 1959*, 73-86; James L. Clifford, "Roger North and Biography," *Restoration and Eighteenth Century Literature: Essays in Honour of Alan Dugald McKillop*, ed. Lois G. Schwoerer (Chicago, 1963), 275-285; James L. Clifford and Paul Delaney, *British Autobiography in the Seventeenth Century* (London, 1969), 149-151.

[19]Roger North, *The Examen: or an Enquiry into the Credit and Veracity of a pretended Complete History* (London, 1740), ii-xix.

[20]See *ibid.*, 93, 115.

[21]*Ibid.*, 340.

[22]*Ibid.*, 458.

[23]*Ibid.*, 352.

[24]*Ibid.*, 418, 516.

[25]Unless otherwise indicated, biographical information on Echard comes from Richard W. Goulding, *Laurence Echard, M.A. F.S.A., Author and Archdeacon* (no place of publication indicated, 1926), and the entry on Echard in the *Dictionary of National Biography* by George Fisher Russel Barker.

[26]Laurence Echard, *The Gazetteer's or Newsman's Interpreter* (London, 1732), vii.

[27]William A. Aiken ed., *The Conduct of the Earl of Nottingham* (New Haven, 1941), 2.

[28]Cited by John Barnard in the Introduction to *Echard's Prefaces to Terence's Comedies and Plautus' Comedies*, new edition (Los Angeles, 1968), 1-4.

[29]Thomas Hearne denounced Echard's *History* as "a most roguish, Whiggish thing, much such as what Kennett writes." See Hearne, *The Remains of Thomas Hearne*, ed. John Russell Smith, 3 vols. (London, 1869) II (April 27, 1718), 62; Victor Wexler calls Echard's *History* "the standard Whig history in the eighteenth century until Tindal's translation of Rapin appeared." See Wexler, "David Hume's Discovery of a New Science of Historical Thought," *Eighteenth Century Studies*, X, 2 (1976/77), 195. On the other hand the *History* was branded as Tory by Edmund Calamy and John Oldmixon, two staunch Whigs; see Edmund Calamy, *A Letter to Mr. Archdeacon Echard upon Occasion of his History of England* (London, 1718); John Oldmixon, *The Critical History of England* (London, 1724). The *History* was endorsed wholeheartedly by two Tory historians, Thomas Salmon and Zachary Grey; see Thomas Salmon, *The Modern History, or the present state of all Nations*, 31 vols. (London, 1724-1738) XXIII, 170, 309; Zachary Grey, *A Defense of Our Ancient and Modern Historians against the frivolous cavils of a late Pretender to Critical History* (London, 1724); The most recent historian to treat Echard as a Whig historian is Deborah Stephan. See Stephan, "Laurence Echard - Whig Historian," *The Historical Journal*, XXXII, 4 (1989) 843-866.

[30]Laurence Echard, *The History of England from the First Entrance of Julius Caesar and the Romans to the conclusion of the Reign of King James II and the Establishment of King William and Queen Mary upon the Throne in the year 1688*, 3 vols. bound as one (London, 1720); 2nd ed., I, unpaginated preface.

[31]See Aiken, "Introduction," *Conduct of the Earl of Nottingham, 1-38.*

[32]Echard, *History*, I, unpaginated preface.

[33]*Ibid.*, 92; II, 411.

[34]Echard, *Appendix to the three volumes of Mr. Archdeacon Echard's History of England* (London, 1720), 31.

[35]For the citations on Henry VII's reign see *History*, I, 247-258.

[36]On Henry VIII see *ibid.*, 264, 274, 284, 287-288.

[37]*Ibid.*, 303, 312-313.

[38]On Elizabeth's reign see *ibid.*, 350-351, 359-360, 375.

[39]See especially *ibid.*, 414-417.

[40]*Ibid.*, 408.

[41]*Ibid.*, 408, 520.

[42]*Ibid.*, 485-486.

[43]*Ibid.*, 540-544.

[44]For Echard's remarks on the radicalization of the opposition see *ibid.*, 544, 614, 620, 634-636, 643; II, 704, 714, 722.

[45]For Echard's discussion of Cromwell see *ibid.*, II, 722-735.

[46]*Ibid.*, I, 734-735.

[47]For Echard's criticisms of Charles II see *ibid.*, III, 806, 905, 908, 937.

[48]For Echard's Tory slant on Charles II see *ibid.*, 803-804, 826, 893, 937, 945.

[49]Echard, *The History of the Revolution and the Establishment of England* (London, 1725), 170, 192-193; *History*, III, 1108, 1150.

[50]*Ibid.*, 1108.

[51]The tales referred to are found in *ibid.*, I, 471; II, 822-823, 827, 833.

[52]Aiken, 27.

[53]Edmund Calamy, *An Historical Account of My own Life*, 2 vols. (London, 1829) I, 408-409.

[54]For Calamy's criticisms of Echard see his *A Letter to Mr. Archdeacon Echard*, 14, 2-24, 5-8.

[55]For Oldmixon's criticisms of Echard see his *Critical History*, 181, 197, 200, 223, 235, 246-247, 266-267, 270-271.

Part Two

The Rise of Whig Historical Writing in the Age of Walpole

Chapter III

Rapin-Thoyras and the Court-Country Historical Debate

i

The history of British historical writing in the second quarter of the eighteenth century is dominated by one man - a Frenchman who wrote his *History of England* in Holland. Paul de Rapin-Thoyras was by far the most popular and celebrated historian of English history on both sides of the Channel, and in the American colonies, prior to David Hume. Voltaire called Rapin's work the only good history of England.[1] It is not difficult to see why it appealed to the French philosophe and anglophile. Rapin glorified the English constitution and mixed monarchy, English rationality and religious tolerance. Rapin's historical method marked a substantial advance over his predecessors. He consulted a wider range of sources and employed them more judiciously. He developed themes and made an effort to interpret the facts rather than simply list them. Although the *History* was written with an unmistakably Whiggish slant, Rapin made a serious effort to expose the partisan distortions that had heretofore so marred historical writing. Finally, Rapin's *History of England* possessed a secular, anti-clerical tone, which distinguished it from the theistic, super-historical themes of previous histories.

Rapin set the standard for British historical scholarship in the age of Walpole. By successfully mapping out new terrain, he undermined the traditional chronicle-compilation form of historical writing. Successive British historians tried to eclipse him. Not until Hume's *History of England* appeared in the 1750s did Rapin fall out of fashion. Of course Rapin's history was not written in an intellectual or ideological vacuum. Like its immediate successors - the histories of Thomas Salmon, John Oldmixon, and Daniel Neal - Rapin's work reflects and illuminates the changing character of early eighteenth-century political thought. In order to fully appreciate the nature of historical writing in this period, we must understand the political and intellectual milieu.

In the second quarter of the eighteenth century, historical writing grew more secular in tone. The shift to naturalistic explanations of causality reflected the ascendancy of latitudinarian and, to a much less

47

extent, deistical ideas.   Erastian religious thought absorbed the new scientific and philosophical ideas, immortalized by Newton and Locke. By the 1720s, writes Margaret Jacob, "the Newtonian Enlightenment was firmly established within the intellectual circles of the British ruling elite."[2] Latitudinarian divines appealed to reason as well as revelation. The deist bogey first rocked the clerical establishment in the 1690s, but it was between 1720 and 1740 that a pamphlet war raged between the deists and their clerical opponents, many of whom were latitudinarians. There was also an international dimension to the growth of rational religion and freethinking.   The · intellectual commerce between England and the Netherlands fostered a steady interchange of liberal Protestant and deistical thought. Rapin-Thoyras, for example, consorted with a variety of freethinkers in The Hague. Lord Bolingbroke met members of a deist lodge in the Netherlands and endorsed their society.[3]

After the reign of Anne the political ideas of Robert Filmer lost their appeal and John Locke gradually came into his own.   Locke's political philosophy was ambiguous and paradoxical enough for political writers of differing viewpoints to invoke his ringing paeans to liberty and property as they saw fit, generally ignoring the more radical implications of his thought. The High Tory doctrines of nonresistance and indefeasible hereditary right were confined to a small Jacobite minority. Most sections of the opposition to Walpole concurred with the Court in endorsing the right of resistance in exceptional cases. However, the political establishment chose to downplay this disquieting legacy of the Glorious Revolution.

The nature of political parties in early Hanoverian England is at present a matter of considerable controversy among historians.   The standard view has been that party conflict dwindled after Anne's reign and that Toryism in particular ceased to count for much in national politics. Within the prevailing Whig consensus the central dichotomy shifted from a Whig/Tory to a Court/Country alignment.   This view has not gone unchallenged. By far the strongest dissent has been registered by Linda Colley. Colley argues that Toryism, far from lingering on as the nostalgic chimera of backwoods squires, was ideologically and electorally dominant in the middle decades of the eighteenth century: "One party government had been superimposed on a two-party, predominantly Tory state."[4]

Although Colley shows the survival, even vitality, of the Tory party, she does not demonstrate convincingly that the polarity between Whig and

Tory was the primary political division of the age. Colley recognizes, in any event, that the Tories employed Country arguments on most of the key issues - opposition to "corruption" and long parliaments, standing armies, stock jobbers, and the pro-Hanoverian foreign policy. The Tories clothed their denunciations of rampant vice and immorality in Country, neo-Harringtonian rhetoric. As Colley points out, most Tories accepted the Toleration Act of 1689.[5] Issues revolving around the status of the Church and Dissent, so crucial to the political identity of the Tories, simply did not rend the nation as they had in the Stuart epoch. The Whig ascendancy is reflected in the historical writing of the period: from the 1720s to the accession of George III only two general histories were published with a distinctly Tory point of view.

The decline of party strife after the Hanoverian accession owed much to the practical consensus that Walpole, above all others, managed to form. The Tories had lost much of their political authority because of the support some of their party had given to the '15 Jacobite Rebellion. Walpole exploited this complicity to the hilt by identifying Toryism with Jacobitism and sedition. At the same time, he skillfully satisfied the fundamentally conservative political interests of the propertied elite, be they Whig or Tory. He conciliated the country gentry by lowering the land tax, by pursuing a relatively cheap, pacific foreign policy, and by maintaining penalties against Nonconformists. He pleased merchants and manufacturers by abolishing export duties and deploying bounties to encourage exports. His adroit manipulation of patronage propitiated many men of property who desired nothing so much as the prestige and fruits of office.

Another reason why Walpole was able to reign supreme for so long was that he faced a badly divided opposition. While many Tories continued to resist Whig latitudinarianism, the radical Real Whigs were pressing for the complete religious toleration of all Protestant Nonconformists. Whereas the Tories hoped to make Parliament an exclusive club for landed gentlemen, Commonwealthmen like John Trenchard and Thomas Gordon wanted to see the franchise extended to encompass men of property outside the charmed circle of landed magnates. Shifting groups of dissident Whigs maneuvered to secure office on their own terms, while Bolingbroke endeavored to fashion a unifying Country ideology. A faction of Jacobites dreamed of restoring the Stuart dynasty.

Despite the relative stability and consensus of British politics in the early eighteenth century, and notwithstanding the factionalism that crippled the opposition to Walpole, one can, nevertheless, discern a central dichotomy between two ideologies or mentalities - the Court and the Country. The newspaper press was the main vehicle for the dissemination of Court and Country political ideas. Country papers like *The Craftsman* and *Common Sense* expressed themes that appealed to both Country Whigs and Tories, including the call for shorter parliaments, the elimination of placemen from the commons, and the disbandment or reduction in size of the standing army. These policy positions came embedded in a "neo-Harringtonian" Old Whig political vocabulary that drew primarily upon James Harrington and the tradition of civic humanism and secondarily upon liberal theorists like Locke and Algernon Sydney.[6] Imbued with a pessimistic view of human nature, Country writers believed that the body politic was easily corrupted through court influence. Walpole's systematic use of crown patronage would reduce Parliament to a rubber stamp and rob the citizenry of their liberty, independence, and civic virtue.

Although the finest writers and ideologists belonged to the Country opposition, there was a distinct Court Whig ideology. Court Whiggism in Hanoverian England was a secularized, more liberal version of the theistic Whig ideology that prevailed in the first two decades of the eighteenth century. Newspapers like the *Daily Gazetteer* and *London Journal* popularized Lockean political ideas, accenting his affirmation of the government's role as the guardian of liberty and, even more so, property. Walpole's press spoke in Lockean terms about the state of nature and the social contract as the basis of civil society, but the Lockean defense of property took precedence over such liberal to radical notions as the natural rights of man, popular sovereignty, and the right of resistance.

Walpole's hired pens defended patronage as a necessary lubricant of the balanced constitution, since king, lords, and commons were interdependent. Otherwise, government would degenerate into chaotic wrangling among the constituent branches, until one power crushed the others and tyranny ensued. To the Country charge that the nation was being beggared by monied men, the Court retorted that the bulk of landed men supported the ministry but that the power of fluid, movable wealth should also be recognized. The Court categorically rejected the Country position that after the Glorious Revolution there were no important philosophical divisions in the nation and that political parties had, in fact, ceased to exist. Quite the contrary, insisted Walpole's propagandists: the opposition was made up of Tory Jacobites whose commitment to divine right kingship, nonresistance, and hereditary right was undiminished.

Court and Country pamphleteers alike found in Rapin's *History of England* a massive armory of historical argument for their war of words. Rapin's evenhanded tone and the wealth of commentary in both the *History* and his *Dissertation upon Parties* (1717) made him acceptable to men of varying political allegiances. If a propagandist looked hard enough he could usually find support somewhere in Rapin (specifically in Nicholas Tindal's translation) for whatever polemical point he chose to make.

i i

Paul de Rapin-Thoyras belonged to that school of emigre French intellectuals, at least nominally Protestant, who found refuge from religious persecution in the Dutch Republic.[7] A professional soldier, Rapin first sojourned to Holland briefly before sailing for Torbay with William in 1688. He subsequently fought with William in Ireland and was pensioned by the crown, serving as tutor to the son of William's Dutch favorite, the Duke of Portland. Portland, a diplomat and ally of the Whigs, possessed a rich collection of historical works that Rapin consulted. Rapin eventually published a *Dissertation sur les Whigs et les Torys* (1717), based substantially on his close observation of court politics in William's reign.

The *Histoire d' Angleterre* was not, however, written under the patronage of Whig politicians. In 1707, when his services as tutor were no longer required, Rapin settled in the Hague, where he began working on his history of England - a project that occupied him the rest of his life. Rapin's career is illustrative of the early Enlightenment; he was a French Protestant who lived in England and the Netherlands and whose works glorified the English polity. In his study of the early Enlightenment Paul Hazard noted that England had foreign "heralds at her disposal ready to trumpet her glories far and wide among the civilized nations of the world,"[8] mainly Huguenot refugees like Pierre Coste, translator of Locke and Newton; Jean Desaguliers, leader of British Freemasonry and champion of the English constitution who traveled between England and the Netherlands teaching Newtonian science and philosophy; and Rapin's fellow historian and annalist of current affairs, Abel Boyer.   Rapin belonged to this group.

The glorification of England and the English constitution by these publicists came in response to emerging Anglophilia on the Continent.   To a growing circle of literati in France, the Netherlands, Austria, Germany, and Italy, England stood as a beacon of light in the darkness of European obscurantism.   A history celebrating the growth of English liberty, toleration, Protestantism, and constitutionalism was bound to find favor, especially if it was written in French, the preeminent language of the age.

Even more than England, the Dutch Republic was a haven for liberal Protestants like Jean Le Clerc, Philippus van Limborch, and Pierre Jurieu, not to mention that skeptical iconoclast par excellance, Pierre Bayle.   It was in this little world of political and religious heterodoxy that Rapin wrote his history.   Rapin was particularly close to Le Clerc, friend, publisher of the *Bibliotheque Ancienne et Moderne*, and translator of John Locke.   It has been suggested that Le Clerc passed on to Rapin Locke's political ideas.[9]   The exact pedigree of Rapin's political philosophy and method cannot be established definitively, but unquestionably he shared the liberal Protestantism and rationalism of Le Clerc and his illustrious friend.   Le Clerc was also a formidable Bible critic, and his influence may well have contributed to the critical, skeptical tone of Rapin's history. Certainly Le Clerc was of great assistance to Rapin in his research.   He had access to many British publications and passed them on to his colleague.

Rapin began his history in 1707 and continued writing until 1724, when he was interrupted by sickness.   He died a year later, at which time the existing published portion ended with the execution of Charles I in 1649.   The remaining manuscript, possibly unfinished, continued the history to the coronation of William and Mary.   The complete work was published in 1727 in The Hague.   The publisher, Alexandre de Rogissart, may have had another author finish Rapin's posthumous draft.

The *Histoire d' Angleterre* met with great success in France and England.   It went through sixteen French editions.   The work was made familiar to English readers by Nicholas Tindal's felicitous translation, published in octavo volumes between 1721 and 1731.   Tindal's edition ranks among the most popular scholarly works of the century.   It was also one of the early serial publications. In order to ensure a profitable return on the sales of expensive, large-scale works and to tap the expanding English reading market, books in the second quarter of the eighteenth century were increasingly sold in fascicles or numbers. Histories were an especially popular commodity, and Tindal's translation alone seems to have contributed significantly to the new sales technique. Newspapers claimed that about fifteen thousand of each number were printed in 1732, even exceeding the subsequent sales of Tobias Smollett's popular history.[10] An issue of the *Grub Street Journal* in 1734 blamed Rapin's *History* for popularizing what it saw as the dubious practice of publishing books serially: A man would spend six-pence for a number of Rapin, "when perhaps his wife and children want a bit of bread, and himself a pair of breeches."[11] Tindal's translation sold so well that an inferior rival translation began appearing in 1732.

Although Rapin lived in England for only a few years, he managed to compile an impressive bibliography for his work. In addition to the books and documents he received from Portland and Le Clerc, Rapin got access to the libraries of Major General von Heiden, commander of the Prussian troops in the War of the Spanish Succession, and Abel Tassin d' Allone, secretary to Queen Anne. Rapin was able to consult a wider range of printed sources than anyone had previously, including works written in Italian, Dutch, and Spanish as well as English and French. Thomas Rymer's *Foedera*, obtained from Le Clerc, was the most substantial new source, and Rapin was the first historian to take advantage of this vast collection of diplomatic treaties and conventions.

What was the most impressive about Rapin's use of sources, however, was not their quantity, but the critical, analytical approach he took to them. For the bulk of his narrative, Rapin relied upon many of the standard works that previous scholars, like Echard, had depended upon. Rapin, however, treated his sources critically and skeptically. He was not satisfied simply to list his sources in the columns of the history - though he did that, too - in the manner of Kennett and Echard et al. Frequently Rapin digressed from his chronological narrative in order to analyze and comment upon previous historians and collectors, exposing their deficiencies, comparing and contrasting different points of view, censuring some authorities and vindicating others. Rapin's novel sensitivity to the differing perspectives, the strengths and weaknesses of his predecessors, derived from his keen awareness of the particular way in which the rise of political parties in the seventeenth century had permeated and distorted historical writing.

Perhaps the best example of Rapin's critical commentary is to be found in his discussion of the historians of Charles I, specifically the Royalist or "Court" historians as he calls them, John Nalson, Thomas Frankland, and Clarendon; and the chief Parliamentarian historian who sided with "the people," John Rushworth.[12] Rapin traces the genesis of political parties to the early Stuart period. These writers were the prototypes of modern Whig and Tory historians. After reviewing the respective interpretations on both sides, Rapin concludes that:[13]

> the histories of the two parties, though founded upon the same facts, are so opposite to one another, that a reader who is not very attentive, or wants leisure to examine what is proposed to him, knows not where he is when he sees this disagreement. For my part, who am not engaged in either of the parties, and aim only at truth, I don't think myself obliged blindly to follow one or other of the two systems.

The two systems consisted of political doctrines that distorted the historians' perceptions of events. Two basic principles underpinned Court historiography: a belief that the king's power was absolute - Rapin exaggerates here - and hence that there was nothing wrong if he chose to rule without Parliament; and the presumption that parliament did not act out of genuine concern for the constitution, but only aimed to stir up the people and ride to power on the shoulders of the mob. On the other hand, Rapin rejects the Parliamentarian "system" that held that the opposition to Charles was a purely defensive struggle to preserve the ancient constitution.

Rapin was particularly concerned with defending the veracity of Rushworth's collection of documents against the mostly false accusations leveled by Nalson. As for Clarendon, Rapin acknowledged that his *History of the Rebellion* was "excellent" in many respects. At bottom, however, it constituted a tendentious apology for Charles I and the Royalist cause. Clarendon's greatest single failing was his virulent anti-Presbyterianism, a vice that he bequeathed to today's "followers of his maxims and principles."[14]

Frequently in the later Stuart section of his narrative Rapin recites various historical explanations of events and then rules on which, if any, he accepts. For instance, he rightly rejects Burnet's claim that the Second Dutch War was fought to eliminate the Dutch defenders of Protestantism while imposing popery on the nation. Chiding the Whig bishop for his overreliance on hearsay evidence, Rapin rejects the stock Whig view that the Tories in James II's reign, spellbound by the dogmas of nonresistance and indefeasible hereditary right, conspired with James II to enslave the nation.[15]

The most detailed and meticulous example of Rapin's critical method is his six folio-page examination of the warming pan theory, that classic bit of Whig mythology which held that the birth of Prince James was supposititious. Scrutinizing the testimony on both sides of the question, Rapin marshals a great deal of evidence to show that there were no grounds for the Whig charge, though he does not categorically rule out the remote possibility that fraud might have been perpetrated. The caliber of evidence that Whig historians like Burnet advance, he points out, was poor - merely rumor and a few odd occurrences surrounding the birth. Commenting on the nature of the evidence in this case, Rapin makes the following observation:[16]

> As the principal design of history is to establish facts that are certain to destroy those that are false; and to inform the readers of the grounds for doubting with regard to such as are dubious, I imagined in an affair so important as this . . . the reader would be glad to know what to rely on.

Here is the voice of skepticism and free inquiry, exploding myths, sifting truth from error.

Rapin's perceptive understanding of modern British politics was shown to best effect in his essay, the *Dissertation on the Rise, Progress, Views, Strengths, Interests, and Characters of the two Parties*, republished and popularized in Tindal's translation. This was Rapin's *piece de resistance*, a shrewdly formulated analysis of British politics and lucid abstract of his *History*. Since the Anglo-Saxon conquest, he writes, England had a "mixed government," with power shared between king and Parliament. This system prevailed until the seventeenth century, at which time James I attempted to roll back the power of Parliament.[17]

The beginnings of political parties, Rapin argues, go back to the reign of James I. The combination of Stuart tyranny and Parliamentary extremism gave birth to Cavaliers and Roundheads, the progenitors of Tories and Whigs. Rapin recognized that the parties were not monolithic. There were absolutist Tories and moderates. The Whigs covered the spectrum from rigid Presbyterians to moderate Church of England members, from extremist republicans to constitutionalists who defended mixed monarchy. Forgoing the partisanship that usually impaired accounts of the Glorious Revolution, Rapin points out that "moderates" from both parties joined together to throw out the tyrannical James II. Moderate Tories like the Earls of Halifax and Danby win Rapin's admiration as well as Whig stalwarts like John Somers and Ralph Montagu.

Rapin's intention was not to glorify the rise of parties. On the contrary, the whole troubled Stuart epoch testified to the factiousness of political parties, not to mention their damaging effects on historical writing itself. Nevertheless, in light of the constitutional issues raised and fought over for the past century, Rapin concluded that the Whigs and Tories would continue to dominate the political landscape. Only a "just and equitable sovereign" might be able to resolve the continuing issues of dispute and put an end to party strife.

Bolingbroke was to develop this theme of the "Patriot King" sweeping away the bickering factions and inaugurating a reign of virtue. The ideas about modern English politics set forth in Rapin's *Dissertation* reverberated in succeeding eighteenth century histories. Although Bolingbroke did not discuss the political dynamics of the Glorious Revolution in any detail, the thrust of his *Dissertation Upon Parties* followed Rapin in presenting it as a bipartisan movement against a popish tyrant. The influence of Rapin can be detected in David Hume's analysis of the rise of political parties and in his picture of the "moderate men" from both parties ejecting James II. No direct line can be drawn between Rapin and the great nineteenth-century historian, Macaulay, who finally restored the Whig interpretation of history to popular favor after its century-long eclipse by Hume. There are, however, notable parallels between the two historians in their discussions of political parties and the Glorious Revolution.[18] Like Rapin, Macaulay wrote in an era of political strife, and he too faulted the partisanship of past historians, Whig and Tory. His heroes of the Glorious Revolution were Rapin's heroes:

trimmers like Halifax and Danby were more admired than Whig zealots like Wharton and Sunderland.

The History of England elaborated upon the ideas originally broached in the *Dissertation*. Throughout the work the narrative focuses on political and constitutional history. There is little discussion of the economy, and less about religion and the Church than in most previous histories. Rapin's treatment of foreign affairs is illuminated by his extensive use of the *Foedera*, but on balance he devotes less space to diplomacy than had Echard. And despite his military background, Rapin was plainly bored with military history. He does not deign to describe battles, observing that "the recital of warlike exploits" was appropriate for teaching "the art of war"; but it was the historian's task to disclose "the causes and grounds of the beginning and continuance of wars, and consequently, the interests, motives, and artifices of the parties concerned, from whence military actions spring."[19]

Even though Rapin was able to step back from the party fray and deliver verdicts on previous historians with relative detachment, the *History of England* has a clear Whig slant. Summarizing the position of both sides in the ancient constitution controversy, Rapin attempts to strike a middle-of-the-road position for himself.[20] He denies the traditional Whig view of Parliamentary powers by plumping for the late origins of the House of Commons. But his entire work rests upon the proposition that English liberty could be traced back to the Saxon constitution. In the end, Rapin was an ancient constitutionalist.

Most of Rapin's *History* was given over to the Tudor-Stuart epoch. The single most important source for his Tudor narrative was Burnet's *History of the Reformation*. Rapin also relied heavily upon the Tudor chroniclers - Polydore Vergil, Edward Hall, Raphael Holinshed, Herbert of Cherbury, George Buchanan, to name the most prominent. Building upon the work of these contemporary annalists, Rapin fashioned a Whiggish narrative, the essentials of which found their way into the histories of Rapin's nineteenth-century Whig successors like Hallam and Froude. Rapin's account of Henry VII and Henry VIII conjures up the image of Tudor despotism. Both rulers were arbitrary and authoritarian, but not positively unconstitutional.

Rapin follows Francis Bacon in portraying Henry VII as a king who wanted, above all else, to secure his throne and make money.[21]   Henry's heavy-handed policies were mild when compared to those of his ruthless son, "the most absolute of all the kings of England since William the Conquerer."[22]   Henry VIII undertook the Reformation purely for reasons of state to increase the power of the crown.   Yet Henry did not really trample on the constitution because Parliament was intimately engaged in legislating the king's reforms.   Rapin never even mentions the dissolution of the monasteries until he comes to Edward VI, a king whose forthright Protestant policies he admires.

Not surprisingly, Rapin's attitude toward Mary Tudor is completely hostile.   Elizabeth, on the other hand, he extols with only a few reservations.   Like her father and grandfather, Elizabeth subordinated religious issues to her concern for royal power and the national security.   She did not squander crown revenues or "lavish her money upon the court-leeches, like her predecessors."[23]   Rapin, however, condemns in no uncertain terms the repression of the Puritans in the last two decades of her reign: "The severity which from this time began to be exercised in England upon the nonconformists produced terrible effects in the following reigns and occasioned troubles and factions which remain to this day, and of which perhaps there will be no end these many years."[24]

Nearly a third of the *History* was devoted to the Early Stuart era. It is with the reign of James I that Rapin begins expanding his narrative, drawing upon the wider range of sources that were available, transcribing them at considerable length.[25]   James I's conception of kingship entailed two unconstitutional innovations: a belief in the inviolability of hereditary succession and the conviction that royal power was absolute. These notions are anathema to Rapin, who maintains that Parliament has always had the ultimate right to "dispose of the crown and settle the succession without any regard to the next heir."[26]   Rapin reiterates the view held by many previous historians that James bequeathed a huge debt to Charles by squandering money on court favorites.   It was James who brought the English monarchy to the brink of ruin.   "Church Puritans" allied with "state Puritans" - all those who cared about the constitution - and together they made up the great bulk of "the people" opposed to the faction at court.

If the decorous mien of Charles I contrasted favorably with that of his boorish father, his concept of government was the mirror image. The financial independence of the crown was crucial if Charles was to dispense with Parliament: hence the noxious financial expedients like Ship Money. Charles trampled upon longstanding consti-tutional liberties.

Proclaiming his impartiality, Rapin apportions blame on both sides for the nation's slide into war after the Long Parliament convened in 1640.[27] He approves Parliament's dismantling of Ship Money, Star Chamber, and the other enormities of Stuart rule, but he cannot condone the aggressive strategies of Pym and his adherents, who aimed to mobilize the populace against the crown. His harshest comments are reserved, not for the Royalists, but for the Independents.[28] Under the guise of defending liberty and the constitution, this power-hungry faction schemed to overthrow the monarchy and rule despotically. Rapin places the blame squarely on the Independents for the execution of Charles I.

Rapin presents the familiar mixed picture of Cromwell, but the Lord Protector's merits far outweigh his defects. Never before was Cromwell depicted so positively in a general history. Granted he had climbed to power ruthlessly and violently, but this was necessary to bring order out of chaos. It was remarkable that "without the advantages of birth or fortune he rose so near the throne that it was in his power to mount it."[29] Rapin gives a perceptive analysis of the disparate political groups in the Interregnum period, and of Cromwell's statecraft in dealing with them.[30]

From Rapin's perspective, the Later Stuarts were no less arbitrary than their immediate predecessors. He gives us the conventional Whig portrait of Charles II: a popish infidel and gull of Louis XIV who planned to destroy Parliament but lacked the enterprise to carry out his designs. Rapin praises the Earl of Shaftesbury and his Country opposition to the Court party. To Rapin, Court and Country were synonymous with Tory and Whig. But Rapin is too good an historian to accept the famous Whig canards: that the Fire of London was started by Papists, the Popish Plot, and - as noted previously - that James III's birth was spurious. While his narrative of Charles II's reign is elaborate, the treatment of James II and the Revolution is cursory and distinctly less satisfactory than the account given in his *Dissertation*. It was very probably compiled after his death and tacked on to the main body of his narrative.

Writing in the intellectual milieu of Bayle and Le Clerc, Rapin did not visualize English history as a morality play, written by God, and portraying the trials and tribulations of the chosen people.   Whereas previous historians endeavored to demonstrate that the nation was endangered by Papists or Puritans, depending upon the author's point of view, Rapin had very little to say about religion and the Church.   In truth, Rapin was not really interested in church history.   His forte was constitutional history, and the scant attention paid to ecclesiastical history was consistent with the Enlightenment's general disinterest in religious controversy.   In his history of Tudor England, Rapin said almost nothing about the burning theological and ecclesiastical issues that polarized the various religious groups.   The Puritans were scarcely mentioned before the reign of James I.   What little he had to say about the clergy was usually critical.   One finds in his history virtually no discussion of the religious disputes between Puritans and Arminians, Presbyterians and Anglicans, Low Church and High Church.

Finally, Rapin made only infrequent references to providence - no more than two or three in the entire Stuart section and none whatsoever in his *Dissertation*.   Not that Rapin disbelieved in providence: he was, after all, a Huguenot, and certainly thought that human history was preordained by God.   But the secular, political orientation of his work makes it clear that Rapin did not believe that history should or could be written to illuminate the workings of providence.   Neither did he put any stock in tales of miracles or supernatural displays of divine power.

Without doubt Rapin's *History of England* marked a substantial advance over previous general histories.   The improvements can be seen in the more critical, penetrating use of sources, in his degree of detachment from party rancor, in his sharp perceptions about the British political system, and in his propensity to explain "the causes and grounds" of events rather than simply to record their occurrence.   It can also be seen in his appreciation of historical change.   Though the theme was not developed as thoroughly and explicitly as it might have been, Rapin's narrative of the seventeenth century is a study of how English politics was transformed. Rapin was less interested in vindicating a particular party than in showing how a new political order had evolved, based upon the fractious but efficacious functioning of two political parties.   By the time of the Glorious Revolution, the counsel of moderate men, committed to the preservation of England's balanced constitution, prevailed in both parties. Age-old liberties had been clarified and consolidated during the course of the seventeenth-century struggle between crown and Parliament.

As guidebooks to the English political system, Rapin's *History* and *Dissertation* were not lost on the continental audience for which they were designed. In particular it has been argued that Montesquieu's view of the English constitution derived mainly from Rapin's *Dissertation*.[31] Given the nature and influence of his works, Rapin deserves to be recognized as an early philosophe, or at least a direct antecedent of the philosophes. It is important, however, not to exaggerate Rapin's modernity. In several important respects his history recalled the traditionalist Echard more than it anticipated the philosophical history of Hume. No matter how perceptive Rapin was about the British political system, the fact was that the *History of England* was political history pure and simple, unleavened by any significant discussion of the economy or cultural history. And although Rapin treated his sources more critically than his predecessors had, he was no innocent in the art of paraphrase and compilation.[32] Rapin did not hesitate to criticize Burnet and other Parliamentarian-Whig historians. The fact, however, that he relied on Burnet more than any other single source suggests one limitation of his work. Despite his air of impartiality, Rapin's allegiances lay with the Whigs, and he was not above rehearsing or even occasionally copying the positions of his forebears.[33]

Rapin was a transitional figure in the history of eighteenth-century historical writing. His *History* commingled traditionalist elements of the compilation-chronicle mode with a more modern Enlightened approach. Writing from the vantage point of a foreigner who had observed English politics firsthand, Rapin was the first historian who appreciated the manner in which English historical writing had been twisted by partisan politics. Paradoxically, however, his moderate, levelheaded Whiggism made him a great favorite during the Whig hegemony of the early eighteenth century.

Rapin did much to shape the course of English historical writing in the second quarter of the eighteenth century. All subsequent historians, up to and including Hume, were responding to Rapin. Even as they criticized his political bias or his dubious credentials as a foreigner, they assumed many of his viewpoints and methods, including his secular orientation and his more explanatory, analytical style. Moreover, the success of Rapin's *History* helped put the Tories on the defensive. The classical Toryism of Clarendon, North, and Echard was no longer in vogue. That erstwhile Tory Lord Bolingbroke buttressed his attacks on Walpole's administration with a Whiggish historical commentary and frequent appeals to Rapin.

i i i

"It is somewhat surprising," wrote the English author of a pamphlet critique of Rapin's *History*, "that the only account of the English affairs which deserves the name of a history should be writ by a foreigner. Most of the English writers seem rather gazetteers and journalists than historians."[34]   Rapin's English audience expressed a rather grudging admiration for the Frenchman's achievement.   Despite this wounded national pride, Tindal's translation immediately supplanted all previous general histories.

The clearest and most immediate manifestation of Rapin's influence in England is to be found in the historical debate conducted in party newspapers during the 1730s. Rapin was cited and quoted more than any other historian. As Isaac Kramnick has shown, he exerted a particularly marked influence on Bolingbroke and the anti-ministerialist position.[35] Court and Country essayists were paid political propagandists who may or may not have believed what they wrote, but who were hired to fashion arguments with which to hammer the opposition. Hence they approached Rapin, like all their sources, with polemical, unscholarly intentions. They ransacked his works for historical arguments and precedents, the value of which was heightened by Rapin's prestige.

There were aspects of Rapin's *History* that Bolingbroke and his circle of *Craftsman* essayists found particularly congenial to their Country outlook. In his *Remarks on the History of England* and *Dissertation upon Parties*, both originally published in the *Craftsman*, Bolingbroke, in effect, fused Rapin's interpretation of history with a quasi-Harringtonian version of English social and economic history. This marked a major conceptual breakthrough. The ministerialist rebuttal to the *Craftsman* also employed a socioeconomic analysis that was considerably more coherent and sophisticated than in previous historical writing. Henceforth social and economic factors figured much more prominently in the general histories - not only in Hume's *History of England*, but in the works of his immediate predecessors William Guthrie and Thomas Carte, and in Catherine Macaulay's popular *History of England*, written to refute Hume. Two of the ablest mid-eighteenth century historians, William Guthrie and James Ralph, were temporarily associated with Bolingbroke's opposition circle of political writers in the early 1740s.

One reason why Bolingbroke's historical writings were criticized by scholars like D. C. Douglas was that Bolingbroke contributed nothing in terms of original research or the critical evaluation of evidence. He contemptuously dismissed the antiquarian scholars as "prating pedants," and there is no denying the fact that his historical essays were propaganda pieces, literary broadsides against his archenemy, Robert Walpole.

What was lost in original scholarship, however, was made up for in Bolingbroke's gift for generalization and explanation. Specifically, Bolingbroke combined a Harringtonian perspective of political power with Rapin's insights into the development of England's political parties.[36] Bolingbroke highlighted the structural, social aspect of history, avoiding providence and the excessive detail of the general histories. Rapin's influence can be seen in Bolingbroke's ancient constitutionalism and in his view that the constitution protected liberty until James I systematically attacked it. He reiterated Rapin's description of James I's reign as the seedbed of political parties and of the Civil War, and, like Rapin, he affirmed that the Glorious Revolution was a cooperative venture between Whigs and Tories. In both his *History* and *Dissertation* Rapin had bemoaned court corruption and the insidious influence of irresponsible courtiers like James I's favorite, the Duke of Buckingham. Bolingbroke and other Country writers quarried Rapin for illustrations of court corruption, drawing the obvious parallel with Robert Walpole and his "Robinocracy."

Bolingbroke also shared Rapin's secular conception of history, though the French historian was not the source of Bolingbroke's skepticism. Isaac Kramnick points to Bayle's influence on Bolingbroke.[37] Certainly he read widely among the works of many late seventeenth-early eighteenth-century freethinkers and deists. Bolingbroke was the first agnostical, "pagan" historian in England. In his *Letters on the Study and Use of History* we hear the voice of eighteenth-century rationalism, the mentor of Voltaire.

There were significant differences in the way Bolingbroke and Rapin interpreted English political history.   Whereas Rapin emphasized the threat to English freedom posed by tyrannical kings, Bolingbroke specified tyranny in the form of "faction" as the great danger.   The struggle between liberty and faction ran throughout English history. Bolingbroke saw the Glorious Revolution as a return to the original Anglo-Saxon constitution.   Rapin, by contrast, considered the Revolution to be a triumph for the old English spirit of liberty, not simply a restoration of the pristine constitution as it was handed down from the Anglo Saxons: Bolingbroke's ancient constitutionalism was, ironically, more Whiggish than Rapin's.

The chief difference was, of course, Bolingbroke's Harringtonian emphasis on economic change, the balance of property, which is nowhere to be found in Rapin. Why did the socioeconomic dimension take hold in the historical writing of the 1730s and continue thereafter at least through Hume's *History of England* in the 1750s?   Clearly one basic precondition was the growing secularization of thought and society. Since neither God nor the Church seemed so omnipresent as they once had, historians could begin exploring natural phenomena, including social and economic change. Two things happened in the course of the 1720s that served to crystallize the neo-Harringtonian ideology and economic interpretation of the Country party. The first was the South Sea Bubble in 1720. After this debacle, investment in the funds declined dramatically, and the monied interest became identified more than ever before with a small parasitic plutocracy.   More importantly, the Bubble temporarily shook what confidence people had grown to have in credit. It cast a cloud over the Whig financial innovations - the national debt, the Bank of England, and the East India Company. The South Sea Bubble seemed a shock of the new, a terrible portent, to many, of what the world of money held in store. As Kramnick puts it: "The ease with which the social order had been threatened and gentlemen made and unmade, would forever be identified with the Bubble and the new commercial order which produced it."[38]   Even though Bolingbroke and his circle advertised themselves as champions of the merchants and all fair-dealing businessmen, monied property - especially in the wake of the Bubble - was seen as ephemeral and intangible. Landed property was the enduring bedrock of society, and historians began to analyze its origins and evolution.[39]

A second development in the 1720s facilitated the rise of a socio-economic interpretation of history: Robert Walpole, largely because of his dexterous disposal of the South Sea scandal, finally rose to power. In the course of the 1720s Walpole not only institutionalized Whig rule, he seemed, from the Country point of view, to institutionalize the rule of money. Corruption, that favorite opposition bugbear, represented the fusion of monied property and politics. "Blest paper-credit," went a line by Pope, "that lends corruption lighter wings to fly."[40]

Bolingbroke's *Remarks on the History of England* and *Dissertation upon Parties* were intended to detail the rise and fall of the landed men in Tudor-Stuart England. Land embodied the spirit of liberty against the forces of tyranny, manifested currently by a parasitic, monied court. Under the ancient constitution of the Saxons the landed order was represented in the House of Commons. The flame of liberty flickered badly after the Norman Conquest but was not extinguished. With the coming of the Tudors in the sixteenth century it again burned brightly. Henry VII was an arbitrary ruler but he encouraged the growth of liberty and the transfer of wealth to the Commons by reducing the power of the nobility and stimulating the economy.[41] The aristocracy's decline and the commons' rise continued in Henry VIII's reign. Overseas trade grew, further increasing the profits and property of the merchants. But the great event of Henry's reign was, of course, the Reformation and, more particularly, the profound impact it had on English landownership. The land transfers following the dissolution finally tilted the balance irrevocably away from the peerage. With her unmatched political acumen, Elizabeth perceived that property and power now rested with the commons. Consequently, she forsook the strong-arm methods of her predecessors. Instead, she pursued a policy of consensus, wooing the commons and "the people" to support her policies.[42]

Harrington had made no attempt to idealize Elizabeth or the supposedly balanced constitution of her reign. But Bolingbroke's analysis was similar to Harrington's in laying the blame on the Stuarts for the breakdown in the established order. Harrington was more of an economic determinist than Bolingbroke. He argued that, given the shift of property away from the nobility to the commons, particularly to the gentry, the prevailing constitution was doomed. Maladroit Stuart policies simply precipitated the final dissolution. Nowhere in Bolingbroke's writings do we find him taking a strictly materialist view of historical change. Even in his discussion of the alterations in land ownership under the Tudors, Bolingbroke holds that the personal capacities and policies of the monarchs played a greater role in effecting these changes than impersonal social and economic forces.

By fashioning the interpretations of Harrington and Rapin into a new country view of history, Bolingbroke strove to lure the Tories away from their traditional Filmerite, High Flying notions of government and history. He combined a Whiggish political narrative with a glorification of landed society, geared to rally Country Whigs and Tories alike behind his new Country party. Thus in his brief discussion of the Later Stuarts, Bolingbroke railed against the popery and tyranny of Charles II and James II with the fervor of any Whig. He even praised the exclusionists of Charles II's reign. In the *Dissertation upon Parties*, published originally in the *Craftsman* during 1733 and 1734, Bolingbroke tried to show that the promise of the Glorious Revolution, to restore age-old English liberties, had been betrayed. The newly established constitutional safeguards were almost immediately undermined by the rise of faction and corruption.

If Bolingbroke could present himself as an Old Whig ancient constitutionalist, Walpole's hired pens quickly demonstrated that they could use traditional Tory historical arguments to good effect. Kramnick has shown how the Court Whigs, in response to the *Craftsman*'s telling essays, temporarily jettisoned ancient constitutionalism and turned to the Tory interpretation of Robert Brady. They countered the Country appeal to a golden age of freedom with the Tory-like assertion that liberty never existed in medieval England: "Reduced to their simplest terms, the historical positions of Bolingbroke and Walpole amount to little more than the simple device of brightening the present day by dimming the past, or vice versa."[43]

Walpole's press, the *Daily Gazetteer, Free Briton*, and *London Journal*, did more than merely rehash the views of Brady and Spelman. Court essayists such as Lord Hervey, Francis Arnall, and James Pitt elaborated upon Bolingbroke's Harringtonian analysis, contributing some original insights of their own. They followed Harrington's position, from which Bolingbroke had deviated, that from Saxon times to 1485 England slept in the darkness of feudalism and serfdom. The first glimmerings of liberty came in Henry VII's reign, at which time property began to shift from the lords to the commons. Walpole's essayists basically concurred with Bolingbroke in their account of the change in land distribution during the Tudor-Stuart era. They shared the Country view that the diffusion of property to the commons meant a growth of liberty in the state, since the commons represented the people. Paradoxically, however, they argued that real liberty did not exist in England until the Glorious Revolution. It was only with this great Whig achievement that the political system was brought into line with the new balance of property. The Revolution Settlement created a new constitutional order designed to defend liberty and property.

Even before Henry VII's reign, in discussing the origins of the House of Commons, Walpole's essayists pointed to economic developments that began slowly to sap the feudal system.[44] The growth of domestic manufactures like wool and tin contributed to the gradual dissolution of feudal tenures. The sixteenth-century price rise and the growth of overseas trade hurt the nobility but benefited those who, "by industry and frugality, became the purchasers of those lands which the lords squandered away in luxury."[45] As property was gradually transferred to the commons and "people" under the Tudors, liberty slowly took hold.[46] By Elizabeth's reign the balance of property had swung decisively in favor of the commons, and by the time the Long Parliament convened in 1640 the people possessed three fourths of the land in the nation. "No wonder then," commented a 1736 issue of the *Gazetteer*, "if they appeared zealous for liberty (which is only the security of property) and in the contentions that followed became able to subdue king, lords, and the Church."[47] Only with the Revolution of 1688 was the promise of liberty finally fulfilled. The "excellency and perfection of the Revolution" consisted in its "distinctly marking out the bonds between prerogative and liberty."[48]

Clearly the Harringtonian, social analysis of the English past was not monopolized by the Country writers. Neither was Robert Brady the only Tory historian to whom the Court writers turned. They frequently cited the "noble historian" Clarendon. How better to vindicate a Whig position - say, aspersions toward the Stuart kings - than to find seemingly corroborative testimony in the most prestigious Tory history? Not surprisingly, Burnet's *History of His Own Time* was also frequently cited.

No historian, however, was referred to as frequently and favorably as Rapin-Thoyras. As has been noted, Rapin's *History* and *Dissertation* lent themselves with particular facility to the Country philosophy that Bolingbroke was fashioning. In response to the *Craftsman*'s continuous citations of Rapin, the Court writers occasionally criticized the French historian. Far more often, however, they praised him and cited him as an authority. Consider the *London Journal*'s comment in September 1732:[49]

> Tis a pleasure to see such numbers of them sold every week. There is no treatise contributes so much to serve the interests of liberty and public virtue, because we see there what the constitution always was; the many alterations and variations from its original foundation, and at last how improved and completed by the Glorious Revolution.

Rapin's *History* stood high in the estimation of Bolingbroke and of Walpole's hired political writers. For all the differences between the *Craftsman* writers and Walpole's publicists, what is most striking about their historical writings is how much they had in common and how markedly their conception of history differed from that of historical writers only twenty years before. One obvious difference is that neither Walpole nor Bolingbroke propagated a Tory interpretation of English history. Country history as enunciated by Bolingbroke was a hybrid, a blend of traditional Whiggish ideas with a Toryish, nostalgic appeal to the virtues of landed society. The *Craftsman* proclaimed himself an Old Whig, championed ancient constitutionalism and the Whiggish Rapin, and denigrated the Stuarts as tyrants and Papists; there was more Whig than Tory in Country history.

Unlike the general histories of the Later Stuart era, the Court and Country historical essayists presented a fully secular view of English history. The economic side of history became far more coherent and developed in the newspaper essays than it had been in previous historical writing. The Court and Country essayists expanded upon Harrington's theme of property shifting during the Tudor-Stuart epoch from the barons and lords to the commons and people. The essays, partisan and polemical, were, nevertheless, elegantly written and occasionally penetrating reflections on English history.

Notes

[1]Quoted in Nelly Girard d'Albissin, *Un Precurseur de Montesquieu: Rapin-Thoyras* (Paris, 1969), 2.

[2]Margaret Jacob, *The Radical Enlightenment: Pantheists, Freemasons, and Republicans* (London, 1981), 94.

[3]*Ibid.*, 112-113, 148, 188-189.

[4]Linda Colley, *In Defiance of Oligarchy, The Tory Party, 1714-60* (Cambridge, 1982), 290. The traditional view of Whig hegemony is set forth in *The Whig Ascendancy: Colloquies on Hanoverian England*, ed. John Cannon (London, 1981).

[5]See Colley, 104-116 on the Tories and the Church.

[6]For discussion of the Country and Court ideologies see W. A. Speck, *Stability and Strife, England, 1714-1760* (Cambridge, Mass., 1977), 229; H. T. Dickinson, *Liberty and Property* (New York, 1977), 121-195; Isaac Kramnick, *Bolingbroke and his Circle* (Cambridge, Mass., 1965); Reed Browning, *Political and Constitutional Ideas of the Court Whigs* (Baton Rouge, 1982).

[7]Bibliographical information on Rapin is drawn from Raoul de Cazenove, *Rapin-Thoyras, sa familie, sa vie, et ses Oeuvres* (Paris, 1866), and from Nelly Girard d'Albissin, *Un Precurseur de Montesquieu: Rapin-Thoyras* (Paris, 1969), 18-25.

[8]Paul Hazard, *The European Mind* (1680-1715), trans, J. Lewis (London, 1953), 69. These "heralds" are described in Hazard, 69-71, and Margaret Jacob, *The Radical Enlightenment: Pantheists, Freemasons, and Republicans* (London, 1981), 122-128.

[9]See d'Albissin, 33, 110-113.

[10]See R. M. Wiles, *Serial Publication in England before 1750* (Cambridge, 1957), 96-97; "Middle Class Literacy in Eighteenth Century England: Fresh Evidence," in *Studies in the Eighteenth Century*, ed. R. F. Brissenden (Canberra, 1968), 57-58.

[11]*Grub Street Journal* number 247 (September 19, 1734).

[12]Paul de Rapin-Thoyras, *The History of England, as well Ecclesiastical as Civil, Done into English from the French, with large and useful notes (and a summary of the whole)* . . . *by N. Tindal*, 2 vols. (London, 1733), 2nd ed., II, 347-350.

[13]*Ibid.*, 349.

[14]*Ibid.*, 650.

[15]*Ibid.*, 745.

[16]*Ibid.*, 768.

[17]Paul de Rapin-Thoyras, *Dissertation on the Rise, Progress, Views, Strength, Interests, and Characters of the Two Parties of the Whigs and Tories*, trans. by Nicholas Tindal (London, 1733).   Originally published in 1717, the *Dissertation* was included and published with Tindal's translation of Rapin.

[18]See Joseph Hamburger, *Macaulay and the Whig Tradition* (Chicago, 1976), 138-139, and Herbert Butterfield, *The Englishman and His History* (Cambridge, 1944), 90-96.

[19]Rapin, History, II, 469.

[20]*Ibid.*, 212-213.

[21]*Ibid.*, I, 675-691.

[22]For Rapin's discussion of Henry VIII see *History*, I, 799-805.

[23]*Ibid.*, II, 65.

[24]*Ibid.*, 141.

[25]Rapin's sources for the early Stuart period included John Rushworth's *Collections*, Bulstrode Whitlocke's *Memorials*, Clarendon's *History*, John Nalson's *Impartial Collection*, Thomas Frankland's *Annals*, Edmund Ludlow's *Memoirs*, Arthur Wilson's *Life of James I*, John Hacket's *Scrinia*

Reserata, Archbishop Spottiswood's *History of the Church of Scotland*, Richard Cox's *Hibernia Anglicana*, and an early volume of *the State Tracts*. Rapin also made good use of Echard's *History*.

[26]*Ibid.*, 160. For James' reign see 159-236.

[27]*Ibid.*, 371-455.

[28]*Ibid.*, 574.

[29]*Ibid.*, 602.

[30]For his discussion of the later Stuart Period, Rapin's principal sources included - in addition to those previously cited, which extended into the late seventeenth century - Thomas Sprat's *History of the Royal Society*, John Strype's *Additions to Stow*, James Welwood's *Memoirs*, Josiah Burchett's naval history, the French ambassador Count d'Estrades' *Letters and Negotiations*, Roger L'Estrange's along with the histories of Burnet, Kennett, and Echard.

[31]See d'Albissin, 123.

[32]Rapin's paraphrasings are sometimes near carbon copies of his sources. Take, for example, Rapin's character portrait of Charles II at the time of the Restoration in 1660. Tindal's translation observes the following:

> He had, besides this, a maxim not much less dangerous, namely, that there was neither sincerity nor chastity in the world out of principle, but that some had the one or the other out of humour or vanity; and believed nobody served him out of love, and therefore he was quits with all the world, and loved others as little as he thought they loved him.

Rapin's diction here nearly duplicates Burnet's description of Charles II:

> He had a very ill opinion of both men and women; and did not think that there was either sincerity of chastity in the world, out of principle, but that some had either the one, or the other, out of humour or vanity. He thought that nobody did serve him out of

love: and so he was quits with all the world, and loved others as little as he thought they loved him.

See Rapin, II, 618; Gilbert Burnet, *The History of His Own Time* (London, 1857), 61.

[33]Rapin was also apparently willing to tailor *The History of England* in order to placate men in authority. In 1719 Rapin wrote to Jean de Roberthon, a counsellor to George I, asking if the *History* could be dedicated to the king. Rapin expressed concern that his unflattering portrait of James I, a distant ancestor of the Hanoverian family, might offend the English king. He offered to suppress his account of James' reign, closing his *History* with the death of Elizabeth, if it would please the king and his ministers. His concerns were apparently unfounded and the *History* was, in fact, dedicated to George I.

[34][William Duncombe], *Remarks on Mr. Tindal's translation of Monsr. de Rapin Thoyras's History of England* (London, 1728), 1.

[35]See Isaac Kramnick, ed., *Lord Bolingbroke. Historical Writings* (Chicago and London, 1972), xviii, xxiii; Kramnick, *Bolingbroke and His Circle* (Cambridge, Mass., 1965), 181, 258. Duncan Forbes, *Hume's Philosophical Politics* (Cambridge, 1975), 240-245.

[36]This point is made by Duncan Forbes; see Forbes, *Hume's Philosophical Politics* (Cambridge, 1975), 240-245.

[37]Kramnick, *Lord Bolingbroke, Historical Writings*, xxviii-xxxix.

[38]Kramnick, *Bolingbroke and His Circle*, 68.

[39]Speck, 225.

[40]Quoted in Speck, 225.

[41]Kramnick, *Lord Bolingbroke, Historical Writings*, 41.

[42]*Ibid.*, 238-244.

[43]Kramnick, *Bolingbroke and His Circle*, 136.

[44]See *Daily Gazetteer* number 353 (August 13, 1736), number 383 (September 17, 1736), number 447 (January 3, 1737), number 633 (July 22, 1737); *London Journal* number 772 (April 13, 1734); *Free Briton* number 248 (August 1, 1734).

[45]*Daily Gazetteer* number 30 (August 2, 1735).

[46]*Ibid.*, number 426 (November 6, 1736).

[47]*Ibid.*, number 24 (July 26, 1735).

[48]*Ibid.*, number 426 (November 6, 1736).

[49]*London Journal* number 696 (September 28, 1732). For other favorable comments on Rapin, see *Free Briton* number 248 (August 1, 1734); *London Journal* number 772 (April 13, 1734); *Daily Gazetteer* number 353 (August 13, 1736); *ibid.*, (September 17, 1736); *ibid.*, number 477 (January 3, 1737).

Chapter IV

The Whig Liberals: John Oldmixon and Daniel Neal

Two historians in the second quarter of the eighteenth century, John Oldmixon and Daniel Neal, articulated a liberal Whig viewpoint that went well beyond the cautious moderation of Rapin and the polemical but establishmentarian commentaries of the ministerial and opposition press. In the histories of Oldmixon and Neal, Puritans and Whigs are presented as valiant defenders of liberty and property against arbitrary princes and a persecuting Church. The right to liberty and toleration is rooted in natural law, as is the right to resist and overthrow arbitrary governments. Both authors were critical of the Church, but Oldmixon was much more secular-minded than the Congregationalist minister Neal. Although the two historians shed light on the popular involvement in politics that had been ignored by previous historians, and Neal's *History of the Puritans* in particular was a work of enduring scholarly merit, neither author matched the level of performance set by Rapin.

i

One infrequent contributor to the *Gazetteer* in the 1730s was John Oldmixon. A perfervid Whig, Oldmixon wrote, among many other works, three folio volumes of sustained historical polemic, in which he glorified his Puritan and Whig heroes and denounced his Royalist and Tory villains. A miscellaneous writer of prodigious output, Oldmixon's career epitomizes the hazardous life and times of the eighteenth-century Grub Street hack.[1] He was born in Bristol, the son of a Dissenting merchant, and first tried his hand in the field of belles-lettres. His attempts at poetry and drama met with little success. A new beginning for Oldmixon came in 1710 when he took up journalism. He became the principal writer of the Whig *Medley,* and as the leading authority on Oldmixon observes, "his vehement prose could match anything Swift, Defoe, or Steele produced at this junction."[2]

After the Hanoverian Accession, however, Oldmixon began a long descent into adversity and neglect. The government appointed him

collector of the customs for the port of Bridgewater in 1716, a post he
disliked because Bridgewater was a hotbed of Toryism and far removed
from London. Apparently Oldmixon bungled his job and lost his pension.
He ran badly into debt, though a grant from the royal bounty in 1735
cleared him of his obligations. In that same year he officially left his post,
having already returned to London some time in the early 1730s.
Throughout the 1720s and '30s Oldmixon was only occasionally patronized
by Walpole and was not one of his regular hired pens.

It was in Bridgewater during the 1720s that Oldmixon took up
history writing. In his *Memoirs of the Press* (1742), written shortly before
his death, Oldmixon recalled how he decided to try his hand at history.
He first entertained the idea of writing a history of the Stuarts in 1717:[3]

> I was impatient to set about the *History of England* while I was in
> that remote corner of the kingdom, having collected materials
> sufficient for it, not doubting but they would enable me to deal with
> these histories, Clarendon's and Echard's, as I had done by the
> *Examiner*, having truth on my side, having a just contempt for the
> poverty of one and the *pussines* (sic) of the other . . . .

Clarendon's *History*, in particular, was so popular and prestigious that
Oldmixon feared maligning it and hesitated to do so for several years.
Finally, in 1724 Oldmixon's *The Critical History of England* appeared.
The book met with considerable success in sales - "thousands dispersed in
a short time."[4]

The *Critical History* lambasted Clarendon and Echard, with occasional
thrusts at Kennett as well. It was fiercely partisan. Oldmixon's ancient
constitutionalism was of the undiluted Edward Coke-James Tyrell variety.
He announced his view that the purpose of history was "to set people
right in that which most concerns them, their religious and civil liberties,
and justify the proceedings of the present age by those of the past."[5]
Specifically, this meant showing how the defenders of the constitution had
historically resisted tyrannical rule, especially by the Stuarts, and exposing
the pseudo-historical propagandists for arbitrary government, like
Clarendon and Echard. It is noteworthy that Oldmixon's complaints
against these historians did not spring solely from partisan motives. He
also assailed the style and form of their massive compilations: "There's

no life, no color, in the dead draughts of your copyers, collectors, and compilers, who have lately usurped the name of historians."[6]

Oldmixon recorded that it took him three years to write the history of the Stuarts, the first of his general history volumes. He claimed that it sold well and "gave the Clarendine history such a blow that it has ever since been low in the market, and is not now named as an authority anywhere out of the hearing of Christ Church bells."[7] Not content with this boast, Oldmixon went so far as to credit his *History of England* under the Royal House of Stuart with the virtual destruction of Jacobitism and Toryism. In actuality, however, this work was never reprinted after the first edition and was not nearly so influential as Oldmixon made out.[8] In this work Oldmixon made his notorious and groundless charge that the Oxford editors of Clarendon's *History* had falsified portions of his text. This provoked a storm of abuse. Despite the obloquy heaped upon Oldmixon for his spurious charge, Queen Caroline reportedly had a Treasury annuity conferred on him as reward for his historical labors. Although it was probably no higher than the hundred pounds per year he had been receiving as a customs official, it enabled him to return to London. Here he could find further materials for his histories.

Oldmixon believed that his move to London, combined with his receiving a pension, gave rise to baseless rumors that he was a court hack. This image of him was no doubt strengthened by the fact that at least twice in the 1730s he criticized Rapin's *History of England* in the *Daily Gazetteer*, making the common complaint that as a foreigner Rapin did not fully understand the English constitution - in other words, that he was not Whiggish enough. At the same time, Oldmixon recommended his own *History of England* as a corrective to Rapin.[9]

In any event, only 350 people subscribed to the *History of England during the Reigns of King William and Queen Mary, Queen Anne and George I* (1735).[10] A still worse fate awaited Oldmixon's final volume, the *History of England under the Royal House of Tudor* (1739). Oldmixon's publishers refused to finance the book unless he could guarantee a satisfactory number of subscribers in advance. In his *Memoirs* Oldmixon said, "This they had not done before, and alleged for reason their doing so now that they did not know whether the prejudices taken against me as a court writer would not hurt the book."[11] Oldmixon further lamented the fact that at about this time his modest Treasury pension was terminated. The upshot was that Oldmixon had to publish the Tudor volume himself, his former publishers Cox and Hett acting only as agents.

Oldmixon was never one of Walpole's regular pens in the manner of Francis Arnall or James Pitt, and he felt he had not been properly rewarded for his heroic services to the Whig cause. At the same time Oldmixon complained about the government's turning a cold shoulder to him in the 1720s and '30s, he, paradoxically, vigorously proclaimed his independence from the court. He dedicated works to a variety of Whigs - Court and Country, ins and outs - including, besides Walpole, the Earl of Sunderland, George Bubb Dodington, the Duke of Argyll, and the Prince of Wales.[12]

Oldmixon, as Pat Rogers informs us, was "a brave and imprudent man, not addicted to trimming his sails."[13] To read Oldmixon's histories is to learn more about the nature of his Whiggery and why his political ideals may have distanced him from the government. An anonymous forward to *Memoirs of the Press*, written after Oldmixon's death, suggested that "the ill treatment he met with was perhaps owing to the freedom with which he asserted some Old Whig principles, not altogether coincident with modern ones." Indeed, the views expressed in Oldmixon's histories disclose a more radical Whiggery, a penchant for the Old Cause, not to be found in the Whiggish histories of the moderate Kennett-Burnet-Rapin variety, or, to a lesser extent, in the Court historical essays. Oldmixon wrote history, he said, to show that "English charters, being founded on the original right of the people, warranted them in resisting arbitrary power, spiritual and temporal tyranny."[14] As works of scholarship, Oldmixon's histories foundered on the reefs of the author's violent Whiggism. They were extensions of his earlier political propaganda. Oldmixon was not really interested in explaining how events unfolded. He wrote to glorify his Whig heroes and their Puritan-Parliamentarian forefathers and to denounce their adversaries: arbitrary kings, including the Tudors, and, more often than not, the Church of England. From the Elizabethan Presbyterians to the Puritan Independents to the eighteenth-century Dissenters, Oldmixon's champions of liberty and property were usually outside the ecclesiastical Establishment. He did not hesitate to chastise earlier historians, be they Whig or Tory, whom he felt were on the side or persecution.

The theme of Oldmixon's Tudor volume, as set forth in his preface, was to show what "mischiefs" and misfortune sprang from the "persecuting spirit."[15] He pictures Henry VIII not as a strong-willed fighter against popery but as a persecuting tyrant. He condemns the notorious Six Articles and the arbitrary power of ecclesiastical courts, "always ready to pick the pocket of sober Christians . . . . How lovingly persecution and tyranny walk hand in hand." Oldmixon pounces on a few sympathetic words by Echard and Burnet toward Mary Tudor, accusing the two clerics of only "pretending to be Protestants." Although Oldmixon admires Elizabeth as a skilled ruler, she does not escape his shafts: she should have encouraged religious freedom and instituted a thorough reformation, but she was duped by the bishops, the main agents of persecution.

In his *History of England under the Stuarts*, Oldmixon declared that his intention was to elucidate the seventeenth-century struggle to preserve "the Protestant religion and liberty."[16] What soon becomes apparent is that to Oldmixon the truest Protestants in the period were the Puritans, who by 1641 were "by much the greater body of English Protestants." He goes so far as to describe episcopacy as a "Romish remnant." The previous Whig historians whom we have considered gave qualified support to the Puritan-Presbyterian wing of the Parliamentarian party, at least up the start of the Civil War. They, however, had nothing but abuse for the Independents. Such is not the case with Oldmixon. Chiding the Presbyterians for being fainthearted and intolerant, Oldmixon contends that the Puritan Independents spoke for the people of England: "This party distinguished themselves by a zeal for a thorough reformation in Church and state, and were, for the most part, republicans."[17] But Oldmixon has no words of sympathy for the Levellers and lays part of the blame on them for the king's death. More guilty, however, were the Cavaliers and king's counsellors who steered Charles on his tyrannical and disastrous course.[18]

In *The History of England during the Reigns of King William and Queen Mary, Queen Anne and King George I* we find that the Puritans have passed on the standard of liberty to their Dissenting heirs. Oldmixon advocates complete religious freedom for all Protestants as a natural right. He scoffs at Kennett's contention that of all the sects, the Quakers were least deserving of toleration, "as if liberty of conscience, to which every man has as natural a right as to the air he breathes, was owing only to the condescension of those who claim authority by such Establishment."[19]

Discussing the issues raised about toleration and comprehension in 1689, Oldmixon assails all "ecclesiastical writers of civil history" in general, and Kennett in particular, because "they distrust the truth and attack everyone in history who goes against the Church."[20]   The fact that Oldmixon completely supports Bishop Hoadly's position in the Bangorian controversy indicates that he did not believe the state should guarantee the special rights and privileges of the Established Church.[21]

Oldmixon always avowed in print that he was a good Church of England member.   But his parents were Dissenters and he was said to have attended Presbyterian and Anabaptist conventicles in Bridgewater. Certainly on the basis of his histories it can be safely concluded that his sympathies rested wholeheartedly with the Protestant Nonconformists and their Puritan forebears.   This reader has not found one positive statement about the institution of episcopacy.   Though we occasionally come across the odd good bishop in Oldmixon's narrative, the hierarchy as a whole is regularly on the side of persecution and tyranny.   This attitude toward the Church distinguished Oldmixon from the Court historical writers. Walpole's journalists advocated religious liberty, but this did not mean complete civil rights for Dissenters or an attack on the privileged position of the Church.

Besides being in the vanguard of liberty, the Puritans and Dissenters in Oldmixon's histories are the most prosperous members of society. Oldmixon is at pains to repudiate the Royalist-Tory image of the Puritans and Parliamentarians in the Civil War as the rabble and dregs of the population.   By the late 1630s the Puritans "had about nine parts in ten of the trade in this country."   The Puritan emigres to America during the Eleven Years Tyranny were "the most quiet, industrious people in the country."[22]   Most of the businessmen and many of the gentry were Puritans, but not the peerage.   Whatever period he is discussing, Oldmixon makes it clear that the "vulgar sort" - laborers and peasants - were in the enemy's camp, manipulated by Papists, Royalists, and Tories.[23]

There are occasional passages in Oldmixon that seem to link the prosperity of the Puritans and Nonconformists in Weberian fashion to a Protestant business ethic.   At one point, for example, he refers to the Dissenters' "sobriety and industry, and the usual effects of them, trade and substance."[24]   The central thrust of Oldmixon's remarks, however, is not that Protestantism fostered business acumen but that Protestantism stood for liberty and that liberty nourished trade.[25]

Oldmixon was no democrat, and he was no less disdainful of "the rabble" than Burnet or Echard had been. However, Oldmixon invoked "the people" - by which he seems to mean all substantial property holders - far more often than earlier historians. He gloried in the people's right to revolt so long as it was not the kind of social revolution he thought the Levellers stood for. He bemoaned, for example, the failure of Wyatt's Rebellion against Mary Tudor.[26] The conventional Whiggery of the day did not exalt Parliament's taking up arms against Charles I, but that is precisely what Oldmixon does. He denounces Echard for holding that it was illegal for the people to rebel against the crown in 1640, "a rare doctrine for the people of this day."[27] Oldmixon's sanction of revolution is indicated by his strongly favorable treatment of that apotheosis of revolution, Oliver Cromwell. The Commonwealth "raised the reputation of England from the lowest depth and disgrace and shame to the highest degree of honor and renown . . . . If we should run back to the origin of the power of all the most famous republics and empires, shall we not find it as criminal as that of the Commonwealth of England?"[28]

Oldmixon was the first historian to praise John Locke, hailing him as "the greatest philosopher of the age."[29] He defends religious liberty in Lockean terms, referring specifically to Locke's *Letters on Toleration.*[30] Oldmixon does not, however, give a Lockean explanation of the Glorious Revolution. That is, he does not suggest that the civil government reverted to the state of nature after James II broke the original contract upon which the state was originally constructed. Rather, the original contract, in Oldmixon's history, was an age-old contract between king and Parliament to uphold the laws and liberty of the realm. Until the seventeenth century it had been regularly reiterated by successive monarchs in the coronation oaths. Oldmixon refers repeatedly to man's natural rights, but he commingles this with appeals to the ancient constitution.

With Oldmixon, even more than with Rapin, we have arrived at a full-blown liberal Whiggism, characterized by an affirmation of the natural right of religious freedom, support for the political rights of the propertied classes including the right of resistance, praise for constitutional monarchy, and for the economic benefits conferred by liberty and Protestantism. To this list should be added the secular, anti-clerical tone of the histories, which is even more pronounced in Oldmixon than in Rapin. Like Rapin, Oldmixon will occasionally bring providence into his narrative. In the preface to his Stuart volume, for example, he submits that "good providence interposed" to deliver the English people from tyranny during the Reformation and the Revolution of 1688.[31] Only on a handful of other instances does Oldmixon appeal to providence, and his conception of divine intervention is more abstract than was customary. God set the general course of history; but Oldmixon rarely falls back upon providence to explain historical events in his narrative. Assailing the notions of providence held by "ecclesiastical" historians, Oldmixon avowed that:[32]

> if I took the same liberty with divine providence as the reverend historians do, I could not avoid applying all the dreadful calamities of this and the following year (1665-6) - war, plague, and fire - to the judgment of heaven, for the lewdness, profaneness, deceit, and cruelty of the times . . . . I always dread to make judgments where it may be heaven left things to second causes, though nothing is more common in Echard and other ecclesiastical writers.

Oldmixon gives no credence whatsoever to the more bizarre tales of the supernatural found in Echard's history, such as his tale of Oliver Cromwell's conversation with the Devil. Oldmixon affirmed that he was "very far from visionary or credulous . . . . I do not think we are justified in imputing to the first cause, what second causes may very naturally produce, which makes me very cautious in interpreting common incidents as judgments."[33]

Oldmixon scorned Church history as a trivial exercise in which general historians should not engage. Even apparently religious disputes were actually secular in nature, "more temporal than spiritual."[34] His curt dismissal of the Convocation controversy indicates this attitude: "I have taken very little notice of the Convocation history of England, it being, as the revenue clerks say, a nil account."[35] When he attacks rival historians such as Echard, Kennett, Zachary Grey, and even sometimes Burnet, it is not only because their political views did not measure up to his Whig purism but because, as "ecclesiastical writers of civil history," they inevitably distorted the truth.[36]

Oldmixon, even more than the party historical essayists, shows how liberal political attitudes had seeped into the historical writing of the 1720s and 1730s. By the exacting criteria of Enlightenment historiography, however - a fully secular, non-providential view of history, an explanatory narrative that conveyed a sense of historical change, an appreciation of social, economic, and cultural history and of the fact that history was more than merely a form of political propaganda - Oldmixon's works do not qualify as philosophical history. They do not represent a significant advance over previous general histories and are certainly inferior to Rapin's *History of England*. Oldmixon possessed a static conception of English history. He reduced the intricate tapestry of historical change to a Manichean struggle between the forces of darkness and light - between the Whigs and their forefathers who stood for the ancient constitution on the one hand and the Tories and their ancestors who championed tyranny on the other. Oldmixon's scheme did not allow for any discussion of how English society and institutions had evolved, beyond making the point that the Hanoverian Whig government now defended and buttressed the time-honored liberties of Englishmen.

Oldmixon was not insensitive to the formal and stylistic drawbacks of historical compilation. He criticized "your copyers, collectors, and compilers" for writing lifeless prose and smothering their narrative in a morass of excessive detail. When denouncing that "sycophant and hireling," William Camden, Oldmixon observes that he typified "the whole herd of heralds, genealogists, monasticists, Gothic antiquaries, pedantic academics, and interested priests."[37] Bolingbroke and any number of philosophes would have said, and did say, much the same thing; they scorned the chroniclers and annalists as pedantic scribblers. Oldmixon admired August De Thou, Francesco Guicciardini, and even Gilbert Burnet for their exemplary prose style.

In his own histories, however, Oldmixon practiced the traditional art of historical compilation, revealing too few flashes of his distinctive, vivid style. Relying upon the familiar printed histories, lives, and collections that previous historians had already, in most cases, made extensive use of, Oldmixon quoted, paraphrased, or plagiarized long extracts.[38] Not surprisingly, he drew heavily upon Parliamentarian and Whig authors, including the republican regicide Edmund Ludlow, whom he admired. The mass of transcriptions and conflated or reworded texts impeded the elaboration of a clear narrative.

Despite Oldmixon's extreme partisanship - or, paradoxically, **because** of it - he managed to make several acute perceptions about English political history.   He shared with Walpole's essayists the Court Whig position that Elizabeth's reign should not be idealized as a golden age of liberty. A skilled statesman, Elizabeth often acted arbitrarily, as when she imprisoned Peter Wentworth and other Parliamentarian critics. Oldmixon recognized what Rapin and earlier historians did not - that Elizabeth was no Parliamentary monarch in the manner of the Hanoverian kings and that the contrast between her government and that of her Stuart successors should not be overdrawn.

Like Rapin, Oldmixon also had a keen awareness of the role of political parties in recent English history, however distorted and tendentious this conception may have been. Unlike Rapin, though, Oldmixon did not recognize parties as an integral part of the constitution. The party alignment shifted in the course of the seventeenth century from Cavalier-Parliamentarian to Tory-Whig.   Oldmixon makes it clear that the "pretended" Country Party under William and Anne was in actuality the Tory Party, masquerading as defenders of the constitution against a tyrannical court. The obvious implication was that the Country opposition to Walpole was also Tory. He brands the Tories as backwoods foxhunters and Jacobites and specifically identifies the *Craftsman* circle as Tory.[39]

John Oldmixon was a liberal Whig, a disciple of Locke. But though an ardent defender of Walpole's government, Oldmixon cannot be pigeonholed as a Court Whig writer. His ancient constitutionalism, his ringing declarations of the people's right to resist and rebel, his scorn for the Church, and his cavalier treatment of moderate Whig historians - all of these positions distinguished Oldmixon's historical and political outlook from that of the establishment Court whigs, that "curious junta of political speculators and speculative politicians, stock-jobbers, officers grown fat on Marlborough's wars, time-serving dependents in the law and the church, and great landed magnates," as a modern radical historian portrays them.[40]

Of course the mere fact that a writer's political views were those of a liberal Whig does not mean he would write successful histories, and Oldmixon did not. History, to Oldmixon, was merely a weapon with which to fight the Tories. The uninspired task of historical compilation was sufficient to this task. There was one way in which a liberal perspective on history could potentially enhance historical inquiry where Toryism could not. Lockean liberalism was secular. Oldmixon shared with Rapin and the Court and Country historical essayists a suspicion of appeals to providence or preternatural power. In his secularism Oldmixon was closer to the Enlightenment school of Hume than to the traditionalist Echard.

Also, like Rapin and, later, Hume, Oldmixon preferred to concentrate on political history rather than on military campaigns, which disinterested him. Although he was sensitive to socioeconomic conflicts in history and duly vindicated the Whig business community and thriving landowners against the improvident and debt-ridden Tory gentry, Oldmixon did not elucidate an economic interpretation of history in the way that the Court and Country writers did. In short, his ponderously constructed compilations, though written by a man whose philosophy was more secular and modern than most of his predecessors, derived their narrative style and form from the pre-Enlightenment conventions of historical writing.

i i

A liberal Whig, Oldmixon claimed that he was loyal to the Church of England, though in fact his heroes were mostly Puritans and Protestant Nonconformists. Daniel Neal's, *The History of the Puritans*, which was for all intents and purposes a general history of England, was also written from a liberal Protestant perspective, but an explicitly Dissenting one.[41] Neal, who subscribed to Oldmixon's histories, produced the closest thing we have to an official Dissenting history of England, one that glorified the contribution of Puritanism to the growth of English liberty.

Born in London in 1678, Neal was educated first at the Merchant Taylors' School and then from about 1696 to 1699 at Thomas Rowe's Dissenting academy.[42] Rowe's school was well known for cultivating the values of tolerance and free inquiry, values extolled by Neal both as minister and historian. Upon leaving Rowe's academy Neal studied for two years at Dutch universities, breathing in the liberal intellectual atmosphere of Utrecht and Leiden. He became an assistant London minister in 1704 and was ordained as pastor at Loriners' Hall in 1706. A prominent London minister, Neal befriended such eminent Dissenters as Phillip Doddridge and Isaac Watts.

Neal was a popular preacher and carried out his clerical duties sedulously. Yet he managed to find time for historical research. His first notable work, the two-volume *History of New England*, appeared in 1720. It won a popular audience in the American colonies, earning Neal na honorary degree from Harvard University in 1721. In 1722 he produced *A Narrative of the Method and Success of Inoculating the Small Pox in New England*, also popular in America, which championed Lady Mary Wortley Montagu's efforts to promote inoculation for small pox against the prejudices of the medical and clerical establishment. Neal's pamphlet caught the attention of Princess Caroline who complimented Neal personally, discussed with him the status of Dissent in England, and introduced him to the Prince of Wales.

The first volume of Neal's *History of the Puritans* appeared in 1732, but the idea of producing such a work was seriously entertained many years earlier by leading Dissenting clergy, including Edmund Calamy III and John Evans.[43] The moving spirit behind the project was Evans, who was inspired by the success of Calamy's *Abridgement of Mr. Baxter's History of His Life and Times* (1702).[44] The plan called for Evans to write the first section of the history, covering the period from the Reformation to 1640, and for Neal to take the final part, from 1640 to 1688. Having collected some of the source materials for the work, Evans died in 1730 and Neal assumed full responsibility.

The years in which *The History of the Puritans* was published coincided with a campaign to repeal the Test and Corporation Acts barring Nonconformists from public and municipal office.[45] Dissenting deputies representing all the Dissenting congregations in and around London began applying to Parliament for repeal in 1732. The first Parliamentary committee to consider the application, lobbied heavily by the Congregationalists, was ineffectual and allegedly bribed by Walpole. Motions for repeal went down to defeat in the House of Commons in 1736 and again in 1739. Almost half a century passed before the campaign for repeal was renewed.

It is apparent from the prefaces to Neal's successive volumes that *The History of the Puritans* was intended as a massive historical argument for the abolition of the Test and Corporation Acts.[46] The Dissenters are described as "his majesty's most dutiful and loyal subjects," unfairly penalized. Neal specifically endorses the ongoing effort "to petition for a repeal or amendment of these acts." He did not confine his brief for religious freedom to the Protestant Nonconformists: "Enthusiasts or Jews have an equal right with Christians to worship God in their own way. . . as long as they keep the peace and maintain no principles manifestly inconsistent with the safety of the government they live under." Since, according to Neal, Roman Catholics at present posed a threat to the state, they should not be granted complete religious toleration.

Although Neal disapproved of the Whig government's continued maintenance of the penal laws, he was nonetheless a firm supporter of Robert Walpole's administration. In a 1733 *A Letter from a Dissenter to the author of the Craftsman* - the main opposition journal - Neal rejected the pseudonymous Caleb D'Anver's call for Dissenters to ally with reformed Tories and join the new Country Party, striving to dislodge the tyrannical Court faction. Extolling the present "free constitution" and Bishop Benjamin Hoadly's latitudinarian views, Neal submitted that the ministerial "friends of liberty" had probably delayed repeal because they feared the Tories would exploit such action to incite "Church in Danger" rioting.[47]

Neal presented the historical case for repeal - and countered the aspersions of pro-Royalist historians like the Earl of Clarendon and John Walker - by depicting the Dissenters' Puritan ancestors as paladins of liberty and the English constitution.[48] "All the arguments against the growth of the prerogative," Neal wrote, "are said to be founded on Puritan principles."[49] Neal differed from other early eighteenth-century historians in treating liberty not as a cornerstone of the ancient constitution or a product of the Glorious Revolution, but as the fruit of Tudor-Stuart Puritanism. Not unlike William Haller in his classic *Rise of Puritanism* (1938), Neal defined liberty as an outgrowth of Puritan individualism. Protestantism, especially Calvinist Protestantism, had libertarian implications because it taught that each individual must seek religious truth in Scripture. Puritanism recognized "the natural right that every man has to judge for himself and make profession of that religion he apprehends most agreeable to truth in the light of Scripture."[50] Here we see the individualist thrust of the Puritan conscience. The state had no business prescribing what was acceptable religious behavior and what was not. The logic of this position led Neal to advocate the separation of Church and state: The Established Church, with its state monopoly on religious observance, should be replaced by an "Official" Church without legal constraints.[51]

The History of the Puritans begins with a relatively brief overview of the Reformation prior to Queen Elizabeth. The Henrician Reformation, Neal argues, derived from personal and dynastic motives, not from religious scruple. The Reformation gradually took a more Protestant direction under King Edward, but was marred from the start by the alienation of Church lands and by religious persecution.[52] Elizabeth's position as Supreme Governor of the Church ran counter to Neal's notions of religious freedom. Her absolute powers were not:[53]

> agreeable with the natural or religious rights of mankind . . . . The powers of the civil magistrate seem chiefly to regard the civil welfare of his subjects: he is to protect them in their properties, and in the peaceable enjoyment of their civil and religious rights.

A successful supporter of foreign Protestant powers abroad, at home Elizabeth was persecutive and arbitrary.

Neal's analysis of Puritanism was his most important contribution to English historical scholarship. He was the first historian to delineate the phases and varieties of Tudor-Stuart Puritanism, describing the Presbyterians, the separatists, and the reformers who wanted changes only in ritual and ceremony.[54] He recounts the stormy history of prophesyings and sabbatarianism, the growth of Puritan lecturers, and Archbishop Laud's efforts to suppress them. The Crown's imposition of the Book of Sports and Puritan opposition to it are duly explained.[55]

Neal's discussion of the Early Stuarts ran to 700 folio pages, forming the centerpiece of his narrative. His interpretation of the period drew upon Rapin's history of England. Neal, who judged Rapin to be "accurate and judicious," adopted the French historian's position that James I bore most of the blame for moving the kingdom toward civil war.[56] Both Rapin and Neal divided the opposition into "church Puritans" ("those who scrupled the ceremonies and espoused the doctrines of Calvin") and "state Puritans" ("those who stood by the law of the land" against James' arbitrary government).[57] By the reign of Charles I, the church Puritans were no longer Presbyterians but supporters of "moderate episcopacy."

The Puritans in Charles I's reign were the "majority of the nation" against the papists and Arminians who backed the king.[58]

"Terrible were the triumphs of arbitrary power," writes Neal of the early Stuart period, "over the liberty and property of the subject."[59] Puritanism was much more than a specific religious movement. Neal presents it as the embodiment of liberty, the spirit of resistance against tyrannical government. His concept of Puritanism was so amorphous that economic and political concerns figure more prominently than strictly religious issues. Economic factors were of primary importance. James I squandered away the patrimony of the crown, leaving his son debt-ridden.[60] In order to become solvent, Charles I resorted to illegal and oppressive financial expedients. These exactions - ship money, purveyances, monopolies - threatened property rights: "No man could call anything his own longer than the King pleased; or might speak or write against these proceedings without utmost hazard of his liberty and estate."[61] Trade was shackled because "almost every branch of it was engrossed and sold by the crown for large sums of money."[62] Puritanism, in Neal's account, is virtually synonymous with liberty, and one offspring of liberty is property. Considering the merchants' opposition to Stuart economic policy, it is not surprising that Neal sees an economic division between Royalists and Parliamentarians: "the nobility and gentry with their dependents being chiefly with the King; the merchants, tradesmen, substantial farmers, and in general the middle ranks of people siding with the Parliament."[63]

Neal's discussion of the Puritan Revolution makes far more of "the people's" contribution to the Parliamentarian cause than was customary in Augustan historical writing. Although he will occasionally scorn the "debauched rabble," Neal recognizes that popular involvement in the Revolution, particularly by the City crowd, was a vital ingredient in the political and military success of Parliament.[64] He praises the apprentices and artisans as valiant defenders of liberty. Drawing primarily upon John Rushworth's *Historical Collection of Private Passages of State* (1659-1701), Neal skillfully details popular political agitation in London during the 1640s. He discusses the "incredible" number of petitions presented to Parliament by representatives of the crowd against the Laudian bishops. He describes the popular disturbances directed against the altar rails and other "popish" innovations in the churches, and also the huge crowds at Westminster who threatened violence toward those M.P.s voting against

Strafford's attainder. Most M.P.s disliked the popular tumults but realized that "their chief strength was among the inhabitants of London" and so did nothing to quell them.[65]

The London crowd consisted primarily of what Neal called "the middle ranks of people": merchants, tradesmen, artisans, shopkeepers, and apprentices - rather than the laboring poor. It is not surprising that Neal endorsed the political agitation of Puritan merchants and artisans when we consider the fact that most Dissenters in the eighteenth century were also middle-class merchants and artisans.[66]

Neal extols the Independents above all other parties in the Revolution because they fought for freedom of conscience. Unlike most historians of his era, Neal lionizes Oliver Cromwell as a thoroughgoing Independent.[67] His Protectorate marked the reign of Independency and "was carried on with the most consummate wisdom, resolution, and success."[68] Whatever strong-arm tactics Cromwell employed were made necessary by the motley league of republicans, Presbyterians and Cavaliers arrayed against him. Cromwell "had a zeal for trade and commerce beyond all his predecessors."[69] The Interregnum was a period of unprecedented virtue and sobriety.[70]

Neal's discussion of the post-Restoration period becomes more superficial, more a scissors-and-paste digest of quotations and recital of facts. He gives a cursory account of the growth of political parties and observes that though the Whigs for the most part were not Dissenters, they nonetheless inherited the liberal Protestantism of their Puritan forbears.[71] Both Charles II and James II pursued tyrannical policies, but James made the fatal blunder of directly attacking the Church, thereby alienating Whigs and Tories alike. While conceding that the Tories cooperated with the Whigs in ejecting James, Neal maligns their motives: the Tories were cynical self-seekers who merely wanted the power and profit of office.[72]

A Dissenting minister, Neal had a providential view of history. The Reformation was of course providential and the Puritans "were glorious instruments in the hands of providence to deliver this nation from anti-Christian bondage."[73] It was due to the "all disposing providence of God" that Charles I was executed. The Cromwellian republic rose and fell according to the dictates of providence. The Dutch War, Great Plague, and Fire of London were "judgments of heaven against the nation" for the debauchery and oppression of Charles II. The Stuarts were "a race of princes raised up by providence to be the scourge of these nations." Above all else the Glorious Revolution stood forth as a miraculous instance of God's intercession in human affairs.

If Neal's frequent references to divine intervention recall the providential history of Laurence Echard, the overall style and method of Neal's history do not. For the most part Neal avoided compilation and laborious transcription. Instead he fashioned a well-written explicative narrative. Certainly no one with Neal's providential view of history and empathy for Puritanism can be classified as a philosophical historian. Nevertheless, Neal's work departed significantly from the pre-Rapin mode of historical writing and anticipated the more modern, Enlightenment style. Far from serving up a narrow political chronicle, Neal constructed a well-written explanatory narrative that threw light on a broad spectrum of historical developments beyond the intricacies of court politics. Neal did not treat Puritanism simply as a religious movement, but as a political and social phenomenon as well. And one does not have to sift through interminable transcriptions or a fatiguing recital of superfluous details in order to grasp Neal's them - the rise of Puritanism and its byproduct, liberty.[74]

Neal obviously had much in common with John Oldmixon. Both were staunch Whigs and exponents of Dissent. Both stressed liberty and religious toleration and maintained that "the people" played an important role in defending liberty and Protestantism. Both vindicated the Protestant, prosperous "middle ranks of the people," as Neal terms the propertied merchants and shopkeepers. Although Neal never invoked Locke by name, he shared with Oldmixon a broadly Lockean political philosophy: the rights of man to liberty, property, and government by consent were rooted in natural law, and the people had the right to resist arbitrary government. Neal and Oldmixon differed from the mainstream Court writers in their anti-establishment tone and their paeans to popular revolt.

92 Augustan Historical Writing

Notes

[1]Unless otherwise indicated, biographical information on Oldmixon is drawn from the following: Pat Rogers, "John Oldmixon in Bridgewater (1716-30)," *Somerset Archaeology and Natural History*, CXIII (1969), 86-98; Pat Rogers, *Grub Street: Studies in a Subculture* (London, 1972), 185-198; John Oldmixon, *Memoirs of the Press* (London, 1742); William Aiken's article on Oldmixon in the *Dictionary of National Biography*.

[2]Rogers, "John Oldmixon in Bridgewater," 86.

[3]Oldmixon, 1742.

[4]*Ibid.*

[5]John Oldmixon, *The Critical History of England, Ecclesiastical and Civil* (London, 1724), 2.

[6]*Ibid.*, 162.

[7]Oldmixon, *Memoirs of the Press*, 42.

[8]It did elicit 658 subscribers, a respectable enough number. Pat Rogers has analyzed the occupational background of the subscribers and found that significantly more merchants appeared on the lists than peers and gentry, traditionally the main subscribers. At least 69 of the 111 lower clergy listed were Dissenters. See Pat Rogers, "Book Subscriptions Among the Augustans," *Times Literary Supplement* (December 15, 1972), 1539-1540.

[9]*Daily Gazetteer* number 284 (May 25, 1736), 383 (September 17, 1736).

[10]Among the subscribers were Speaker of the House Arthur Onslow, dissident Whig leader George Bubb Dodington, hymn writer Isaac Watts, and the Secretary of War, William Yonge.

[11]Oldmixon, *Memoirs of the Press*, 58.

[12]Rogers, *Grub Street*, 191.

[13]*Ibid.*, 185.

[14]Oldmixon, 41-42.

[15]The discussion of Tudor persecution is drawn from Oldmixon, *The History of England during the Reigns of Henry VIII, Edward VI, Queen Mary, Queen Elizabeth, Including the History of the Reformation of the Churches of England and Scotland* (London, 1739), 5, 42, 116, 154, 292, 410-419, 609.

[16]The following discussion of Stuart persecution and Puritanism is from John Oldmixon, *The History of England during the Reigns of the Royal House of Stuart* (London, 1729), vi, 2-3, 54.

[17]*Ibid.*, 298.

[18]*Ibid.*, 338-339, 364-365, 380.

[19]Oldmixon, *The History of England during the Reigns of King William and Queen Mary, Queen Anne and George I* (London, 1735), 191.

[20]*Ibid.*, 34.

[21]*Ibid.*, 640.

[22]*Ibid.*, 131.

[23]*Ibid.*, 210, 353.

[24]See *The History of England during the Reigns of King William and Queen Mary, Queen Anne and George I* (London, 1735), 6, 12.

[25]"Ever since the Reformation," Oldmixon wrote, "trade has not been at all in favour with the enemies of spiritual liberty, which is the life of industry, as that is the life of trade." See Oldmixon, *The History of England during the Reigns of King Henry VIII, Edward VI, Queen Mary, and Queen Elizabeth* (London, 1739), 227, 464.

[26]Oldmixon, *The History of England during the Reigns of King Henry VIII, Edward VI, Queen Mary, and Queen Elizabeth* (London, 1739), 227.

[27]Oldmixon, *Stuart*, 207.

[28]*Ibid.*, 411.

[29]Oldmixon, *The History of England during the Reigns of King William and Queen Mary, Queen Anne and George I*, 150.

[30]Oldmixon, *The History of England during the Reigns of King William and Queen Mary, Queen Anne and George I*, 299.

[31]Oldmixon, *The History of England during the Reigns of the Royal House of Stuart*, iii.

[32]*Ibid.*, 521.

[33]*Ibid.*, 611.

[34]*Ibid.*, i.

[35]Oldmixon, *History of England during the Reigns of King William and Queen Anne*, 534.

[36]*Ibid.*, 34. Zachary Grey wrote no general history but attacked Oldmixon and Daniel Neal in pamphlets.

[37]Oldmixon, *Tudor*, 377.

[38]A diligent compiler, Oldmixon did not hesitate to transcribe his sources without attribution. In the *History of England during the Reigns of King William and Queen Mary, Queen Anne and George I*, Oldmixon relied upon the annals of his fellow Whig Abel Boyer. Boyer wrote the following about the Land Qualification Bill:

> Men, who by their natural and acquired abilities, experience, and skill in business, are the fittest to serve their country in Parliament, may happen to be excluded; and men of ever so indifferent parts chosen, if but qualified in land . . . . It may prove a great detriment to trade, by excluding the proper trustees for it, and committing the protection of it to the landed men only, which is a great alteration

of our constitution, it being originally intended that corporations should be represented by some of their own party.

Oldmixon follows Boyer almost verbatim:

Men who by their natural and acquired abilities and skill in business are the fittest to serve their country in Parliament, may happen to be excluded, and men of mean parts chosen, if but qualified by having land only. Thus it may prove a great detriment to trade, by excluding the proper trustees of it, and committing the protection of it to none but landed men, which is a great alteration of our constitution, it being originally intended that corporations should be represented by some of their own body.

In his preface Oldmixon acknowledged his debt to Boyer but never indicated that his transcriptions were lifted almost word for word from Boyer. See Abel Boyer, *The History of Queen Anne* (London, 1735), 489; Oldmixon, *The History of England during the Reigns of King William and Queen Mary, Queen Anne and George I*, I, 459.

[39]Oldmixon, *History of England during the Reigns of King William and Queen Mary . . .*, 220, 616, 621, 799.

[40]E. P. Thompson, *Whigs and Hunters: The Origins of the Black Act* (London, 1975), 195.

[41]Daniel Neal, *The History of the Puritans, or Protestant Non-conformists from the Reformation under King Henry VIII to the Act of Toleration under King William and Queen Mary: with an account of their Principles; their attempts for a further Reformation in the Church; and the Lives and Characters of their most considerable Divines*, 4 vols. (London, 1732-38), 2 vols. (2nd edition, London, 1754). The second edition is employed here.

[42]Biographical information on Neal is drawn from Joshua Toulmin, "Life of the Author," in Daniel Neal, The History of the Puritans, 3 vols. (London, 1822), I, xvi-xxvii; and from James Bass Mullinger in the *Dictionary of National Biography*.

[43]See the article on Evans in Alsager Vian, *Dictionary of National Biography*; Edmund Calamy, *A Letter to Mr. Archdeacon Echard upon occasion of his History of England* (London, 1718), 13.

[44]Toulmin, xiii.

[45]See Michael R. Watts. *The Dissenters: From the Reformation to French Revolution* (Oxford, 1978), 485-486.

[46]See Neal, *History*, I, ix-xv; II, xvi-xx.

[47][Daniel Neal], *A letter from a Dissenter to the Author of the Craftsman* (London, 1733), 20-28. "As long as there is a Protestant Dissenter in England," wrote Neal in his *History*, "there will be a friend of liberty and our present happy constitution." See Neal, *History*, I, ix.

[48]For Neal's comments on Clarendon and Walker, see *History*, I, xiii, 733-734, 782; II, vi-vii, 102, 659.

[49]*Ibid.*, I, 477.

[50]*Ibid.*, 161.

[51]*Ibid.*, 6-12; II, 429.

[52]*Ibid.*, I, 52-53.

[53]*Ibid.*, 88-89, 256, 361-366, 402 for Neal's judgments on Elizabeth.

[54]For Neal's discussion of Elizabethan Puritanism, see especially *ibid.*, 97, 102, 161-175, 210, 230, 233-255.

[55]Neal was among the first historians to make use of Simond D'Ewes *Journals of all the Parliaments during the reign of Queen Elizabeth* (1662). He also used Gilbert Burnet's *History of the Reformation in England* to a good effect, and he gained access to manuscript materials in Cambridge University dealing with the Puritan movement during the Reformation.

[56]Neal, *History*, I, 471, 715; Rapin-Thoyras, II, 185, 204, 213-214.

[57]Neal, *ibid.*, 492; Rapin-Thoyras, 178, 214.

[58]See Neal, *ibid.*, 492, 715.

[59]*Ibid.*, 518.

[60]*Ibid.*, 471.

[61]*Ibid.*, 539-540.

[62]*Ibid.*, 608.

[63]*Ibid.*, 805.

[64]On Neal's discussion of popular involvement in the Revolution, see *ibid.*, 661, 693, 750-753, 765-766, 782.

[65]*Ibid.*, 753.

[66]See Watts, 346-371. In terms that call to mind the twentieth-century debate over the relationship between Puritanism and capitalism, Neal will occasionally link Puritanism with the business virtues of frugality and discipline. Referring, for example, to the Puritans in Elizabeth's reign, he notes that "they were circumspect as to all excesses of eating, drinking, apparel, and lawful diversions, being frugal in housekeeping, industrious in their particular callings, honest and exact in their dealings, and solicitous to give everyone his own." See Neal, I, 399; II, 564.

[67]Neal, *History*, II, 201, 543-544, 549.

[68]*Ibid.*, 378.

[69]*Ibid.*, 422, 469.

[70]*Ibid.*, 494-495, 564.

[71]*Ibid.*, 718.

[72]*Ibid.*, 805.

[73]On Neal's appeals to providence, see *ibid.*, I, 79-80; II, vii-viii, 378, 382, 651, 656, 791-794.

[74]The *History of the Puritans* provoked a series of rejoinders.   Isaac Maddox produced an 85-page *Vindication of the Government, Doctrine, and Worship of The Church of England during the Reign of Elizabeth* (1733) at the suggestion of his patron, Edmund Gibson, Bishop of London. Zachary Grey, also encouraged by Gibson - as well as Thomas Sherlock, Bishop of Salisbury - wrote three pamphlets attacking Neal's *History.*   See Isaac Maddox, *A Vindication of the Government, Doctrine, and Worship of the Church of England during the Reign of Queen Elizabeth* (London, 1733); Zachary Grey, *An Impartial Examination of the Second Volume of Mr. Daniel Neal's History of the Puritans* (London, 1736) - the first of three such *Impartial Examinations*; John Nichols, *Literary Anecdotes of the Eighteenth Century*, 9 vols. (London, 1812-1815) XI, 540; Norman Sykes, *Edmund Gibson, Bishop of London, 1669-1748* (London, 1926), 142.

Chapter V

Thomas Salmon: The Tory Rebuttal to Rapin

One thing that Rapin, Oldmixon, Neal, and the newspaper essayists had in common - none would accept the label of Tory historian.   Even Bolingbroke and his circle called themselves Old Whigs.   And, in fact, none of these writers **were** Tory historians.   They did not romanticize the Stuarts and were certainly not Jacobites.   Neither did they vindicate the Tory Party of the Later Stuart era.   They duly praised liberty and limited monarchy and rejected the "slavish" notions of divine right kingship and passive obedience.

The decline of Tory historiography reflected the changing political and ideological currents since the Hanoverian Accession and the ascendancy of Robert Walpole.   Between the appearance of Laurence Echard's history (1707-18) and Thomas Carte's English history in the late 1740s, only one distinctly Tory general history was published.   This was Thomas Salmon's arch-Tory *History of England* (1732-34), written as a refutation of Rapin-Thoyras.   In the gallery of little-known, overlooked historical writers of the eighteenth century, Salmon is perhaps the most obscure.   Though several of his works sold exceedingly well, Salmon (1679-1765) attracted little attention from contemporary commentators or historians.

Information on Salmon's background is scant.[1]   We know that he was not of gentle birth and was mainly self-educated.   He traveled extensively abroad.   As a young man he apparently resided twice in India, serving as a soldier connected with the East India Company.   He claimed to have witnessed Thomas Pitt's purchase of his great diamond in 1700.   Salmon also soldiered in Flanders during the War of the Spanish Succession.   During the 1720s and '30s he was purportedly the proprietor of two coffee houses, first in Oxford, then in London.   It was while managing these establishments that he wrote his major work, *The Modern History, or the Present State of all Nations* (1724-38).[2]

It was Salmon who began compiling the *State Trials*, the first edition of which appeared in 1719.   Of the works he actually wrote, rather than edited, *A New Geographical and Historical Grammar* was probably the most popular. First published in 1749, Salmon's *Grammar* went through its thirteenth edition in 1785. That its circulation was far-reaching is indicated by the fact that Harvard, Yale, and other American universities used the *Grammar* as a standard text in the mid-eighteenth century, until it was replaced by William Guthrie's *Grammar* (1770).[3] The prestige accorded Salmon's *Grammar* is evidenced by its receiving the royal privilege, granting Salmon and his publishers exclusive copyright privileges for fourteen years. Salmon intended this work, a compendium of historical, geographical, and miscellaneous information, for young readers and for all those who hesitated to take on the multi-volume folio histories. The author's wide-ranging and sharply observed descriptions of foreign places were clearly written from the parochial, ethnocentric perspective of an Englishman taking stock of strange and exotic lands, some of which Salmon himself visited. However, there was also a cosmopolitanism, a broadminded appreciation of cultural differences in Salmon's reportage that came to characterize much of Enlightenment thought. Salmon made this explicit:[4]

> As I am a citizen of the world, I look upon all men as my brethren, and have long endeavored to set them right in their notions of one another. I am extremely concerned to see almost every people representing the distant nations as barbarous and treating them as such.

Salmon's brand of High Toryism is set forth in the work for which he is perhaps best known today, *An Impartial Examination of Bishop Burnet's History of England* (1724). In this vituperative polemic Salmon idealized all the Stuart monarchs and excoriated their antagonists - Puritans, Dissenters, Whigs. Salmon's broadside was a well-written, often telling rejoinder to Burnet. It pointed out how Burnet held diametrically opposite positions during the course of his career, how he overlooked the contradictions and vacillations of Whig politicians over the years, and how much his narrative was based upon hearsay or simple gossip. Salmon often drive home his points with a sharp sense of irony. Burnet's air of self-importance, his tendency to exaggerate his own role in the course of events, made him an easy target for Salmon's barbs.[5]

Next to *The Modern History*, Salmon's most important work was *The Review of the History of England* (1722). This historical brief was intended to refute both the theory of elective monarchy and the conquest rationale used by some Whigs and Tories to justify William III's kingship. Throughout the work Salmon was at pains to demonstrate that the royal prerogative has always been strong and that "the people" have never possessed any discernable voice in Parliament or the counsels of government. He assumed the traditional Tory disdain for ancient constitutionalism and emphasized that when the barons and clergy in the Middle Ages claimed to "stand up for the people's rights tis plain they only mean themselves and their particular interests."[6]

The ideas and themes set forth in Salmon's *Impartial Examination* and *Review* were elaborated upon and expanded in *The Modern History*, specifically in the one extended historical section of the work, *The History of England*. Published serially between 1724 and 1738, *The Modern History* eventually ran to 31 octavo volumes. It was an ambitious synthesis of travel literature and world history. All indications are that this was a very popular work. Salmon originally intended merely to review several travel books to gauge their veracity and explode fabulous tales. However, the work met with such great success - according to Salmon 14,000 volumes printed in less than five years - that he decided to undertake a wide ranging improvement of "our modern history."[7] *The Modern History* was translated into four languages and advertised in many newspapers.[8]

The late seventeenth and early eighteenth centuries saw the growth of a large market for books of travel, responding to the seemingly insatiable public curiosity about far-away lands and peoples. An interest in exotic cultures and a growing recognition that non-Europeans were not some inferior species came to characterize Enlightenment attitudes about the extra-European world. The Enlightenment's uniformitarian view of human nature held that people were everywhere fundamentally the same but that climatic and geographical influences produced political and cultural differentiation between Europeans and non-Europeans.

Moreover, an effort was made in the Augustan age to apply critical methods to the travel exotica that had gradually accumulated over the past two centuries, to distinguish fact from fancy and demolish fabulous and apocryphal tales. In *The Modern History* Salmon set out to dispel myths and provide his fellow countrymen with a more realistic and sympathetic portrayal of foreign cultures and customs. The voyages of exploration and discovery, Salmon observed, took place "at a time when superstition and ignorance overspread even this part of the world, and every romantic tale was greedily swallowed by great and small, even by the clergy as well as laity." Gripped by superstition and sheer ignorance, missionaries and explorers, Salmon believed, had perpetuated incredible tales. Even Francis Drake and Walter Raleigh pretended to have met "giants, cannibals, [and] wizards."[9]

Ignorance and misconceptions fueled hostility between peoples, and this Salmon strove to counteract. He maintained:[10]

> that human nature was everywhere the same, allowances being made for unavoidable prejudices, occasioned by custom, education, and savage principles . . . . And as I have observed on other occasions, nothing has contributed more to render the world barbarous than their having been taught from their cradles that every nation almost but their own are barbarous.

To a considerable extent, Salmon lived up to his cosmopolitan ideals, though there is a probably inevitable ethnocentrism about the work as well. He made it clear that he regarded England as the greatest nation, but he also evinced an unusual respect for and dispassionate interest in foreign cultures. Salmon shared the Enlightenment's growing inquisitiveness about the social and cultural life of foreign peoples. Scorn "the people" as he may, Salmon avowed his intention to correct the deficiencies of most histories that are:[11]

> usually taken up entirely with the actions of the prince and of some great men about him, the splendour of his court, his wars or negotiations with foreign powers; the bulk of the people have scarce a page afforded them . . . insomuch that these works may with propriety be styled the history of the king than of the nation.

The Modern History was the first English work to scrutinize exhaustively a wealth of travel books, in the neighborhood of 200. The work was partially original, based on Salmon's conversations with "public ministers, travellers, or merchants in the countries treated of" and upon his own travels.[12] He also compiled and rewrote portions of the travel books, separating the wheat from the chaff, weaving his sources into a composite picture. Salmon sprinkled his narrative with many allusions to classical historians. He was an impressive autodidact.

The Modern History was not written simply to explode myths and diffuse knowledge in the philosophical spirit of the eighteenth-century Enlightenment. Salmon had his own political axe to grind. In the opening preface to *The Modern History* he launched a diatribe against the government for not aggressively expanding England's overseas empire.[13] This became a common Patriot-Tory complaint against Walpole, as was Salmon's charge that an elite circle of company directors profited unduly at the expense of the trading companies generally and the nation as a whole. He also complained in his preface that the spirit of self-interest prevailed over concern for the nation's welfare, the South Sea Bubble being the most notorious example of this mercenary age. Later in the same volume Salmon presented a summary description of contemporary England. He expressed the views of a thoroughgoing Country Tory: the court was in danger of becoming absolute through corruption and influence; the gentry, one fifth of whom were badly in debt, grew increasingly corrupt as the court tempted them with titles and bribes; the Church was sorely weakened by rampant vice and by the fact "that everyone is at liberty to dissent from it."

The History of England offers an historical exposition on these Tory themes. Although it was published serially between 1732 and 1734 as octavo volumes 17 to 27 of *The Modern History*, *The History of England* clearly differs in style and substance from *The Modern History*. It was the one extended historical section of Salmon's magnum opus and was above all else a fiercely Tory political history. One can read volumes of Salmon's accounts of Africa, Asia, and the Americas and find few clues to the author's political predilections. Such is not the case with *The History of England*. Although his English history was certainly no court annal, neither did it delve into the social and cultural life of the people, their manners and mores, as did the complete history.

The History of England was clearly written as a massive refutation of Rapin-Thoyras. Having previously dissected the first prestigious Whig history, that of Gilbert Burnet, Salmon now took up his pen against the most formidable historian of the era. In his introduction, Salmon denounces Rapin for being a Presbyterian, a republican, and a revolution-ist.[14] However, he goes on to charge that Rapin did not even write the history to which his name is given. He makes the patently ridiculous charge that the entire history was compiled by a cabal of Dutch Calvinists,

French Huguenots, English Presbyterians, and Scotch Cameronians, bent on fomenting revolution.[15]

Salmon's *History* encompassed the entire span of time from the Romans to the end of Queen Anne's reign. Most of the work centered on the Stuart epoch. Salmon's intention was to vindicate the Stuarts from the aspersions of Rapin and other critics. Predictably he extolled the Cavalier and Tory adherents of the Stuarts and blamed the Puritan-Dissenter-Whig axis for fomenting factiousness and rebellion. The only serious charge that could be leveled against the Stuart princes was that they did not act promptly enough to suppress these malcontents. Salmon kept clear of Jacobitism and consistently justified the new dynasty, but his romanticized image of the Stuarts bears many similarities with the Jacobite history of Thomas Carte.

Along with his apologia for the Stuarts, and for their imperious conception of the prerogative, Salmon strove to vindicate the traditional ruling order of nobility and gentry. The aristocratic order governed paternalistically and benevolently, exuding virtue and public spiritedness. The opposition to the Stuarts constituted a faction of social upstarts.

The entire pre-seventeenth-century portion of Salmon's history was designed to show that English monarchs traditionally exercised their prerogative at least as rigorously as the Stuarts. Naturally Salmon stakes out a Tory position on the ancient constitution question, following Robert Brady to the letter. In his account of the Tudors, Salmon emphasizes their despotic methods of governance. He reiterates the conventional wisdom that Henry VII depressed the nobility and elevated the commons.[16] Henry VII was positively benign compared to his heir. Salmon depicts Henry VIII as a ruthless pillager of the nation who enjoyed unlimited power. Under Henry, "a man might be orthodox in his opinions one day, and burnt for the same principles the next."[17] Salmon disputed the apologists for Henry who argued that he did nothing contrary to law: "Having no laws cannot be a greater misfortune than laws thus strained and perverted." More than a century before J. R. Green propounded the classic Whig portrait of Tudor despotism, Salmon said very much the same thing. The Henrician Reformation was above all else a grab for power and wealth by the king.

Salmon did not admire what he saw as the ultra-Protestantism of Edward VI, and he restates the familiar depiction of Mary as a tyrant. Where he broke new ground was in his treatment of Elizabeth. Ironically, Neal and Salmon, writing from very different political viewpoints at almost the same time, arrived at similar conclusions about Elizabeth's reign. Like Neal, Salmon made good use of Strype's annals to present a relatively complete and vivid picture of Elizabethan Puritanism. However, whereas Neal wanted to show how his Puritan forbears had been mistreated by the Virgin Queen, Salmon wanted to exculpate the Stuarts by debunking Elizabeth and demonstrating that the people's pretensions to curb the prerogative had no basis in history. It had been a standard Royalist-Tory refrain that the Early Stuarts merely carried on the tradition of Elizabethan statecraft, but Salmon was the first to specify the ways in which continuity existed between Elizabeth and James and the first to ground his discussion in historical documents. Elizabeth, he pointed out, had created monopolies, imprisoned M.P.s, and bequeathed a war and large debt to her successor.[18] As we might expect from a geographer and world traveler, Salmon paid more attention to England's growing interaction with the non-European world than had previous historians. He took the time to describe the magnificent voyages of discovery by Drake and Raleigh.[19]

Salmon's fairly complex picture of Elizabethan Puritanism is gone in his treatment of the Early Stuarts. He submits that James I's only failings were in not suppressing the opposition immediately and in plunging the nation deeper into debt by lavishing money on his favorites.[20] Otherwise the Puritan "faction" were all to blame. Power-hungry malcontents, they conspired to overthrow the monarchy by refusing to grant subsidies to James and Charles. Salmon depicts the Great Rebellion as the classic example of what can happen when proto-Whig, social-contract notions of the state were put into practice. He assails Rapin as the historical apologist for both the Revolution and the seditious philosophy that informed it. The Puritan "faction" believed that "the two Houses had a right to resist by the fundamental laws of the land; and the authors of Rapin say that by the King's invading the subject's liberties and properties, the government was dissolved, and the people were at liberty to settle what government they pleased."[21] Actuated by this philosophy, the Parliamentarians in the Revolution were intent on plundering the propertied elite. Their campaigns of pillage and terror in Royalist areas "gave the nobility and gentry terrible apprehensions of what they were to expect from their usurpers."[22]

Salmon's condemnation of Cromwell is unqualified.[23]   Charles II, on
the other hand, he admires in all respects, except for his excessive
forbearance, for which Salmon blames the Earl of Clarendon.   Clarendon
was too moderate for Salmon's taste and "was far from being partial to
the King's side."[24]   Salmon depicts the Country or Whig party as standard
bearers of the Parliamentarian Old Cause.   Fortunately, the Church's
emphasis on passive obedience and the loyalty of the Tory gentry averted
a repetition of 1640.

In his account of the Glorious Revolution, Salmon upholds passive
obedience and nonresistance but separates himself from the nonjurors and
Jacobites.[25]   It was James' attack on the Church that forfeited his right
to the throne.   In justifying the new dynasty, Salmon takes the position of
some Tories during the Revolution that James automatically disqualified
himself from being king by embracing popery.   However, there was no
election of a new monarch by Parliament, no altering of the constitution,
and no principle of hereditary rule.

It is Salmon's history of England after the Glorious Revolution that
most clearly shows his Country-Tory support for the landed men against
the nouveaux riches monied men.   Already by 1690 the position of the
gentry had deteriorated as they were hit hard by new taxes.[26]   In the early
1690s the Bank of England and national debt were established.   Henceforth the "monied men" grew rich, lending at exorbitant interest rates.
They "purchased the estates of the gentry, eaten up by taxes and interest
money."[27]   The joint-stock companies, argues Salmon, subverted the
constitution.   They also led inevitably to the South Sea Bubble, in which
thousands of families were ruined.   Linked to the joint-stock companies
were the wars of the League of Augsburg and the Spanish Succession.
The Bank of England was established as a finance institution to meet the
steep costs of William's war against France.   Salmon was one in a long
line of Tory writers who accused the Whigs and stock jobbers of
deliberately promoting unnecessarily long and expensive continental wars
in order to beggar the gentry with the high land tax and to enrich
themselves on the exorbitant interest paid to meet war-induced debts.[28]

Salmon's account of English history after the Glorious Revolution
diverges from the Country interpretation in two major ways.   Firstly, the
Country publicists maintained that the Revolution of 1688 resolved the

substantial differences between Whigs and Tories; and consequently, genuine political parities, divided on issues of principle, no longer existed. As an unreconstructed Tory, however, Salmon sees the contention of Whig and Tory political parties as the key to understanding modern British politics. The division was clearcut. On one side, the Tories: loyal defenders of Church and throne, of landed society and the public interest. On the other side, the Whigs: a faction of self-seeking revolutionists and upstart monied men, void of virtue and public spiritedness. And Salmon virtually identifies the Whigs with the Puritans, remarking that "they (the Whigs) murdered King Charles."[29]

Secondly, like any good Tory High Flier, Salmon champions the powers and privileges of the Church in post-Revolutionary England.[30] He explicitly concurs with Burnet that the nation was falling under corruption and immorality during William's reign. He differs from Burnet, however, in perceiving this vice as a result of the breakdown in the monolithic state church, the final blow to which came with the dissolution of Convocation after Anne's reign. He, naturally, reviles Dissent and Dissenters, shocktroops of the Whigs.[31]

Salmon was primarily interested in battering the Whigs and did not undertake extensive research or tap a rich vein of new sources.[32] *The History of England* is a straightforward political history, concentrating on developments at court. Salmon devoted considerable attention to the financial revolution and its socio-political repercussions, but on the whole, socio-economic and culture developments were no less subordinate to his political narrative than they were in the history of this immediate Tory predecessor, Laurence Echard.

Nevertheless, we should not overlook the notable formal and substantive differences between Salmon's work and that of the pre-Rapin historians of the later Stuart era. For one thing, his histories - the *Review*, *Impartial Examination*, and *Modern History* - were simply more readable than the traditional folio compilations. Salmon designed the *Modern History* to appeal to a wide audience. He occasionally interpolated lengthy extracts from other works, but generally he avoided transcriptions and paraphrasings. He was not primarily a compiler. Whether exploding mythical tales about foreign lands or confuting Burnet and Rapin, Salmon revelled in the role of critic. Almost by definition this critical function demanded more of Salmon than simply relating an interminable series of discrete events. He relied more on explanation and generalization than most previous historians. Rather than bury his points in a mass of documentary extracts, Salmon utilized the evidence to substantiate his criticisms and rebuttals.

Once one penetrates the veil of polemical bombast it becomes clear that Salmon formulated some impressive counterarguments to Rapin. He scrutinized the documents and found what he wanted to find: that the Tudors, especially Henry VIII, stretched and perverted the law and that the contrast between Elizabethan liberty and Stuart tyranny was much overdrawn. Rapin said next to nothing about Puritanism, but Salmon - along with his ideological opposite Daniel Neal - was the first generalist to discuss the doctrine, discipline, and organization of Elizabethan Puritanism. Although Salmon lacked Rapin's even-handed tone when discussing political parties, he shared with Rapin a keen awareness of the fact that modern English politics was virtually unintelligible without taking the Whigs and Tories into account.

Salmon was a Tory High Churchman, and we might expect he would adhere to a providential conception of history a la Clarendon and Echard. In fact, allusions to providence and divine intervention are rare, and there are no supernatural tales such as Cromwell's conversation with the Devil. Considering the fact that Salmon wrote his *Modern History* partly to dispel the fantastic yarns that had accumulated about far off climes, it is not surprising that he showed no inclination to perpetuate similar tales at home.

* * * *

Salmon's works illustrate the changing character of historical writing in the quarter century after the Hanoverian Accession. While he wrote to attack the quasi-Lockean, liberal interpretation of history, which he identified with Rapin-Thoyras, his own writings show some of the stylistic and methodological innovations that came increasingly to characterize early-eighteenth-century historiography, particularly the trend toward explanation rather than compilation and the rise of a more secular conception of historical change.

On one level, British historical writing from Salmon to Hume can be regarded simply as a collective attempt to supersede the Frenchman, Rapin, and his particular interpretation of English history. Only Hume in the 1750s finally succeeded in replacing Rapin as the standard authority. Rapin's *History of England* was not only the most popular and celebrated history to date, in style and method it marked a significant advance over previous histories. Keenly sensitive to the distorting effects of party politics on historical writing, Rapin was the first general historian to evaluate earlier histories critically, denoting the particular way in which an author's political bias determined his interpretation of events. He made more of an effort to analyze and explain in his narrative, though he also compiled and elaborated facts in inordinate detail.

Rapin was a Whig moderate who extolled not resistance and revolution, but moderate men and gradual change to preserve liberty and property. As Herbert Butterfield pointed out more than 40 years ago, Rapin was among the intellectual founding fathers of the modern Whig approach to history and politics. Rapin was cited approvingly by Court and Country writers in the Augustan newspaper debates. The Court essayists in particular, however, and, even more so, the pro-Court historians Neal and Oldmixon fashioned an even more fully liberal interpretation of English history. Their works affirmed "the people's" right to resist, the natural right to religious freedom, the ultimate sovereignty of Parliament, and the economic benefits conferred by liberty and Protestantism.

Polemical motives continued to take precedence over dispassionate inquiry in determining the historian's particular interpretation of events. Insofar, however, as one byproduct of liberal Whiggery was a more secular world view, the rise of Whig historical writing contributed to the formation of a more rationalistic, modern style of history. Invocations of supernatural and preternatural power declined in the early Hanoverian period. Historians were more inclined to work under the assumption that people made their own history and that it was for theologians to speculate on the super-historical imponderables of God's will and his relationship to humanity. It followed logically from this "philosophical" perspective that natural causes had to be discovered in order to explain the course of events. One of the reasons why Rapin's analysis of the Glorious Revolution was more complex and penetrating than Laurence Echard's was that he did not simply dispose of the event as a miraculous, ultimately unfathomable manifestation of providence. Historians were less willing to make the factual evidence conform to some divine plan.

The more critical, rationalistic outlook of this period also contributed to the reaction against historical compilations. One sees in the works of Rapin, Salmon, and Neal a more discriminating, discerning use of sources, though they were certainly not free of the traditional methods. In these histories, as in the newspaper essays, there is appreciably more analysis and explanation, less transcription and conflation of sources.

Part and parcel of the trend toward a more secular, analytical historiography was the growing interest in the economic side of history. During the 1730s the socio-economic interpretation found expression in the quasi-Harringtonian analysis of the Court and Country newspaper essayists. It has been suggested that the economic dimension featured prominently in the 1730s particularly because the aftermath of the South Sea Bubble and the "corrupt" Robinocracy stirred up bitter debate over the role of credit and money in English society. Neal and Oldmixon, moreover, helped broaden the scope of history because their anti-Establishment perspective led them to look beneath the upper crust of society and discuss popular involvement in politics. Not until the 1740s and '50s do we find a coherent, well-formulated social and economic interpretation in the general histories.

Recognizing the differences between historiography in the age of Anne and the age of Walpole, one must not exaggerate the modernity of the latter school. The providential explanation shaped Daniel Neal's narrative. Oldmixon assiduously practiced the art of historical compilation. The general histories were all political narratives, with social, economic, and cultural themes relegated to the periphery. The 1720s and '30s were years of transition in the evolution of eighteenth-century history writing. It was not until mid-century that the first famous examples of Enlightenment history appeared. Hume's *History of England* and Robertson's *History of Scotland* were both published in the 1750s, as were Voltaire's *Essai sur les Moeurs* and *Siecle de Louis XLV*. Rapin and his immediate successors, however, were the first historians whose works reflected the "philosophical" intellectual currents of the early Enlightenment. Bolingbroke, whose interpretation of English history owed much to Rapin, is now regarded by scholars as a major influence on Voltaire. The impress of Bolingbroke was also felt on English historical writing in the 1740s.

Notes

[1]Biographical information on Salmon comes from Cornelius Neale, *The Life of Thomas Pitt* (Cambridge, 1915), 242; (Francis Palgrave), "Hume and his Influence upon History" in *Quarterly Review* CXLIII, (March 1844), 545; and from the *Dictionary of National Biography* article on Salmon by Thompson Cooper.

[2]See Salmon, *The Modern History, or the Present State of All Nations* 31 vols. (London, 1724), I, preface, n.p., for Salmon's lavish dedication to Pitt, and *A Review of the History of England* (1724), I, dedication to Capel Berrow. Salmon dedicated volume II of the *Modern History* to Charles Boon, one of his military commanders in the East Indies, who he acknowledged as his patron.

[3]William Warntz, *Geography Now and Then* (New York: 1964), 22-24.

[4]Thomas Salmon, *A New Geographical and Historical Grammar* (London, 1749), unpaginated preface. Among Salmon's other works was *A Short View of the Families of the Present English Nobility* (1751), during the composition of which Salmon applied to many peers for information about their families. Like *A New Geographical and Historical Grammar*, several of Salmon's books were spin-offs from the *Modern History*. This was the case with his *Present State of the Universities*, written "to treat of the education of our nobility and gentry in those celebrated seats of learning." Another digest of factual information drawn from the *Modern History* was *The Modern Gazetteer, or a Short View of the General Nations of the World*, a topographical and geographical dictionary. Salmon also wrote *The Chronological Historian: Containing a Regular Account of all Material Transactions and Occurrences, Ecclesiastical, Civil, and Military from the Invasion of the Romans to the fourteenth year of George II* (1723). This was simply a chronology, a list of dates and events stretched over two volumes and seven hundred pages.

[5]Thomas Salmon, *An Impartial Examination of Bishop Burnet's History of His Own Time* (London, 1724) 2 vols., II, 943-944. Consider, for example, Salmon's sarcastic comments about Burnet's description of how grandly he was received by the French government and nobility after the increasingly repressive policies of James II forced him to live abroad:

All men stood amazed: The world was struck at the approach of
Gilbert Burnet as if some prodigy of nature had appeared.   All
princes joined in proclaiming his uncommon worth.   We knew not
how to value him: a prophet has no honor in his own country.

[6]Thomas Salmon, *A Review of the History of England as far as it relates to
the Titles and Pretensions of our several Kings* (London, 1722-24) 2 vols., I,
xiv.

[7]Salmon, *The Modern History*, IX (1729), unpaginated preface.

[8]The success of *The Modern History* is indicated by the fact that a
separately published edition of *The History of England*, published in 1734,
received the "royal privilege," granting Salmon and his publishers sole
printing and vending rights.

[9]*Ibid.*, XXVII (1735), 1-3.

[10]*Ibid.*, I, unpaginated preface.

[11]*Ibid.*, IX (1729), unpaginated preface.

[12]*Ibid.*, XXVII (1735), 6.

[13]Salmon's attacks on the government are to be found in *ibid.*, I,
unpaginated preface, 200, 315, 318-319.

[14]*Ibid.*, XIX (1733), 404.

[15]*Ibid.*, XVI (1732), x-xii.

[16]*Ibid.*, XVII (1733), 368.

[17]*Ibid.*, XIX, 280.   On Henry VIII see 183, 229, 377.

[18]*Ibid.*, XX, 138, 140, 156-159; XXI, 31.

[19]*Ibid.*, XX, 156-159.

[20]On James I's reign see *ibid.*, XXI, 32, 53-55, 87, 136-137, 286-287.

[21] *Ibid.*, 262.

[22] *Ibid.*, 312, 335.

[23] See *ibid.*, XXII, 186.

[24] On Charles II's reign see *ibid.*, XXII, 251, 312-313, 412-413; XXIII, 125-126.

[25] *Ibid.*, XXIII, 431-440.

[26] *Ibid.*, XXIV, 41.

[27] *Ibid.*

[28] On the consequences of the wars against Louis XIV see *ibid.*, XXIV, 154, 167; XXV, 102, 402, 421, 455; XXVII, 99.

[29] *Ibid.*, XXVII, 230.

[30] For Salmon on the Church see *ibid.*, 398-399; XXVII, 100-105, 120-121, 128.

[31] Salmon has nothing but praise for Sacheverell and his infamous sermon. The popular acclaim for Sacheverell after his trial, followed by the 1710 Tory electoral victory, testified to the fact that "the people" naturally supported their Tory overlords, despite the Whigs' self-image as the "voice of the people." Salmon makes the apposite point that when the Whigs eventually took power after the Sacheverell riots they jettisoned much of their libertarian rhetoric and enacted "statutes against the rabble; and, indeed, a Whig shifts his principles (if they deserve that name), with more ease than he does his clothes." See *ibid.*, XXVI, 83; XXVII, 133.

[32] Salmon mainly consulted the more familiar printed sources available - Bacon, Strype, Godwyn, and Camden on the Tudors; Temple, Burnet, Whitlocke, and Warwicke on the Stuarts. He also used Rymer's *Foedera*, D'Ewes *Journal* and additional collections of proclamations, statutes, and other state papers.

Part Three

History and Ideology after the Fall of Walpole

Chapter VI

Thomas Birch and the Historians

It is generally recognized that Enlightenment historical writing blossomed in mid-eighteenth century Europe. Christian-humanist historiography had already been disparaged by critics like Pierre Bayle, Fontenelle, and Lord Bolingbroke, but the "new history" first found its voice on the Continent in Voltaire's *Siecle de Louis XIV* (1751) and, especially, in his *Esai sur les moeurs* (1753). These works broke with traditional historical writing by transcending the standard political, diplomatic, and military narratives to treat social, cultural, and economic history. Bolingbroke's historical essays probably helped shape Voltaire's cognizance of economic and cultural history, his preference for modern over ancient history, and his distaste for detail and excessive erudition.[1] Voltaire's appreciation of economic forces in history was perhaps his single most important contribution to the development of historical writing. He did not formulate any theory or mechanism to explain historical change, but as J. Brumfitt points out, "in the emphasis he places, particularly in his later years, on economic causes, he appears to serve as a link between Machiavellian realism and nineteenth-century theories of economic determinism."[2]

In addition to the new style of history that Voltaire made fashionable, mid-eighteenth-century Europe witnessed the emergence of sociological, "philosophical" theories of historical development. In *Esprit des lois* (1748) Montesquieu set forth a deterministic view of historical causation, arguing that every country's history is the product of underlying social and economic conditions.[3] The philosophers of the Scottish Enlightenment - John Millar, Adam Ferguson, David Hume, Adam Smith, and William Robertson - were much impressed by Montesquieu's sociological method. Focusing on the economic side of history, the mode of production, the Scottish philosophes delineated four stages of history from primitive, pre-agricultural societies to contemporary commercial civilization.[4] Two products of the Scottish school, Hume and Robertson, wrote narrative histories. They leavened their accounts of political and diplomatic affairs with intermittent commentaries about art, manners, and, above all, economics.

Hume was the only author of an English history who is regularly placed in the pantheon of the Enlightenment. His *History of England* enjoyed far more popular and, on the Continent, critical success than any previous general history of England. Hume's towering reputation and the success of his *History* have thrown a shadow over the historiography of the 1740s, the decade before his *History* appeared, obscuring the fact that the fifth decade of the eighteenth century saw a rich efflorescence in English historical writing.   By overlooking or treating superficially Hume's immediate predecessors, scholars have tended to exaggerate his originality.

Four major histories of England appeared, or began appearing, in the 1740s. There was Nicholas Tindal's *Continuation of Rapin's History of England* (1744-47), published simultaneously in folio and octavo editions, which took Rapin's narrative from the accession of William III to the death of George I. James Ralph's *History of England during the Reigns of King William, Queen Anne, and King George I with an Introductory Review of the Reigns of the Royal Brothers, Charles and James* (1744-46) was a three-volume folio work that never in fact got beyond William's reign. Two large general histories of England, by Thomas Carte and William Guthrie, were works of considerable scholarship and erudition. Carte's *History* was published between 1747 and 1754, Guthrie's between 1744 and 1751.

Production of these new histories was made easier by the growing number of documentary collections that appeared in print during the 1730s and '40s. One such work, the *Ormonde Papers* (1739), was edited by Carte and printed in conjunction with his *Life of Ormonde*.   The indefatigable Thomas Birch, about whom more will be said presently, edited one of the most important collections of state papers to be published in the first half of the eighteenth century, the *Thurloe Papers* (1742). This seven-volume work consisted mainly of official letters dating from the Interregnum period and was transcribed by Cromwell's secretary John Thurloe. Birch gleaned the documents from private collections, including the library of Lord Somers and the manuscripts of Richard Rawlinson, an antiquarian scholar and collector. Birch also wrote *An Historical View of the Negotiations between the Courts of England, France, and Brussels, from the year 1592 to 1617* (1749), which was comprised largely of hitherto unpublished state papers. Another major collection dealing with the Early Stuarts was *The Earl of Strafford's Letters*, published in two folio volumes in 1739. The *Sidney Papers*, (1746) a collection of letters and state papers written and compiled by the Sidney family, encompassed the late Tudor-early Stuart period. Other documentary collections included the *Burleigh Papers* (1740) and Patrick Forbes' *Full View of the Public Transactions in the reign of Elizabeth* (1740-41), which assembled state papers pertaining mainly to Anglo-French relations between 1558 and 1663. Finally, two famous collections of manuscript selections drawn from the capacious libraries of Robert Harley and John Somers were published at this time: The *Harleian Miscellany* (1744-46) and the *Somers Tracts* (1748-52).

Supplementing these collections were the lives, memoirs, and histories of specific reigns or topics, particularly Sarah Churchill's *Account of the Conduct of the Dowager Duchess of Marlborough* (1742), the posthumous works of Roger North - the *Examen* (1740) and the *Lives* of his three brothers (1742-44) - and the aforementioned *Life of Ormonde* by Thomas Carte. By the fourth and fifth decades of the eighteenth century, historians had begun to utilize foreign documents much more extensively than they had previously because important new sources were coming into print. Jean Dumont's *Corps Universel Diplomatique* had appeared between 1726 and 1731, a valuable addition to the treaties of Rymer. A five-volume *Supplement* to Dumont, edited by J. Rousset de Missy, came out in 1739. The fourteenth and final volume of Guillaume de Lamberty's *Memoires* appeared in 1740. Also important were the letters of two French diplomats in England during the reigns of James I and Charles II - La Boderie (1750) and Godefrey L. Comte D'Estrades (1743). Finally, as mid-century approached we see for the first time an effort to collect and publish Parliamentary proceedings and debates on a fairly large scale: Richard Chandler's *History and Proceedings of the House of Commons*, 1660-1743, printed in fourteen volumes between 1742 and 1744; E. Timberland published in eight volumes *The History and Proceedings of the House of Lords from . . . 1660 to the Present Time* (1741-42); the anonymous *Journals of the House of Commons, 1547-1714* began appearing in 1742; in 1752 the *Parliamentary of Constitutional History of England from the Earliest Times to the Restoration of Charles II* was begun with the ubiquitous Thomas Birch as principal compiler. In the late Augustan period, printed sources were still far more accessible to historians than manuscript materials. This continued to be the case even after the Harleian, Camden, and Sloan libraries were merged in 1753 to form the British Museum Library - the first major public library in England.

The fact that many new sources had become available since the publication of Rapin's *History* made it seem all the more urgent to Englishmen that the Frenchman's history should be replaced by an up-to-date, authoritative, and thoroughly English work. Moreover, in an age when history shaded almost imperceptibly into political propaganda, it was a matter of some importance to the various political factions that the historian who succeeded in dethroning Rapin, or of continuing his history, should be of the right political stripe. As will be shown, Tindal, Ralph, Guthrie, and Carte were patronized by competing political interests and wrote from differing political perspectives.

In order to appreciate the political connections and ideology of these historians, it is necessary to understand the political situation in England after the fall of Walpole.[5] Between 1742 and 1746 England experienced considerable ministerial instability. At the time of Walpole's resignation, three major political groups existed - those Court Whigs who had supported Walpole to the end, the Country Whigs, and the Tories. The latter two groups can be subdivided. The Tories were split between Hanoverians and Jacobites. The Country Whigs were an even more disparate group: about eighty M.P.s were Independents with little desire for court favor. About fifty others wanted places and were divided into two competing factions - the Carteret-Pulteney group on the one hand and those politicians who were identified with the Prince of Wales and the Duke of Argyll on the other. When Walpole left office George II chose the Carteret-Pulteney "new Whigs" to join with the Old Corps of Walpole adherents and together secure a Parliamentary majority. Owing to Carteret's diplomatic failures, however, the new Whigs were discredited by 1744. They were replaced as allies of the Old Corps by those Country Whigs such as the Earls of Chesterfield and Harrington, who belonged to the Prince of Wales' circle, along with several Tories. This amorphous collectivity made up the so-called Broad Bottom Administration. The combination of "new allies" - those Country Whigs who had broken with the Prince of Wales - and Old Corps formed the ingredients for ministerial stability. Not until 1746, however, when George II's hopes of reinstating Carteret were shattered by the refusal of the other political groups to work with him, when the few Tory aspirants for office had either sold out to the Whigs or resigned from the government out of principle, and when William Pitt entered office for the first time, was the alliance between Old Corps and new allies cemented. The rule of the Pelhams endured until Henry Pelham's death in 1754.

The ideological divisions that had gradually narrowed during Walpole's tenure converged still further after his fall. Many Country politicians quickly jettisoned their high-minded rhetoric and joined the scramble for office. They shattered the illusions of those men of principle in the opposition to Walpole - men who sincerely wanted to end corruption, check the purported depredations of monied men, and reduce or abolish the standing army.[6]

The Pelhams maintained the Robinocracy even though its eponym had departed. Their hand was strengthened by the ruthless suppression of the '45 Jacobite Rebellion, which finally eliminated Jacobitism as a serious political threat. They also worked to reconcile conflicting political and economic interests in the City, specifically between the great financial corporations and aldermen on one hand and the smaller businesses and Common Council on the other. Repeal of the City Elections Act in 1746 served this end. The Pelhams, and the Newcastle-Pitt administration that succeeded it, presided over what W. A. Speck calls "the making of the English ruling class." "No longer riven by bitter party strife or rent by conflicting economic interests," he observes, "the aristocracy and gentry, together with merchants, plutocrats, and leading professional men, amalgamated to form a narrow oligarchy which controlled all the levers of power, at the center and in the provinces."[7] This ruling class, and the politicians that represented it, held sway with something approaching serene tranquility until the 1760s. Then, George III affronted it; radicals and reformers began to challenge it.

Political developments in the decade after Walpole's fall were reflected in the histories under consideration. Until 1746 politics was in a state of flux with several factions maneuvering for power. Tindal, Carte, and Ralph-Guthrie were all sponsored by rival political groups. However, with the histories of Guthrie and David Hume, we see the production of two establishment histories in which the traditional Whig/Tory Court/Country polemics are largely absent.

i i

There is clear evidence that in the 1740s historians were hired by specific political factions to produce partisan histories. Thomas Carte was a Jacobite historian, sponsored by Jacobite chieftains like John Hynde Cotton and the Duke of Beaufort. William Guthrie and James Ralph collaborated on a Country Whig historical project, patronized by George Bubb Dodington and the Earl of Chesterfield. The author of the *Continuation of Rapin* was patronized and supervised by members of the Hardwicke family and other staunch Court Whigs.

Although the *Continuation* was written nominally by Nicholas Tindal, the Hardwicke papers in the British Library reveal that Thomas Birch was in fact the main author. The *Continuation* is one case where extensive documentation exists detailing how the actual composition of the work was tailor-made to meet the specifications of politicians. The correspondence between Birch and Philip Yorke in the Hardwicke papers also sheds light on Ralph, Guthrie, and Carte, who were working simultaneously on rival histories for competing political factions.

Samuel Johnson described his friend Birch with characteristic wit: "Tom Birch is brisk as a bee in conversation, but no sooner does he take a pen in his hand then it becomes a torpedo to him and benumbs all his faculties."[8] Birch was a prosaic stylist and lacked the historian's gift for interpretation and generalization. He was a skilled, if pedantic, collector, compiler, and editor. He cannot, therefore, be classified as an exemplar of Enlightenment historical writing. But his contribution to British historical scholarship should not be slighted. No one in the eighteenth century contributed more to the raw materials of history, to the disclosure and methodization of documents without which the celebrated works of writers like Hume and Robertson might never have been written - or at least not written so well. Birch did much to advance the state of British biography by writing over 600 new lives for the expanded translation of Bayle's *Dictionary*, published in 1734-41. In addition to the *Thurloe Papers* and *Historical View of the Negotiations between the Courts of England, France, and Brussels*, he compiled a *Life of Archbishop Tillotson* (1752-53), *Memoirs of the Reign of Queen Elizabeth* (1754), *History of the Royal Society* (1756-57), and the *Life of Henry, Prince of Wales* (1760), to mention only several of the most important works. Birch was also one of the principal early benefactors to the British Museum and one of its most active trustees.

Birch was a sort of literary man-about-town with a special gift for cultivating the friendship of eminent men of letters, many of whom he assisted. At one time or another he offered his services to Alexander Pope, Samuel Richardson, William Robertson, David Garrick, Benjamin Hoadly, William Warburton, and Samuel Johnson. Warburton told Birch that "I know no one who so well understands our literary history, and no one is so communicative and ready to oblige your friends as yourself."[9] Birch was one of Johnson's best friends, particularly in the late 1730s and early '40s when Johnson was writing the Parliamentary debates for the *Gentleman's Magazine*. Birch himself occasionally advised the editor, Edward Cave, on details of the debates and other matters.

Birch was also a friend of Philip Yorke - the Earl of Hardwicke and Lord Chancellor of England - and of the Yorke family. From 1732 onward he was patronized by Hardwicke.[10] His services included supplying frequent letters to Hardwicke's son, Philip, on literary topics and public news. When this correspondence began in the early 1740s, Philip was a young Member of Parliament who had been pensioned as Teller of the Exchequer in 1738. He was a major literary patron and minor historical writer.

William Coxe noted nearly two centuries ago that the *Continuation* was primarily written by Birch, with considerable assistance from Philip Yorke and his younger brother Charles and from Horace Walpole.[11] The Birch-Yorke correspondence reveals unmistakably that the Yorkes directed and abetted Birch in the composition of this work. Birch and his coadjutors fashioned a Court Whig history, acutely conscious of the fact that their political rivals were also producing partisan histories.

Birch specified that he wrote the *Continuation* of Rapin between autumn 1743 and spring 1746. "You know," wrote Philip Yorke to his client, "one recommendation of your history with us is to be its par-tiality."[12] Philip and his brother supervised Birch in order to ensure the history's Whiggism. When Charles gave Birch portions of the Somers and Burnet papers that were in his possession, Philip Yorke commented that they would enable Birch to "paint the conduct of the Tories in its true colours."[13] In a letter to Yorke dated July 21, 1744, Birch referred to his patron as "the master of my scheme, and I believe have read more of the printed numbers than I have."[14] Three months later he informed Yorke, "I have followed your advice in being most literal of my quotations from all the best Whig pamphlets during King William's reign."[15] In addition to supplying Birch with source materials, the Yorkes occasionally checked to see how he was proceeding on the history and even wrote whole pages for him to insert.[16]

Two eminent Whigs assisted Birch. Speaker Onslow gave him access to letters of Richard Hill, the diplomat, and George Rooke, the Tory admiral. Apparently Horace Walpole had a large say in determining what went into the Hanoverian volume. Philip Yorke arranged for Birch to consult Walpole about the reign of George I. He told Birch to write a "general account" of George I's reign for Walpole's inspection: "You must ask his leave to take notes in writing of what he tells you, and then digest it in your own words into the body of the history." He directed Birch to visit Walpole several times on this matter.[17]

Though Birch took orders from the Yorkes first and foremost, he had to answer to two other overseers. One was Tindal. No doubt the *Continuation* bore Tindal's name because his popular translation of Rapin augured well for the supplement. However, he appears to have played an important editorial role, a position that clearly set him at odds with Birch and the Yorkes.[18] References to Tindal in the Birch and Yorke letters are almost invariably negative. Charles Yorke complained to his brother in October 1744 about Tindal's penchant for cutting Birch's text, "not reflecting that the book is good for nothing unless it be a full compilation. Birch behaves pitifully in it. I tell him that he is not bound to endure these chains, but he smiles upon them as he does upon everything."[19]

As if it were not enough that Birch had to please both the Yorkes and Tindal, he also had to serve his publishers, John and Paul Knapton. Already in December 1742 John Knapton was advising Birch on how to construct the history. He instructed him, among other things, to quote from Rapin occasionally and to insert a paper that he, Knapton, had written.[20] Charles Yorke called Birch Knapton's "slave" and protested that he was not providing him with enough source materials.[21]

Given the tangled, committee-like manner in which the *Continuation* was produced, and Birch's leaden style, it is not surprising that the work is without literary distinction. Although the *Continuation* abjured providence, it was not an innovative history and cannot be presented as an example of Enlightened historical writing. It was simply a compilation in the tradition of Echard and Oldmixon.

The only manner in which the *Continuation* differed from many of its predecessors was in its secular analysis and detailed coverage of economic developments. Birch devoted much space to describing and lauding the new financial institutions and condemning the Tories for resisting them.[22] The basic thrust of the history, detected amidst a maze of facts, was to show how the unexampled benefits conferred by the Whigs in 1688-89 were successfully defended against the Tories during the reigns of William and Anne and firmly secured by Whig statesmen under George I. The Whigs are uniformly cast as champions of liberty, property, and Protestantism; the Tories as a cabal of tyrants and crypto-Jacobites. Religious themes play a very secondary role in the narrative, with virtually no references to divine providence.

Although the *Continuation* was assembled with little sense of style or a clear narrative thread, it does contain an impressively comprehensive catalogue of information about foreign and domestic political developments, more so than any other eighteenth-century work dealing with the Late Stuart-Early Hanoverian period. It has been of enduring value to scholars. William Coxe, William Lecky, Winston Churchill, and George Macaulay Trevelyan all found it a valuable source for their own works.

The letters Birch and his young patron exchanged during the 1740s are sprinkled with frequent negative references to their three historian rivals, James Ralph, William Guthrie, and Thomas Carte. In September 1744, Philip Yorke asked Birch how Ralph was proceeding on "his counterpart to your history."[23] Like Birch, Ralph was at work on a history of England, designed to encompass the reign of George I. Ralph's history was part of a Country Whig historical project patronized by George Bubb Dodington and the Earl of Chesterfield.[24] Guthrie was to take his *General History of England* down to the Glorious Revolution and Ralph was to cover the post-Revolutionary decades.

Between the late 1730s and early 1760s Ralph and Guthrie were probably the two foremost political journalists in England. Both had written on and off for two leading opposition journals, *Common Sense* and *Old England*. Dodington and Chesterfield hired Ralph and Guthrie to write their latest newspaper, *Old England*, at about the end of 1742. Like *Common Sense*, it reiterated the Country arguments originally set forth in the *Craftsman*. The histories of Ralph and Guthrie were conceived, at least in part, as extensions of their anti-ministerial propaganda, presented in a more scholarly vein.[25]

Birch kept Philip Yorke abreast of his rivals' activities.[26] In July 1743 Birch informed his patron that "their Proposals are not yet made public, but I am told express a sovereign contempt for all their predecessors, without the least exception to Rapin-Thoyras."[27] A couple of months later he expressed his doubts whether either of the histories would ever actually see the light of day.[28] Birch belittled their prospects of obtaining firm sponsorship or finding a significant reading market. All indications are that Guthrie and Ralph met with few buyers and very little press reaction either in England or abroad.[29]

Neither Ralph nor Guthrie conformed to the Court Whig rendering of English history, but they were certainly not Tory historians. However, one full-blown Tory history did appear almost contemporaneously with Birch's *Continuation*. This was the Jacobite Thomas Carte's *History of England* (3 vols., 1747-54). The chief promoters of this venture were the country's leading Jacobites, including John Hynde Cotton, the Duke of Beaufort, and Watkin Williams Wynn.[30] However, Carte did more than elicit individual sponsors. In 1744 he obtained subscriptions from the London Court of Common Council and from the company of Grocers and Vinters, from the Goldsmith's Company, from several Oxford Colleges, and from the chapter of Durham. The history that finally emerged was a curious mixture of learned scholarship and unabashed Jacobitism, propagating a High Tory, Filmerite conception of monarchy, and implicitly supporting the King over the Water. This was too much for Carte's non-Jacobite subscribers, many of whom withdrew their backing when the first volume appeared.

Birch knew Carte well. In the 1730s they had worked together on the Society for the Encouragement of Learning, an organization that tried to publish scholarly books that the ordinary run of booksellers would avoid.[31]   Birch must have respected Carte's scholarship because he acknowledged the assistance Carte had provided him on the *General Dictionary*.[32] By the time Birch began writing the *Continuation of Rapin*, however, he was clearly at odds with Carte. The first reference to Carte in the Birch-Yorke letters comes in the fall of 1742. Birch was appalled that Carte had applied to be keeper of the Cotton Library and took issue with "a loose pamphlet of his."[33] The pamphlet to which Birch referred, *A Full Answer to the Letter from a Bystander*, was an anti-ministerial propaganda piece in which Carte flailed away at the rise of standing armies and the overweening power assumed by the crown since the Revolution of 1688. Several weeks later Birch reported on a personal encounter with Carte:[34]

> I saw him on Saturday last and told him before a large company my sentiments of his pamphlet and the grounds of them in very plain terms which would have provoked an innocent man, but threw him into confusion. His performance has met with vast applause from the Tories, who appear now a set of men to me who are capable of believing everything that will suit their prejudices; but a few instances in itself will show you how unfit a person he is to write our history, or to be entrusted with the Cottonian Library, which he is vigorously soliciting. Astonishing impudence.

A week later, Birch vowed to expose Carte's *Full Answer* in a broadside of his own, but one never came forth.[35]

Volume I of Carte's *History* was devoted to the medieval period and did not extend to the controversial Tudor-Stuart epoch. Nevertheless, readers had no difficulty finding manifestations of Jacobitism. One assertion in particular was seized upon by critics. Buried in a footnote was an anecdote in which the Pretender administered the royal touch, successfully, to cure the King's Evil. Birch echoed the views of many in denouncing this story as an "absurd romance."[36] Carte's succeeding volumes were not attacked, simply ignored. Birch commented in the summer of 1750 that he could find no bookseller or gentleman who owned a copy of Carte's second volume.[37]

Although the opposition Whigs Ralph and Guthrie held little in common with the Tory Carte, there is nothing in the correspondence between Birch and Yorke to indicate that they actually differentiated between the political allegiances of Ralph and Guthrie on one hand and Carte on the other. A letter from Yorke to Birch in July 1744 expresses their attitude:[38]

> I do not think any court pension was worse bestowed than the City's liberality to Carte, which reflects as much on their taste as patrons as their loyalty as good subjects; so that I am a little puzzled to believe that Sir J. B. could be at the bottom of it. I hope the next step they take of the literary kind will be to appoint Guthrie their historiographer.

Birch and Yorke were outraged at the City's decision to grant Carte fifty pounds a year for researching and writing his history. So was Horace Walpole, who denounced the Common Council's support for this "Jacobite parson" as "surveyors of common sewers turned supervisors of literature."[39] "Sir J. B." of the letter must be Sir John Barnard, the City leader in Parliament. The day before Yorke wrote this letter, Birch wrote that Sir John Barnard was behind the subscription.[40]

Yorke's sarcastic gibe about making Guthrie City historiographer is consistent with Birch's comments testifying to Guthrie's City appeal. Guthrie's "only patrons and purchasers," he submitted in 1744, were the Independent Electors of the City of Westminster - an opposition group, supported by middle-class tradesmen and lawyers.[41] Except for the biggest financiers and merchants, City businessmen generally supported the shifting groups of dissident Whigs and Tories who comprised the opposition to Whig administrations.[42]

The Birch-Yorke correspondence discloses the manner in which history was written to serve political interest groups. It also documents the production of a specific Whig compilation. Politicians, publishers, a ghostwriter, and the nominal author were all involved in the composition of the *Continuation of Rapin*. Birch's rivals, however, Guthrie, Ralph, and Carte, were not content to simply conflate and paraphrase texts. Their scholarly narratives departed markedly from the compilation format.

Notes

[1]J. Brumfitt, *Voltaire, Historian*, 2nd ed. (London, 1970), 167.

[2]For Bolingbroke's influence on Voltaire, see Isaac Kramnick, *Bolingbroke and his Circle: the Politics of Nostalgia in the Age of Walpole* (Cambridge, Mass., 1968), pp. 137-187; "Introduction," in Lord Bolingbroke, *Historical Writings*, edited and with an Introduction by Isaac Kramnick (Chicago, 1972), xi-liii.

[3]See David Carrithers, "Montesquieu's Philosophy of History," *Journal of the History of Ideas*, January-March, 1986, XLVII, no. 1, 61-80.

[4]On the Scottish Enlightenment, see Anand C. Chitnis, *The Scottish Enlightenment, A Social History* (London, 1976); R. H. Campbell and Andrew S. Skinner, editors, *The Origins of the Scottish Enlightenment* (Edinburgh, 1982); Istvan Hont and Michael Ignatieff, editors, *Wealth and Virtue: the Shaping of Political Economy in the Scottish Enlightenment* (Cambridge, 1983); Ronald L. Meek, *Social Science and the Ignoble Savage* (Cambridge, 1976). Richard B. Sher, *Church and University in the Scottish Enlightenment: The Moderate Literati of Edinburgh* (Princeton, 1985).

[5]See J. B. Owen, *The Rise of the Pelhams* (London, 1956).

[6]See J. H. Plumb, *England in the Eighteenth Century* (London, 1950), 105.

[7]W. A. Speck, *Stability and Strife: England, 1714-1760* (Cambridge, Mass., 1977), 164.

[8]Quoted in James Boswell, *The Life of Samuel Johnson*, 6 vols., ed. George Birbeck Hill (London, 1887), I, 159.

[9]John Nichols, *Illustrations of the Literary History of the Eighteenth Century*, 8 vols. (1817-58), II, 136.

[10]*Ibid.* (1812), V, 284.

[11]William Coxe, *Memoirs of the Life and Administration of Sir Robert Walpole, Earl of Oxford*, 4 vols. (London, 1798), I, xviii-xix.

[12]BL. Add. MS. 4260. f. 24.

[13]Yorke to Birch, Aug. 6, 1744, BL. Add. MS. 35396. f. 236.

[14]Birch to Yorke, July 21, 1744, BL. Add. MS. 35396. f. 224.

[15]Birch to Yorke, Oct. 6, 1744, BL. Add. MS. 35396. f. 264.

[16]Yorke to Birch, Aug. 6, 1744, BL. Add. MS. 35396. f. 236.

[17]Yorke to Birch, July 24, 1745, BL. Add. MS. 35396. f. 296.   Walpole offered to help Birch on the *Continuation*; Walpole to Birch, Aug. 5, 1745, *The Letters of Horace Walpole*, ed. Peter Cunningham, 9 vols. (Edinburgh, 1906), V, 87.

[18]In August 1743, when Birch was gathering materials for the history, Tindal advised him what points he should address in "our history," including the characters of great men, foreign affairs and treaties and "the origin of the Bank and other funds." Tindal to Birch, Aug. 23, 1743, BL. Add. MS. 4319. f. 157.

[19]Charles Yorke to Philip Yorke, Oct. 22, 1744, BL. Add. MS. 35360. f. 139.

[20]John Knapton to Birch, Dec. 10, 1742, Dec. 21, 1742, Oct. 7, 1743, Dec. 9, 1743, BL. Add. MS. 4312. ff. 30, 33, 34, 35.

[21]Yorke, June 7, 1744, BL. Add. MS. 35360. 128; Oct. 22, 1744, BL. Add. MS. 35360. f. 139.

[22]At one point Birch observes that the East India Company's ability in 1698 to raise two million pounds in three days "surprised and amazed the whole world . . . .   It gave the neighboring nations an astonishing image both of the opulence of England, and the strength of the government." There is a long history to this quotation.   Citations in several early-eighteenth-century histories indicate that it came originally from Abel Boyer's *Annals of the Reign of King William III* (1702-03).   Kennett employed exactly the same language in the *Complete History* (1706).   And in his *History of England during the Reigns of King William and Queen Mary, Queen Anne and George I* (1735), Oldmixon submitted that the two

million raised by the New East India Company "surprised and amazed the whole world. And as it greatly mortified all those that were assured his majesty would be disappointed of this supply, so it gave our neighboring nations an astonishing image both of the opulence of England and the strength of the government." All these Whig compilers, then copied from each other - without quotation marks - plaudits for the new Whig trading-financial company. See Nicholas Tindal, *The History of England, by Rapin de Thoyras. Continued from the Revolution to the Accession of George II*, 13 vols. (London, 1744-47), XVIII, 418; White Kennett, *A Complete History of England*, 3 vols. (London, 1719), 2nd ed., III, 750; John Oldmixon, *The History of England during the reigns of King William and Queen Mary, Queen Anne and George I* (London, 1735), 177; see Tindal, XVIII, 277-82 on Montagu and the Bank.

[23]Yorke to Birch, Sept. 17, 1744, BL. Add. MS. 35396. f. 256.

[24]See Robert W. Kenny, "James Ralph: An Eighteenth Century Philadelphian in Grub Street," *The Pennsylvania Magazine of History and Biography*, LXIV (1940), 218-242; John Burke Shipley, "James Ralph: Pretender to Genius" (Ph.D. Dissertation, Columbia University, 1963), 403-405.

[25]See Shipley, 318-323, 376-378; Laurence Hanson, *Government and the Press, 1695-1763* (London, 1936), 119.

[26]During the 1730s Birch had been a good friend of Ralph's, before the latter cast his fate with the opposition to Walpole. Birch helped him to get some works of fiction published and seems to have lent him money as well. He also knew Guthrie from the 1730s when both were associated with Cave and the *Gentleman's Magazine*. By the early 1740s, however, there was clearly no love lost between the ministerial Whig Birch and "that noble pair of historiographers," as he called Ralph and Guthrie; 172-183, 190-193; see Shipley, 318-323, 376-378; Laurence Hanson, *Government and the Press* (London, 1936), 119; on Birch's connections with the Gentleman's magazine, see James L. Clifford, *Young Sam Johnson* (London, 1955), 186-187, 198, 202, 242, 250.

[27]Birch to Yorke, July 9, 1743, BL. Add. MS. 35396. f. 120.

[28]Birch to Yorke, Aug. 20, 1743, Add. MS. 35396. f. 134.

[29]In September 1744 Birch reported that "Ralph's Supplement, notwithstanding the splendid appearance of Lord Somers' and Lord Halifax's names in the advertisements" - references to the unpublished papers of Somers and Halifax - "meets with so cold a reception, which by no means answers the expense, and is expected by the booksellers, who are the best judges of the fate though not the merit of the books, to expire even before it reaches the reign of Charles II." Birch to Yorke, Sept. 22, 1744, BL. Add. MS. 35396. f. 257. By "supplement" Birch meant that Ralph's work was, like his own, a supplement to Rapin's *History of England*.

[30]See the following chapter for information on the production of Carte's history.

[31]See Clayton Atto, "The Society for the Encouragement of Learning." *The Library*, XIX (1939), 263-281.

[32]Carte gave Birch information on the Earl of Clarendon and Rapin-Thoyras. Ironically, the only evaluative comments that Birch wrote in his *Dictionary* profile of Rapin were the harsh criticisms Carte had leveled against him in the 1738 proposals for his projected history.

[33]Birch to Yorke, Sept. 2, 1742, BL. Add. MS. 35396. f. 53.

[34]Birch to Yorke, Sept. 30, 1742, Add. MS. 35396. f. 70.

[35]In February 1743, however, Birch did send Carte a thirty-nine page textual comparison between Carte's *Life of Ormonde* and his *Full Answer* to show how the latter's discussion of Charles II's reign completely contradicted what he had written earlier in the *Life*. To drive home his point that the *Full Answer* whitewashed Charles II, Birch even transcribed the critical descriptions of Charles found in Echard, a historian "unsuspected of any prejudice to the memory of Charles II." Subsequently, in 1747, Birch wrote a trenchant little volume demolishing Carte's specious claim in his *Life of Ormonde* that the Earl of Glamorgan had forged the commissions from Charles I entitling him to negotiate with the Irish Catholics to raise an army behind the back of Ormonde, the Lord Lieutenant. Hume partially backed Carte's version in his *History*, and the issue of Glamorgan's commission continued to be debated into the early nineteenth century; see Birch to Yorke, Oct. 7, 1742, Add. MS. 35396. f. 75; Birch to Yorke, Feb. 2, 1743, Bod. Lib. Carte MS. 260. ff. 2-23; Birch,

An Enquiry into the Share which King Charles I had in the Transactions of the Earl of Glamorgan (London, 1747).

[36]Birch to Yorke, Aug. 13, 1748, BL. Add. MS. 35397. f. 142.

[37]Birch to Yorke, July 14, 1750, BL. Add. MS. 35397. f. 261; Birch to Yorke, Oct. 20, 1740, BL. Add. MS. 35397. f. 307.

[38]Birch to Yorke, July 29, 1744, BL. Add. MS. 35396. f. 229.

[39]Birch to Yorke, July 28, 1744, BL. Add. MS. 35396. f. 229; Walpole to Horace Mann, July 2, 1744, *The Correspondence of Horace Walpole*, 42 vols. ed. W. S. Lewis, George L. Lam, C. H. Bennett (New Haven, 1948), XVIII, 480.

[40]Birch to Yorke, July 28, 1744, BL. Add. MS. 35396. f. 229.

[41]Birch to Yorke, Sept. 22, 1744, BL. Add. MS. 35396. f. 257; Birch to Yorke, July 11, 1747, BL. Add. MS. 35397, f. 53.

[42]See Lucy Sutherland, "The City of London in Eighteenth-Century Politics" in *Essays Presented to Sir Lewis Namier*, eds. Richard Pares and A. J. P. Taylor (London, 1956), 49-74; Eveline Cruickshanks, *Political Untouchables: The Tories and the '45* (London, 1979), 41.

Chapter VII

Thomas Carte and the Historical Mind of Jacobitism

The commercial and critical success enjoyed by Birch's *Continuation* indicates that the compilation was still a popular form of historical exposition in mid-eighteenth-century England. This style of writing had begun to change, however, even before the *Continuation of Rapin* was published. As we have seen, the historical essays of Bolingbroke and other political writers in the 1730s and the histories of Neal, Salmon, and Rapin himself marked a significant advance in critical method and narrative fluency.

Thomas Carte was certainly no compiler. Scholarly and erudite, Carte conducted extensive research and interspersed his narrative with learned disquisitions on sundry topics. When he began his *A General History of England* in the late 1730s he was already a scholar of note, well versed in British and Continental sources. Subsidized by politicians and corporations, Carte possessed the time and resources to accomplish his ambitions: to produce an authoritative history of England and knock Rapin from his pedestal. In the end, however, Carte utterly failed to provide a valid alternative to Rapin. For all the scholarly pyrotechnics, his basic premise was preposterous. From pre-history to the seventeenth century, from the Druids to the Stuarts, Carte maintained, English kings had justly exercised a high prerogative, based on divine ordination and indefeasible hereditary right. Accordingly, he glorified the Stuarts and implicitly condemned the Hanoverian constitution as a perversion of fundamental law. Carte was the official historian of the Jacobite faction in England. He and his Jacobite backers aimed to replace the Whiggish Rapin with a historical justification of their cause. Carte's show of scholarship and his perspicacious criticisms of Rapin were undone, ultimately, by his dogmatic Jacobitism. To read Carte is to gain insight into the historical ideology of Jacobite Toryism during the years of political instability surrounding the '45 Rebellion.

Educated at both Oxford and Cambridge, Carte was a nonjuring cleric whose life was devoted chiefly to scholarship.[1] He first attracted attention in 1714 with a published sermon exculpating Charles I from the spurious charge that he instigated the Irish Rebellion and "massacre" of

1641. There is no evidence that Carte participated in the 1715 Jacobite Rebellion, but he was secretary to Francis Atterbury during the 1722 Jacobite conspiracy, in which Atterbury was implicated, and was rumored to have incited Jacobite riots at the county elections of that year. He escaped prosecution only by fleeing to France. Princess Caroline secured permission for Carte to return to England in about 1730.

Shortly thereafter Carte set to work on his first major historical work, the *Life of Ormonde* (1735-36). James Butler, the 2nd Duke of Ormonde, had replaced Marlborough as Commander of the Forces during the War of the Spanish Succession. He was a renowned Jacobite Tory and had fled to France along with Bolingbroke in 1715 to join the Pretender. The 3rd Duke of Ormonde hired Carte to undertake the biography. When volume I appeared, Ormonde complimented Carte on his work and thanked him for vindicating "my grandfather from malicious false accusations."[2] The *Life of Ormonde* was a panegyric, but it was based upon extensive research.[3] Among the subscribers to this work was none other than the Pretender, James III. Carte sent him a copy.[4]

Carte's narrow escape from criminal prosecution had done nothing to blunt his appetite for intrigue. From the early 1730s to his death in 1754 he went on plotting, zealously and indiscreetly, for a Jacobite invasion. The high esteem in which he was held by the Jacobite chieftains for his historical gifts did not extend to his amateurish excursions into the murky world of political conspiracy. Publicly, Carte's trips to Paris in these decades were taken to conduct research on his *History of England*. But, he combined his historical inquiries with fruitless intrigue.[5]

It was while on one trip to Paris in 1739 that Carte, through an intermediary, was made a messenger from Walpole to the Pretender in Rome.[6] Walpole's agent in Paris, David Avery, told Carte that Sir Robert was facing political disaster at home and was, consequently, willing to consider a Stuart restoration on condition that James not tamper with the Church and that he guarantee safe conduct to the Hanoverian family. Carte, who appears to have believed this concoction, relayed this message to the Pretender. Supplied with James' response, Carte then followed Avery's instructions and met secretly with Walpole.

Carte's meeting with Walpole speaks volumes for the dexterity with which the prime minister could manipulate his political antagonists. It also illustrates Carte's guileless devotion to his exiled king. After handing Walpole a letter "from the King my master," which promised to preserve the Church and safeguard the Hanoverian family, Carte was completely taken aback by his host's reaction. Showing no interest in the letter, Walpole began bombarding Carte with questions: What intelligence had he gathered about the possibility of a Jacobite invasion? Did he think a war with France was on the horizon? What was the Pretender's opinion of Bolingbroke? When Carte refused to answer this line of questioning, Walpole proceeded to threaten him with arrest and, at the same time, offered him a handsome annuity. Carte rejected Walpole's blandishments and left fearing imminent arrest. A warrant was in fact issued for Carte's arrest that year on suspicion of concealing arms, though he was not taken into custody. In 1744 Carte was incarcerated briefly on the same charge.

Carte's Jacobitism, then, was more than an intellectual position, expressed in his writings. He practiced Jacobite politics and wrote Jacobite history with as much political commitment as Lord Bolingbroke or John Oldmixon. Carte also employed his pen in Tory pamphleteering. The essentials of Carte's historical ideology can be found in *A Full Answer to the Letter from a Bystander* (1742), a rejoinder of more than a hundred pages to a Whig broadside, and in *A Full and Clear Vindication of the Full Answer to the Letter from a Bystander* (1743). These tracts make it clear that Carte saw the English Revolution of the mid-seventeenth century as the crucial determinant of recent English history. It was:[7]

> the detestable Rebellion of 1642 . . . (the unhappy consequences of which the nation still feels) that ruined the patrimony of the crown, and entailed upon all posterity a burden of taxes necessary to enable the Prince to subsist, and repair the alienations which that Rebellion and the usurptions which followed it, had produced.

The Parliamentary taxation that had replaced the traditional revenues of the crown was, Carte believed, exiguous and, at the same time, oppressive.[8] Most of the *Full Answer* was devoted to an attack on standing armies and the exorbitant expense of maintaining them.

It was while working on his *Life of Ormonde* that Carte began plans to write his major work, the *History of England*. Carte's *History*, wrote a detractor after volume I appeared, was "the joint labor of the whole Jacobite Junto."[9] This was an exaggeration, but certainly Carte's principal backers were Jacobites. From the start Carte envisaged a Society for an History of England (modeled after the recently disbanded Society for the Advancement of Learning), which would finance his history. The first of several papers by Carte, aimed to drum up subscribers to his *History*, was published in March 1736. His *Proposals for Removing the Impediments of Writing a History of England* argued for a new history that would tap hitherto unexplored sources. Carte clearly designed this piece to attract men of all political viewpoints who were dissatisfied with Rapin's hegemony. He took the Frenchman to task, not for his Whiggism, but because his research was so limited. Rapin, he submitted, had never consulted the journals of either House, or the documents in the Paper Office and Cotton Library. Although better than his predecessors, Rapin was a foreigner who really knew nothing about England except the "modern notions" he picked up in coffee houses. Carte also made the apposite point that "writers as have presumed the venerable name of historians" merely compiled "memorials of public facts" and placed too much stress on the "military exploits of our ancestors." What was sorely needed was a good "civil history." "An history of our constitution, laws, usages, customs, and manners, with the various sudden or gradual alterations which these have undergone in the course of time, and the effects thereof on the nation, is still wanting."[10] Hume and Voltaire said much the same thing.

Carte wrote letters containing the substance of his *Proposals* to various personages. Some of Carte's letters were quite specific about the ulterior motives for his *History*. In a draft of one letter Carte speaks of having his history serve the clergy, "whose rights and privileges are nowadays either little understood or little minded. Nothing can clear up their rights and privileges but going through our records in the manner I propose."[11] Hence, Carte wrote, he had applied to cathedrals for subscriptions. The Chapter of Durham, for one, had subscribed 20 guineas a year.

In April 1738 Carte published another advertisement for his *History*, a ten-page *General Account of the Necessary Materials for an History of England*.[12] By the summer of 1738 at least fifteen people had subscribed ten and twenty pounds apiece toward the *History*. Carte was not satisfied with that rate of progress. In July he complained to this friend Corbet Kynaston, a fellow Jacobite who had helped organize the Fifteen Rebellion:[13]

If anything could surprise me it is the backwardness of the Tories to encourage a work necessary for the clearing up of that constitution for which, in other cases, they so much contend; and which will be a standard perhaps forever, since in all probability nobody will ever be at the pains hereafter of going through that infinite number of records that I shall do. But they are fonder, I see, of paying for the support of Old Whig papers, stuffed with quotations out of Rapin, a violent enemy of the Church and monarchy, than to encourage a work which would make everybody ashamed of quoting him, and enable everybody that wishes well to his country to know, defend, and support their true rights and privileges; for at present they are not known enough to be defended, and disputed privileges are really none.

This excerpt lays bare the deep-seated political motives that actuated Carte in his historical labors: Rapin should be replaced because his *History* was a storehouse of political and ideological ammunition for the Whigs, whether they be Country Whig or Court Whig. Carte's scorn for the Old Whigs reflects his concern that the Tories were being lured away from the fold by Bolingbroke and his allies. Carte's *History* would help prevent further defections.

Carte may have been disappointed with the financial backing in this early stage, but he was receiving advice and assistance on his labors from various scholars and politicians, including Thomas Baker (a distinguished antiquarian scholar), Zachary Grey (the Tory antagonist of Oldmixon and Neal), and a Jacobite leader, John Hynde Cotton.[14]

The Society for an History of England, comprised of those who were subsidizing Carte, did not meet for the first time until February 14, 1744.[15] A seven-man committee was established to manage the Society, with the Earl of Ailesbury, a Jacobite, serving as president. The committee agreed to meet once a month, and the Society as a whole once a year.[16] The Society convened near the Cotton Library in London, in the same house that had accommodated the defunct Society for the Encouragement of Learning. Society records list twenty-six subscribers as having attended the first meeting. Subscriptions ranged between ten and twenty pounds per person per year, with a few members exceeding that amount. Among the subscribers were Watkin Williams Wynn, owner of large Welsh estates and a preeminent Jacobite chieftain; John Hynde Cotton, the top Jacobite in Parliament, briefly a member of the Broadbottom ministry, a close friend of Carte; and Alderman William Benn, another City leader, Lord Mayor in 1747, active in Jacobite plotting.[17]   When we add the Duke of Beaufort and the Earl of Orrery to this list, it becomes clear that virtually all of England's Jacobite chieftains sponsored Carte's *History*, though there is nothing to substantiate one critic's charge that the committee of the Society actually revised the *History* before it was published.[18]

Besides the aforementioned individuals there were also institutional subscribers.[19]   Oxford was an eighteenth-century hotbed of Toryism, and five Oxford colleges subscribed in 1744:   Trinity, New, Brasenose, Magdalen, and Lincoln.   Later that year the Goldsmith's and the Grocers and Vinter's companies subscribed twenty-five pounds each.   Carte's biggest coup came in July 1744 when the Court of Common Council of the City agreed to subscribe fifty pounds a year for seven years.

As noted earlier, Carte's first volume incited a storm of abuse with its distinct Jacobite tone, its graceless reference to the Pretender touching for the King's Evil.   The City promptly withdrew its subscription. Pamphlets poured scorn on the hapless scholar.   Whereas the first volume had been published by the Tory bookseller J. Hodges, volumes II and III were privately printed.[20]   These last two volumes never appear to have reached the booksellers' shelves.   References to Carte down through the years regularly allude to the work having fallen into immediate popular neglect.[21]   Nevertheless, the Oxford colleges continued to subscribe, as did the Chamber of London.   The Society minutes do not, in fact, indicate a substantial falling off in subscriptions to the *History*.[22]

Like so many of his contemporaries, Carte crowded his *History* with detail, yet his theme stood out in bold relief.   Carte wanted to glorify the Stuart monarchy and the conception of Church and state that it symbolized.   Had Charles I in particular succeeded in neutralizing his opposition, he would have made England safe for Church, king and aristocracy - safe from the pretensions of Parliament and the depredations of Puritans. Carte envisaged a form of aristocratic paternalism in which the nobility ruled benevolently over the deferential freeholders and merchants beneath them.   In his basic interpretation, then, Carte did not move beyond the traditional Tory apologies for the Stuarts.   But he grounded his discussion in much more extensive documentation than did all earlier Royalist-Tory historians, he informed it with a more coherent and thoroughgoing economic analysis, and he embellished it with learned disquisitions on specific issues.

The great bulk of Carte's research and original scholarship was devoted to the Tudor-Stuart period. His medieval narrative followed Robert Brady's definitive Tory interpretation faithfully. It served Carte's purpose in his account of sixteenth- and seventeenth-century England to paint the Tudors in dark colors, thereby making the Stuarts appear more lustrous by comparison. Repeatedly in his efforts to palliate the Stuarts Carte made farfetched claims that flew in the face of all the known evidence.[23] In the case of Henry VII this took the form of whitewashing that stock villain, Richard III, and trotting out Perkin Warbeck as the right and true king. Carte thus undercut the legitimacy of Henry's rule and endorsed the claims of the Pretender to the throne. The parallel with George II and James III was obvious. While Carte did not go so far as to support Mary Queen of Scots' claim to the throne, he nonetheless idealized Mary as a woman of spotless virtue, incapable of plotting against Elizabeth.

Carte could find no words of praise for Henry VII. The first Tudor oppressed the populace and depressed the nobility for his own financial advantage.[24] By contrast, Henry VIII was painted in relatively soft colors.[25] Carte accepts Henry's explanation at face value that it was pangs of conscience that made him seek an annulment and ultimately break with Rome, but he explains the dissolution of the monasteries as a straightforward grab for riches. Carte points to a cruel and arbitrary streak in the king, the most notorious example being the "cruel six articles," which laid down draconian punishments for heresy. In the end, nonetheless, Carte rates Henry as a great king, more just than unjust, and rightly esteemed for throwing off the Romish shackles.

Curiously, Carte does not fault the more radical Edwardian Reformation, and his vehement denunciation of Queen Mary would satisfy the most ardent Whig.[26] He presents a mixed assessment of Elizabeth, much more critical than the conventional Whig encomiums.[27] Elizabeth paled in comparison with her irreproachable Scottish cousin. On the positive side, she rescued the Church, refused to devalue the currency, built up the navy, encouraged commerce, supported the United Provinces, and curbed the power of Spain. On the other hand, she treated the nobility shamelessly, not offering them enough employments at court and charging them exorbitantly whenever she stayed with them on her progresses around the country. Her war with Ireland toward the close of her reign ran England into debt. She put offices up for sale, thus planting the seeds of future corruption. Finally, Elizabeth plundered the Church and failed to stamp out Puritanism.

Elizabeth bequeathed to her successor a depleted treasury and a Church and crown threatened by Puritanism. Carte admires James I for what he sees as his reassertion of royal prerogatives. The problem was that James' words were not matched by deeds.[28] Carte admires his ringing declarations of divine right and the repressive measures taken against the Puritans. But James was not a suitable candidate for glorification. He appeared to be personally offensive and dependent upon dissolute favorites. The king's greatest failing was in not living up to his high sense of prerogative by exerting strong-arm methods to crush his enemies, the Puritans.[29]

From the time of Clarendon onward, historians, Whig and Tory, had usually treated Charles I more sympathetically than James I. By the reign of Queen Anne, Charles was on the way to becoming the royal martyr and a Tory hero. As Richard Ollard has eloquently shown, the passage of time gradually softened Charles' blemishes, shaping him finally into a saintly image.[30] With Carte we have gone as far as possible in this direction. The king is canonized. A model of piety, Charles "used none of Elizabeth's arts of courting them [the people], proposing to deserve their love by solid virtue, by the justness of his administration, and by the peace, plenty, and fidelity they enjoyed under his government."[31]

The execution of Charles I changed the course of English history. Because the divinely appointed prince had been murdered in the name of the English nation, England was made the target of divine retribution:[32]

We are as reasonably and surely justified in deeming the calamities which are the natural consequences of any unlawful action to be the judgment of God upon it, as we are in imagining that our eyes were given to us to see with or the sun was made to give light to the world.

Carte submitted that the "want of virtue and public spirit, the irreligion, immorality and corruption which reign too generally throughout these nations" could "be traced to the execrable murder of King Charles and the subversion of the constitution at that time, as naturally and surely as a stream may to its fountain." It is a measure of Carte's devotion to the Stuarts that for the remainder of his narrative, describing the years 1649 to 1654, he concentrates his discussion on the trials and tribulations of Charles II in exile, with only a few perfunctory remarks about the epoch-making events at home. Although he intended to take his history down to the Glorious Revolution, Carte died in 1754 before it even reached the Restoration.

There was nothing startlingly original about Carte's assessment of the Tudor-Stuart monarchs. Only differences in emphasis distinguished his interpretation from that of his Tory predecessor, Thomas Salmon. It would be incorrect, however, to dismiss Carte's *History* as simply a well-researched version of the traditional Tory history of England. Underpinning this conventional political chronicle of the various reigns was a quasi-Harringtonian, social and economic interpretation, considerably more coherent and developed than previous Tory histories.

The English Revolution did more than destroy Charles I and put an end to virtue and public spiritedness in England. It issued the final death blow to the traditional nobility. In a long passage about the "state of the Lords" in 1640, Carte reviews the decline and fall of the English peerage:[33]

The Lords at this time were so much different from the old barons, who made in former days so great a figure in England, as the modern Romans are from the ancient. Their dignities had ceased for some ages to be an incident of their tenures. The old heroic race of nobility, honored for their great qualities, noble sentiments, military glory, large estates, number of vassals, and unbounded hospitality, . . . had been in a manner extinguished by the civil wars between the houses of Yorke and Lancaster. The few remaining families had been trepanned into forfeiture by the craft of Henry VII, cut off by the violence of Henry VIII, discountenanced, burdened, depressed, or crushed by Queen Elizabeth.

Who, then, are the nobles of contemporary England?

Such as had got large shares of Church lands into their possessions, or had served for a time in any office about the court; secretaries, lawyers, and all that acquired fortunes in any other manner, began to fancy themselves entitled to a peerage, as if honours were of course to follow riches.   Hence arose another spirit in people ennobled by titles.   A selfish temper, confirmed by habit, and encouraged by rewards due only to distinguished merit, was not to be curbed by a pompous title.   The men continued as they were before the change of their name.   Zeal for the public good and the glory of their country gave way to private interest and the lust of power.   This quest of profitable offices and beneficial grants, the amassing wealth by profits oppressive to the people, got the better of those generous sentiments which a course of military service and an emulation of the glory of great ancestors seldom failed to inspire.

What these extracts describe in essence is the fall of the feudal nobility, the "old heroic race" whose titles derived from feudal tenures and military service, and the rise of nouveaux riches aristocrats, nobles in name only.   These upstarts, Carte argues, carried with them those contagious vices of profiteering and self-seeking.   For age-old mutual obligations between people they substituted the cash nexus.   Carte has no use for those modern values that we might today label as middle class. A career open to talents, for example, the "rewards due only to distinguished merit," only encouraged "a selfish temper" in the new nobility.[34]

Carte's ruminations about the state of the nobility on the eve of the English Revolution spell out in summary form what he had been discussing, intermittently, throughout his Tudor-Stuart narrative: namely, the decline of the aristocracy and aristocratic values and the concomitant rise of the commons.   Henry VII set out to cripple the nobility, thus enhancing his own power.[35]   Carte says surprisingly little about the social consequences of Henry VIII's policies, suggesting that the nobility made a resurgence but that the dissolution ultimately diffused property to the commons.[36]   Elizabeth depressed the nobility.   She stooped to court the commons as a counterweight to the aristocracy, was too lenient toward the Puritans - lower-class enemies of the nobility - and destroyed the flower of English nobility supporting Mary Stuart.   Like Cardinal Richelieu in France, Elizabeth reduced the nobility from territorial magnates with troops of retainers to impoverished courtiers.[37]

When James I assumed the throne in 1603, he inherited not only a steep debt from his predecessor but also a badly depleted aristocracy. James was not the man to ameliorate this situation. Prodigal by nature, he inflated the peerage by selling off titles to the highest bidder:[38]

> Thus favourites and monied men came to be ennobled . . . . This debased and weakened the nobility, the bucklers of the crown, so that Charles found none to stand between him and the people; and the royal interest in the house of peers was sunk in a multitude of titles.

What is striking about Carte's socioeconomic interpretation is the fact that he took the stock Country-Bolingbrokian image of *nouveaux riches* courtiers and monied men climbing to power over the bodies of the landed aristocracy and set it back from post-Revolution of 1688 to pre-Revolution of 1640. Carte was the only Augustan historian to do this. It reflected the High Tory and Jacobite belief that the mid-seventeenth-century conflagration with its "martyrdom" of Charles I formed the critical juncture in English history.

As we might expect, Carte discussed the Puritans primarily in terms of social class, though unlike most previous historians he did not ignore Calvinist doctrine. On the whole, however, Carte's examination of Puritanism was only marginally better than earlier historians and was distinctly inferior to Daniel Neal's treatment of the subject. According to Carte, the Puritans were not, in the main, those insidious "new persons" and "monied men" who infiltrated the ranks of the aristocracy. They were, rather, the "common people" - represented in the House of Commons - who in fact opposed both the landed and monied interest. The thrust of Carte's remarks is that certain elements of the parvenu aristocracy and much of the business community inflamed the lower classes with republican, revolutionary notions - Puritanism.

Carte first mentions the Puritans in connection with the return of the Marian exiles, inculcated with Calvinist religious thought. Denouncing Calvin's "absurd doctrines of necessity, absolute predestination and reprobation," he submits that the Calvinist style of church organization appealed especially to the common people, though he does not say precisely why.[39] Elizabeth "left that turbulent set of men in a condition that enabled them to distress her successor throughout his reign, and, in that of his son, to subvert the monarchy as well as the episcopacy, liturgy, and the whole constitution of the Church of England."[40]   When James I assumed the throne the Puritan-dominated commons took the offensive and refused to grant him the subsidies he needed.   "The Puritan faction in the House wanted to keep the King necessitous, that they might the easier carry their point in depressing the royal prerogative."[41]   The Puritans' anti-monarchical principles were imbibed by hypocritical self-seekers who saw the destruction of the monarchy as a means to advance their own ambitions and lust for power.   Carte believed the Puritans intended to "destroy the weight of all the landed and monied interest in the kingdom."[42]

Earlier Tory historians had referred fleetingly to the changing balance of property, but Carte was the first to make social change, specifically the decline of the aristocracy and the rise of the commons, a key facet of his overall interpretation.   In so doing he incorporated into his general history some of the neo-Harringtonian themes delineated in the Court and Country historical essays of the 1730s.   There was nothing scientific or detached about Carte's social analysis.   It was built into his whole partisan theme - to champion the Stuarts and the traditional landed order over which they had presided.

Carte shared the Harringtonian consciousness that we find in the other histories written at around mid-century - Ralph, Guthrie, and Hume. Moreover, unlike the *Continuation of Rapin* and so many previous histories, Carte's *History of England* avoided compilation.   Steeped in original sources, Carte abstained from synthesizing secondary historical works. Although his central themes were polemical and fundamentally wrongheaded, Carte's erudition is plainly evident.   No other Augustan history contains so many learned digressions or scholarly exegeses.[43]   For example, Edward VI's succession as a minor is made the occasion for a four-page disquisition on the subject of when a monarch may legally assume his majority.   When Carte takes up the controversial issue of Ship Money in Charles I's reign, he defends its legality by discoursing at length (twelve pages) on the medieval precedents.   In order to expose the illegality of the Long Parliament's attainder of Strafford, Carte again launches into an historical review of attainders.   The subject that Carte took up in the greatest detail was the intrigue, both foreign and domestic, of Mary Queen of Scots.   He studied valuable and hitherto unexplored foreign manuscripts, the most fruitful of which were the diplomatic papers of Antoine, Francois, and Gilles de Noailles, in possession of the Noailles family, in Limousin, France.[44]

A reading of Carte's *Proposals* alone makes it clear that he understood the deficiencies of British historical writing - the partisan distortion; the shallow research; the annalistic, compilation style; the overemphasis on military events at the expense of political, social and economic developments. In a limited way Carte's *History* atoned for some of these inadequacies. This is the case especially with respect to Carte's style and method. He chose to explain, not compile. He saturated his narrative with factual detail, as was customary, but wrote with a distinctive voice and thematic clarity. He explored certain issues and events in greater depth than had heretofore been the case, based upon his wider range of sources. Finally, he brought to his *History* a quasi-Harringtonian awareness of social change.

Ultimately, however, Carte could not transcend the limitations of traditional Augustan historical writing and the Christian humanist genre to which it belonged. He followed the conventional practice of denouncing partisanship and protesting his impartiality, but he was an active Jacobite whose *History* was sponsored by the Jacobite leaders and produced to serve the Jacobite cause. *The History of England* bears all the hallmarks of ideological distortion and special pleading. Furthermore, the very nature of Carte's ideology impeded the elucidation of a fully secular and mundane history. Carte resorted to providential explanations less than Clarendon or Echard, but the High Tory philosophy to which he adhered included a providential conception of history - a history in which God sent forth omens and dispensed rewards and punishments and in which the divinely ordained king possessed miraculous curative powers.

Carte's *History* was the most ambitious attempt to date to produce a definitive history of England, one that would at once furnish all the correct political lessons to be drawn from the English past, be an authoritative work of scholarship, and also be widely read. Unfortunately for Carte and his party, their old-fashioned, unreconstructed Toryism had lost most of its credibility by the mid-eighteenth century. What can be called the classical Royalist-Tory period of English historiography, from Clarendon to Carte, had drawn to a close. The Tories could no longer offer a serious alternative to the conventional Whig version of history as set forth in Rapin's *History of England.*

Even without the Jacobite slant, Carte's *History*, with its dry scholarly style and abstruse digressions, was not the stuff of which best sellers were made.   Given a lively narrative and a more palatable interpretation, nonetheless, the Whig hegemony could be broken. Even before Carte's posthumous last volume appeared, Hume's controversial first volume was published.   It soon became the most popular history of any kind ever published in England.   Before considering this successful challenge to Rapin, however, two far less famous works should be addressed.

Notes

[1]Unless otherwise noted, biographical information on Carte comes from the *Dictionary of National Biography* article on him by Evelyn Shirley Shuckburgh.

[2]Ormonde to Carte, Dec. 30, 1735, Bod. Lib. Carte MS. 227. ff. 111-112.

[3]See Carte letter to unnamed correspondent, Aug. 25, 1736, Bod. Lib. Carte MS. 203. f. 21.

[4]See Thomas Carte, *The Life of James, Duke of Ormonde*, 4 vols., orig. pub. 1736 (Oxford, 1851) I, iv.

[5]James II and his agents treated Carte politely but did not include him in their machinations.   As one Scottish conspirator put it, they "knew too well the indiscretion and heat of his brains, to which the warmth of his heart could only reconcile a fool."   Carte's liaison with other amateur plotters in the late 1730s and early 1740s, most notably with the two sisters of John Edward Oglethorpe, impeded rather than helped the Jacobite cause.   See Patricia Kneas Hill, *The Oglethorpe Ladies* (Atlanta, 1977), 88; see also pp. 80-92 generally on Carte's plotting.

[6]The account of Carte's mission is drawn from Carte's journal, BL. Add. MS. 34522. ff. 4-14; see also Hill, 82-83.

[7]Carte, *A Full and Clear Vindication of the Full Answer to the Letter from a Bystander* (London, 1743), 94-95.

[8]Carte, *A Full Answer to the Letter from a Bystander* (London, 1742), 101, 147, 184-185.

[9][Samuel Squire] Duncan Macarte, pseud., *A Letter to John-Trotplaid, Esq., author of the Jacobite Journal, concerning Mr. Carte's General History of England* (London, 1748), 14. Squire was a historian and Carte's chief critic. His principal work was a medieval history, *An Enquiry into the Foundation of the English Constitution* (1745). He also wrote a *Historical Essay upon the Balance of Civil Power in England* (1748). Both these works presented a strongly Harringtonian version of English history. For a detailed discussion of Squire, see Reed Browning, *The Political and Constitutional Ideas of the Court Whigs* (Baton Rouge, 1982), 117-150.

[10]John Nichols, *Literary Anecdotes of the Eighteenth Century*, 9 vols. (London, 1812-16) II, 485. The "Proposals" are printed in Nichols, 484-485.

[11]Carte to Ker, Oct. 1738(?), Bod. Lib. Carte MS. 240. ff. 332-342, 344-345.

[12]Besides reiterating most of his original proposals, this ten-page pamphlet cited some political advantages to be gained by producing a new English history. His *History* would detail:

> what changes have happened in our courts of judicature, in our maxims of law, and in our methods of justice; . . . and what effects have followed such deviations from the old rules; and thus by the experience of former ages they will be instructed how to reform what is or shall be amiss, and to do it in the safest and most effectual manner by returning to the old rules established by the wisdom and warranted by the practice of their ancestors.

See Carte, *A General Account of the Necessary Materials for an History of England* (London, 1738), 9.

[13]Carte to Kynaston, July 4, 1738, Nichols, *Illustrations of the Literary History of the Eighteenth Century*, 8 vols. (London, 1817-58) V, 60-68.

[14]Baker, a nonjuror, told Carte he would gladly solicit subscriptions for him and said that manuscripts at St. John's Cambridge were open to him. Grey assured Carte he would search among the manuscripts in the Cambridge Library.

Carte also received assistance from Richard Rawlinson, an antiquarian scholar who promised to subscribe to and promote Carte's *History*; George Jeffreys, a playwright and hanger-on of the Duke of Chandos, who supplied Carte with manuscripts; Thomas Sheridan, a schoolmaster and old friend of Swift. Carte consulted about various points of English history with Cotton, the Duke of Chandos (a Whig), and the Earl of Middleton. Bod. Lib., "E. Edwards Calendar of the Carte Papers," LIV, 121, 176; Carte MS. 136. f. 261, MS. 227. f. 222, MS. 232. f. 47, MS. 231. f. 62, MS. 237. f. 3.

[15]The Society minutes constitute Bod. Lib. Carte MS. 175, and the discussion of Society meetings, unless otherwise noted, is drawn from this document. Information on the political allegiances of the subscribers comes mainly from Eveline Cruickshanks, *Political Untouchables: The Tories and the '45* (London, 1975), Linda Colley, *In Defiance of Oligarchy, The Tory Party, 1714-60* (Cambridge, 1982), and the *Dictionary of National Biography*.

[16]As it turned out, however, only about a half dozen usually attended each of the Society meetings. Besides Ailesbury, members of the committee included James Edward Oglethorpe, founder and former governor of the Georgia colony. A one-time Jacobite who had supported Atterbury in the 1722 Conspiracy, Oglethorpe had forsaken "the Cause" for a staunch Hanoverian Toryism, though he remained close to his sisters and other Jacobites. Another committee member was Edward Gibbon (father of the historian, Tory M.P.), City alderman, and probably a Jacobite. There was also George Heathcote, a powerful City leader, who had converted from radical Whig to zealous Jacobite in 1741. Another Tory alderman, John Blackford, was the Society's trustee. The Society's funds were lodged with Child's Tory banking house in Blackford's name. Blackford would soon become Lord Mayor. Given the illustrious City figures who participated in the Society, it is easy to understand why Whigs like Birch and Horace Walpole were irate.

[17]Other subscribers included John Bosworth, chamberlain of the Corporation of London, a Jacobite; Samuel Pennant, City alderman, an opposition Whig; Charles Leigh, M.P. and a wealthy Jacobite landlord; John Cotton, like his namesake, a Jacobite.

[18][Samuel Squire], *Remarks upon Mr. Carte's Specimen of His General History of England, very proper to be read by all such men as are contributors to that work* (London, 1748), 49-50.

[19]It should be pointed out that Carte did not shrink from soliciting subscriptions from eminent Court Whigs. He wrote a long letter to the Duke of Newcastle reiterating the arguments he had made in the original proposals about the urgency of producing a new history of England.

[20]Colley, 280.

[21]Carte's *History* also may not have sold well simply because it was too expensive and was not marketed properly. One critic said as much. Samuel Squire expressed the wish "that it had not been quite so dear; that it had been hawked about the streets in six-penny numbers, as seems to have been the author's original intention . . . ." Macarte, 36. On Carte's lack of commercial success, see Nichols, *Literary Anecdotes*, II, 497-498; C. H. Firth, "The Development of the Study of Seventeenth-Century History," *Transactions of the Royal Society*, VII (1913), 37.

[22]The Society met for a second time in February 1744 and then did not meet again until July 4, 1745. The minutes indicate that Carte had gained access to the Treasury offices. Moreover, the Earl of Ailesbury had prevailed upon Lord Edgcumbe, Chancellor of the Duchy of Lancaster, to examine historical documents deposited in the Duchy offices. At the Society's annual meeting in 1746, on February 12, the Earl of Orrery replaced the deceased Ailesbury as president. And in May 1747, the 4th Duke of Beaufort, another top Jacobite, whom Horace Walpole described as "the head of their party," took the reigns as president from Orrery. A committee of the Society met nine times in 1748, six times in 1750, five in 1752, once in 1753, and for the last time on January 28, 1754. Furthermore, the minutes of the Society do not suggest a sharp decline in annual contributions until the last two years. Subscriptions usually ran between four and five hundred pounds but fell to about 150 pounds in

1753, the final year. See Carte MS. 175. ff. 10, 13, 24; Walpole's opinion of Beaufort is quoted in Cruickshanks, 73.

[23]The far-fetched claims enumerated are to be found in Carte, *History*, I, 854, 866; II, 591-619; *Ormonde*, III, 418.

[24]On the nature of Henry VII's rule, see *History*, II, 836, 846, 866-867.

[25]On Henry VIII see *History*, III, 101, 136, 149-151, 194-196.

[26]*Ibid.*, III, 235-309.

[27]*Ibid.*, III, 325-353, 700-703.

[28]See *ibid.*, 729, 747; IV, 127-134, on James I.

[29]*Ibid.*, III, 726.

[30]Richard Ollard, *The Image of the King* (London, 1979), 183-198.

[31]Carte, *History*, IV, 609.

[32]*Ibid.*, 609-610.

[33]*Ibid.*, 301-302.

[34]*Ibid.*, II, 836, 846, 866.

[35]Carte saw the elimination of Mary Stuart's rich aristocratic supporters Norfolk, Northumberland, and Westmorland as "the finishing stroke to the power and glory" of the old nobility. Clearly Carte imbued his Harringtonian interpretation with a strong pro-Stuart coloring. See *ibid*.

[36]*Ibid.*, III, 194-196.

[37]Again it took no special acumen for readers to draw the obvious parallel with that dire vortex of corruption in Hanoverian England - the Whig court. See *ibid.*, III, 701; see also 359-396, 700-701.

[38]*Ibid.*, IV, 302; see also 127-134.

[39]*Ibid.*, III, 396.

[40]*Ibid.*, III, 703; on Elizabeth and the Puritans, see also III, 495, 541; IV, 4-5.

[41]*Ibid.*, III, 747; see also IV, 1-2.

[42]*Ibid.*, IV, 312. The success of the Puritans in bringing about the over-representation of the small boroughs in the early-seventeenth century, Carte argues, endured to the present day. The consequences of this electoral system were corruption and the oppression of landed society by the venal monied men. At this point in his narrative, Carte deplored the rise of the corrupt monied interest and extolled the landed interest as the natural foundation of the state. Machiavelli, he notes, described land as the original basis of government. In every European state, the "original constitution" admitted no other "representatives than of the landed gentry and freeholders . . . ." This state of grace could be restored in England by "giving the landed interest a greater power and influence in Parliament than they have at present." A law mandating land qualification, Carte submitted, would extrude the monied men and "put a stop to corruption grown so general." See *ibid.*, IV, 5-6.

[43]For the specified digressions, see *ibid.*, III, 198-201; IV, 245-258, 346-347; on Mary Queen of Scots, see III, 400-490, 603-619.

[44]The correspondence of these ambassadorial brothers shed light on court politics under Mary Tudor and Elizabeth and on the plots directed against them. Carte also studied the dispatches of other ambassadors deposited in Parisian archives, including those of Du Bellay (1527-29), La Mothe-Fenelon (1568-75), Comte de Beaumont (1602-05), and La Broderie (1602-11). On his trips to France, moreover, Carte made abstracts of nearly one thousand treaties and transactions between England and France, preserved in the *Chambre des Comptes*, and in the possession of the Parlement of Paris. Carte's account of Mary Queen of Scots was constructed partly on the basis of the correspondence between Mary and Elizabeth stored in the Paper Office. He also used the archives in the Cotton Library, the Exchequer Office, the Tower, and the Office of Rolls. He studied (in manuscript) the rolls and journals of Parliament, King

Edward VI's journal, in addition to innumerable printed lives, memoirs, and histories.

Chapter VIII

James Ralph

In the early 1740s James Ralph and William Guthrie set out to do for the Country Whigs what Carte had done for the Tories: to produce and English history that would finally take the place of Rapin. Commercially they failed almost as completely as Carte. If we judge them on their merits, however, they belong in a different class from their Jacobite rival and from their predecessors generally. True, they elucidated their histories in no less exhaustive detail. And for most of their careers they were paid political propagandists with little sense of historical detachment. Nevertheless, they broke the mold of traditional Augustan historical writing. Their histories were anti-clerical, if not positively anti-Christian, and they spurned providential explanations of historical change. They made a sustained effort to evaluate critically Whig and Tory party historians. They also carried over into their histories the Harringtonian consciousness of social and economic change that had characterized Bolingbroke's historical writings.

To students of English literature Ralph is known (along with Oldmixon, whose career resembled Ralph's own in many respects) as one of Alexander Pope's Dunces, a failed poet and playwright turned successful political journalist and reputable but commercially unsuccessful historian.[1] Neither the place nor date of Ralph's birth is definitely established. He was born circa 1705 in either London or Philadelphia. He lived as a youth in Philadelphia, and as a clerk in the early 1720s he befriended Benjamin Franklin. In his *Diary* Franklin described Ralph as ingenious and shrewd, genteel in his manners and extremely eloquent: "I think I never knew a prettier talker."[2]

Accompanied by Franklin, Ralph emigrated to London in about 1724, seeking fame and fortune as a poet. But his poetry was dismissed or ignored by his contemporaries and by posterity. Pope's attack in the *Dunciad* alone seems to have destroyed Ralph's prospects in his chosen career. Ralph next tried his hand at drama and criticism. In the early 1730s he collaborated on several theatrical productions with a rising young literary star, Henry Fielding. The moderate success enjoyed by their plays seems to have benefited Fielding alone. By 1736 Ralph operated as an aid to Fielding in the management of the Haymarket Theatre. Then in 1737 the government closed down the Haymarket due to Fielding's theatrical salvos against Walpole.

Up to this point in his life Ralph had suffered the classic symptoms of the struggling Grub Street hack. He was fighting poverty through most of the 1720s and '30s.[3] It was his political journalism that finally brought Ralph financial security. He began writing occasionally for newspapers in the early 1730s, contributing to the Court journals, the *Weekly Register* and *Daily Courant*. The first definite political writings that can be attributed to him can be dated to 1737, when he went to work covering Parliament for the anti-ministerial *Universal Spectator*.[4] Henceforth Ralph would write strictly for anti-Court newspapers. By the early 1740s, at the latest, Ralph's financial troubles were a thing of the past. After a two-year stint on the *Universal Spectator*, he resumed his collaboration with Fielding, this time as co-editor of a new opposition Whig journal, the *Champion*. Ralph was responsible for most of the political essays. He lambasted the government for its inept handling of the War of Jenkins' Ear, as well as for the usual court evils: corruption, vice, standing armies, et cetera. Ralph went on writing political broadsides for the *Champion* until 1744. In 1743 he produced *The Critical History of the Administration of Sir Robert Walpole*, a compilation of anti-ministerial extracts from newspapers and pamphlets. During these years he came into his own and found his metier, political polemics.

In 1739 Ralph was contributing essays to *Common Sense*, by this time the leading opposition newspaper.[5] The paper was patronized by the Earl of Chesterfield, himself an occasional contributor, and conducted chiefly by Charles Malloy and William Guthrie. In 1743 Ralph and Guthrie joined forces to bring out *Old England: or the Constitutional Journal*. Guthrie was principal author. Chesterfield co-sponsored this preeminent Country Whig paper with George Bubb Dodington.[6] Ralph had come under Dodington's patronage in 1739 or 1740 and was to remain his client for the next decade. Ralph and Guthrie stopped work on *Old England* in the autumn of 1744, at which time they were writing their histories. Both histories were patronized by Chesterfield and Dodington and were initially cooperative extensions of Ralph and Guthrie's political propagandizing.[7] Ralph's *History* was published serially between 1744-46.

When Dodington joined the Broadbottom administration in 1744, Ralph was pensioned by the Treasury at 200 pounds per year. However, Ralph temporarily deserted Dodington in 1747 and joined the Prince of Wales and his opposition circle. He soon became chief writer and editor for another anti-ministerial newspaper, the *Remembrancer*. Before long he reenlisted Dodington in the opposition camp. But Frederick's death in 1751 shattered plans for a concerted opposition movement against the administration.

A dexterous political operator, Dodington quickly maneuvered back into the Pelham administration. Henry Pelham, however, felt nothing but hostility for the man who had been pillorying his ministry remorselessly for years: he refused to pension Ralph, despite Dodington's pleas. The only problem was that Ralph had established himself, along with Guthrie, as the most formidable propagandist since Bolingbroke. He inflicted too much damage with his pen to be kept out in the cold. Having abandoned the *Remembrancer* after Prince Frederick's death, Ralph joined another dissident Whig faction led by the Duke of Bedford. This alignment produced yet another propaganda journal, the *Protestor*. It was the *Protestor*, with Ralph at the helm, that poured out a torrent of abuse against the Jewish Naturalization Bill of 1753, the most controversial issue to develop between the fall of Walpole and the succession of George III. Ralph and his propaganda mill played a critical role in getting the bill repealed.[8]

By now it had become obvious that Pelham's policy of scorning Ralph held no prospect of silencing this bothersome gadfly. Newcastle persuaded his brother to pension Ralph, and in 1753 Ralph was given the generous Treasury pension of 300 pounds a year simply to keep quiet. Henceforth Ralph wrote semi-annual thank you letters to Newcastle and occasionally proffered a little political advice. He stopped all political pamphleteering. The only regular writing chores that he engaged in were as a literary reviewer in the *Monthly Review*. And in 1758 he published what is probably his best known and certainly best selling work, the *Case of the Authors by Profession or Trade stated*, a diatribe, discussed below, against the modern system of publishing.

Sensing a change in the political wind, Ralph began to cultivate the friendship of the Earl of Bute in the late 1750s. No sooner had George III taken the throne than Ralph was pensioned for the last time by Bute, that bete noir of his opposition Whig masters. *The Case of the Late Resignation* (1761), an assault on William Pitt, was Ralph's last contribution to political polemics. Stricken with gout, the tireless warhorse of political journalism was about to launch still another newspaper, this one pro-Bute, when he died in 1762.

"My brain such as it is," Ralph once wrote, "is my only estate."[9] Unlike the clerical historians who held the field in the first tow decades of the eighteenth century, Ralph was an "author by profession," a label apparently coined by Guthrie.[10] For most of his life he was a professional writer without other means of support. It would be a mistake, however, to assume that he was an unprincipled hack who simply hired himself out to the highest bidder. True, he served at various times both the Court and the Country. The fact is, however, that virtually nothing in print of a political nature from a Court Whig point of view can be definitely attributed to Ralph. Country themes are discernable throughout the corpus of his works. Take for instance his most influential book, the *Case of the Authors by Profession or Trade stated* (1758), written while he was on the Treasury's pay list. What we find in this work, once we peel away the layers of personal recrimination and sour grapes, is a meditation on the degrading effects on authorship produced by the rise of monied wealth and the growing commercialization of society.

Probably no single work had more of an impact on nineteenth-century conceptions of authorship and publishing in Augustan England than Ralph's *Case of the Authors*. Its essence was reiterated in Goldsmith's *Essay on the Present State of Polite Learning in Europe*, plagiarized in Isaac Disraeli's *Calamities of Authors*, and made the conventional wisdom in a famous 1831 essay by Lord Macaulay in the *Edinburgh Review*.[11] Ralph's basic argument was that after the munificent aristocratic patronage of the seventeenth century, writing in the present century had become a business in which the booksellers reaped all the rewards. The writer was cruelly exploited, yet if he demanded a just return for his labors he was universally stigmatized as a venal, money-grubbing hack. Ralph bemoaned the fact that "money, however acquired, is at the summit, and public spirit underfoot."[12] He cited John Oldmixon as a classic example of how the writer was debased and exploited by mercenary booksellers: his employers had him "labour at the press like a horse in a mill, till he became as blind and wretched."[13]

The Case of the Authors was Ralph's best-written work, a scintillating and impassioned cry against the degraded state of letters in the new monied world. Next to the *Case* and his *History*, Ralph's most effective book was *The Other Side of the Question* (1742), a telling Country Whig critique of Sarah Churchill's memoir, *An Account of the Conduct of the Dowager Duchess of Marlborough*. Although it ran to more than 450 pages, *The Other Side* was not a scholarly work based on documentation. It does, however, vividly convey Ralph's Country analysis of Queen Anne's reign, a period not covered in his *History*. Sarah, Ralph argues, and to a lesser extent her illustrious husband, were archetypical courtiers, power-hungry self-seekers. To counterbalance the Whig Churchills, Ralph depicts Tories like William Sacheverell as equally objectionable.[14]

Although inferior to both *The Case of the Authors* and *The Other Side of the Question*, Ralph's *Of the Use and Abuse of Parliaments* (1744) offers perhaps the clearest exposition of Ralph's Country philosophy. More than 700 octavo pages in length, the work reviewed the history of Parliament from the seventeenth century onward, showing how "through the craft and perfidy of kings, the degeneracy of mankind, and the extinction of that noble spirit which accompanies liberty," Parliaments invariably become corrupt and tyrannical.[15] Ralph supports the Parliamentarian and Country Whig movements to check overbearing Stuart power, but he follows the conventional Country line in arguing that royal "influence" and arbitrary power actually increased after the Glorious Revolution. The Convention Parliament missed the opportunity to reform the constitution by eradicating placemen and insisting upon frequent Parliaments. Furthermore, the government began running up huge debts in William's reign. England would never prosper until the bulk of them were paid off.[16]

The modern Whigs, Ralph contends, had betrayed all their principles. Referring to the arrest of an opposition newspaper publisher during George II's reign, Ralph comments sarcastically, "So extremely tender were these worthy Whigs both to the liberty and property of the subject."[17] Ralph closes his volume with a Lockean, democratic-sounding appeal to the people against a corrupt Parliament and administration. The authority of Parliaments is not unlimited, he warned. Should the House of Commons surrender "the public liberties into any hand whatsoever" the people have a right to refuse obedience, in which case "the delegation they had would be dissolved: that consequently all power would return in the hands of those who gave it."[18]   Similar attitudes appear in Ralph's *History of England*.   It is not surprising that the liberal Whig Charles James Fox and the radical republican Thomas Hollis both admired the work greatly.[19]

Ralph's magnum opus was misleadingly titled *The History of England during the Reigns of King William, Queen Anne, and King George I, with an Introductory Review of the Reigns of the Royal Brothers Charles and James*. Actually, Ralph never got beyond William's reign. This may have been partly because, like Macaulay after him, his history swelled in size far beyond his original expectations. The introductory review of Charles and James alone numbered a thousand folio pages. Moreover, all indications are that the *History* sold poorly, although it was marketed by subscription in numbers.[20]   Only one edition of the *History* was published and it provoked virtually no comment in the press. Finally, by 1749 when the last numbers of volume two appeared, Ralph was busy at work writing the *Remembrancer* and may well have had his hands too full with this latest project to continue the *History*.

Several qualities of Ralph's *History* distinguished it from its predecessors and marked it as a product of emerging Enlightenment culture. There was first of all the author's relative impartiality.   His Country outlook, though scarcely objective, equipped him to see through the spurious rationalizations of Whig and Tory party historians.   Secondly, Ralph wrote from a thoroughly secular and anti-clerical perspective. Nothing in his narrative suggests that he saw the hand of God shaping the course of events, no indication that the Glorious Revolution was to be regarded as some miraculous instance of divine intervention. An admirer of Bolingbroke, Ralph probably shared his deistical philosophy, as he did his Country ideology. Reportedly Bolingbroke so admired Ralph's *History* that he recruited him for the Prince's faction.[21]   Like Bolingbroke, Ralph informed his history with a socioeconomic, Harringtonian dimension. And Ralph was the first historian to trace the roots of the Glorious Revolution, in copious detail, back to the reign of Charles II. And more than Rapin, Ralph went to great lengths to explain the European background of the Revolution.   In this endeavor he used many heretofore neglected documents. No one employed them more critically and meticulously.

Ralph's *History* detailed the themes he had addressed in his political pamphleteering. It showed how the champions of liberty against tyrannical administrations quickly shed their libertarian guise upon taking office and put on the armor of tyranny and corruption. In addition, the history set out to demonstrate that the tyranny of faction was more oppressive in post-Revolutionary England than before 1688. Even during the Exclusion crisis, for example, when the liberties of the nation were imperiled by the crown, the situation was less ominous than in Ralph's time: "Though more stress was laid on the prerogative in those days, it had less of real power for its support" - no Riot Act, no series of Parliamentary acts to secure the succession, no tyranny of corruption, standing armies, or monied men.[22]

Of all the accretions of royal power, it was the "dominion rising from money" that Ralph seems to have believed was most important; the financial revolution was a prerequisite for the transformation in English politics and society that took place during the reign of William III. It opened the door for those financiers who controlled the new corporations - the Bank of England and new East India Company - to reduce Parliament to a rubber stamp by corrupting the politicians. The new system of patronage - "corruption" - sprang from the massive infusion of money into politics. The "monied men" who dealt in corporate stocks and bonds were servants of the crown. William became "lord of the cash of the kingdom."[23] The "new system" worked out in the Revolution Settlement paved the way for the tyranny of money, and "as surely as power follows property, the power of the crown would increase with the revenue it had distribution of, and that the manager would in the end be the master."[24] Ralph makes several rather elliptical references to the need in 1689-90 for a degree of electoral reform to deprive "worthless, insignificant, venal boroughs."[25] Failure to modify the franchise, Ralph argues, contributed to the growth of corruption and tyranny. Those who had a "natural interest in the soil" lost ground politically and economically to the monied men. From his remarks elsewhere it is clear that by "natural interest" Ralph had in mind the landed gentry - a characteristic Country attitude. Ralph exaggerates the impact of the financial revolution on land distribution, submitting that the "extortioners and usurers" acquired more estates in a few short years than at any similar span of time since the dissolution of the monasteries.[26]

It was not only the traditional landed order that suffered from the growth of the financial sector. Legitimate commerce was also set back. Here the war against France played a key role. Not only did it necessitate enormous loans, but it made international trade a more risky proposition. Consequently, merchants estimated that it was "more profitable to traffic in government securities." A massive disinvestment in trade was followed by commercial stagnation. Meanwhile "a new species of dealers (since better known by the name of brokers and stockjobbers)" enriched themselves merely by buying and selling stocks for others.[27] Like the neo-Harringtonians studied by J. G. A. Pocock, Ralph regarded fluid capital as fictitious, insubstantial wealth. Whereas landed property fostered virtue in society, monied property generated vice. By the end of William's reign, the poisonous fangs of corruption and vice had sunk deep into the fabric of society.

Although Ralph shared the Country Whig and Tory view that corruption and tyranny actually worsened after the Revolution of 1688, he did not idealize the Stuarts. He depicted Charles II and James II as tyrants and dupes of Louis XIV. The Earl of Shaftesbury and his Country associates may have been hypocritical self-seekers, but they nonetheless "served to awe the throne and keep the flame of liberty alive among the people."[28] They had the support of high-minded country gentlemen. Unfortunately, the Revolution of 1688 failed to reduce "the power of the clergy which had so often been collegu'd (sic) with that of the crown to the oppression of the subject."[29] But the greatest single failing of the Convention Parliament was its inability to forbid standing armies.[30]

Ralph's credentials as a Country writer were impeccable. Why then should his *History* be regarded as any less partisan than those of his predecessors? For one thing, Ralph's Country vantage point enabled him to make shrewd perceptions about the distortions of traditional party historical writing. The great block to historical writing "is the misfortune of almost every Englishman to be attached to some one part or faction."[31] Page after page of Ralph's *History* exposes the errors and misrepresentations of his forebears, Whig and Tory alike. He dislikes the two major historians of Queen Anne's reign, White Kennett and Laurence Echard, one Whig the other Tory. He classifies Echard as one of the "idolators of the prerogative" and chastises him for describing "with an air of triumph" the servitude of Parliament to James II in 1685.[32] Ralph upbraids Kennett, Echard, and Gilbert Burnet for accepting at face value William III's declarations that he only descended on England to save the expiring liberties of the nation.[33]

When Ralph wrote his *History*, Burnet's *History of His own Time* was still the most famous study of the Later Stuarts and Glorious Revolution. Probably for this reason Ralph criticized Burnet more than anyone else. Ralph disapproved of the Bishop's anecdotal style, observing that he was "outdone by no one in credulity."[34] He rightly faulted Burnet's assertion that the anti-Court politicians in the Convention Parliament were in league with James II. He chided Burnet "and the rest of our general historians" for not discussing the bill to establish the Bank of England. He picked out factual errors, pointing out, for instance, that the Sacheverell Bill in 1690, designed to proscribe the Tories, was not, as Burnet reported, carried by a great majority in the Commons; it was repeatedly defeated there.[35] Like Thomas Carte, Ralph was well aware of the stylistic and methodological shortcomings of earlier historians: "All our histories," he submits, "are indeed little more than transcripts from one another."[36] He pointed out specific examples of this in the works of Burnet, Tindal, Kennett, Oldmixon, and Abel Boyer.

The Country slant of Ralph's *History* made for some historically suspect positions - the assertion that "tyranny" increased after the Glorious Revolution, the excessively negative account of the financial revolution, the characterization of William's war against France as an utter waste of money and lives. On balance, however, Ralph's ability to pierce the cloud of ideological distortion thrown up by Whig and Tory party historians meant that he could explicate a significantly more fair-minded and historically valid narrative. He dismissed the stock canards perpetuated by partisan histories such as the Popish Plot and the Rye House Plot.[37] He ridiculed the notion that the birth of James III was spurious; the tales that were circulated "were neither over-decent, well bred or charitable: a pillow, a dropsy, a tympany, a cushion, the Queen's maladies, the King's crazy constitution, were the favourite topics of the wit and humour of the day."[38]

Ralph produced the most subtle and detailed history of the Glorious Revolution to appear before Macaulay, not excluding Burnet and Rapin. Previous historians had written about how the arbitrary measures of Charles II laid the foundation for the headlong attack against Parliament and the constitution launched by Charles' brother. Ralph, however, explained in detail how the growing authoritarianism of Charles II, combined with the growing servility of Parliament and people, almost enabled James II to succeed in his designs of erecting a French style monarchy. The royal assault on charters and corporations, the efflorescence of Filmerite, high prerogative theories of government, the subordination of foreign policy to Louis XIV's absolutistic priorities - these prepared the way for the obsequious Church and Parliament that greeted James II when he took the throne.

Ralph prefigures some modern authorities, most notably J. R. Jones, in arguing that James very nearly succeeded in revolutionizing the English monarchy. In 1685 "his people were indeed in the condition of the lion in the fable: they had fallen in love with the prerogative, and to make their courtship more acceptable, they had consented to have their teeth drawn and their nails pared."[39] The bulk of Parliamentarians very nearly went along with James. It was only the king's ultimate ineptitude, the belated resistance of the Church, the diplomatic situation and clever opportunism of William, and the courageous opposition of a few principled politicians that at practically the last moment swung the balance against James.

Ralph chided "our common historians" for neglecting the European background of the Revolution.[40] He recognized the central fact that William of Orange wanted above all to have England and its resources lined up against France in order to preserve Dutch independence, not English liberty. He rejected the common myth that William was the great deliverer of the nation who swept onto the stage of history to rescue the English people from popery and slavery. William assumed "the glorious name of deliverer; while the part he really played was consummate politician. If that is not panegyric, it is truth."[41] Ralph explained the diplomatic conditions that led to the League of Augsburg and war with France, but exaggerated English deference to the strategic interests of Holland.

One reason Ralph was so well aware of his predecessors' deficiencies was that he undertook a thorough and scholarly study of the available evidence. He examined hundreds of documents - not only printed sources, but manuscript materials as well. Among the latter were the papers and collected pamphlets of John Somers (some of which would go to make up the *Somers Tracts*) and the letters, journal and collections of the Earl of Halifax.[42] Printed sources were still of much greater importance than the manuscript, and Ralph consulted more than a hundred books.[43]

Ralph's judicious use of sources and his sensitivity to the pitfalls of historical compilation bear witness to his critical and discerning mind. His was a rationalist, thoroughly secular mind.[44] The *History of England* contains but one allusion to providence, the remark that it was the "unsearchable ends and purposes" of providence that wafted William to Torbay.[45] The whole tenor of Ralph's *History* makes clear that it was not within the historian's compass to meditate upon "unsearchable ends." He has no patience whatever with references to preternatural power in history. At one point he comments upon a tale circulated by the Country party at the time of the Exclusion Crisis that a "spectre" appeared warning Charles not to move the Parliament out of London: "Those who depend upon the people for support must try all manner of practices upon them; and such fooleries as these sometimes operate more forcibly than expedients of a more rational kind."[46]

The "philosophical" historians of the Enlightenment have been fairly criticized for their hostile and ahistorical treatment of religion and the Church. Ralph cannot be acquitted of these charges. The Church of England crops up in his narrative infrequently, only to be denounced for its servility to crown and court. Ralph castigates the bishops for hypocritically switching from champions of nonresistance to exponents of rebellion against James II.[47] Ralph's disinterest in religious questions is evidenced by a terse comment on the Convocation of 1701:

> The bare mention that Convocation was suffered to sit as long as the Parliament sat is all that is necessary for this work: the effects of the Lower House to re-establish the power of the Church and the disappointments they met with belonging more properly to the writer of ecclesiastical history.

Details, declared Voltaire, are the vermin that destroy history. More than 2,000 folio pages in length, Ralph's *History* is nothing if not detailed. It contains long transcriptions from gazettes and state documents, though far less so than previous histories. The wealth of detail works against the kind of pellucid, highly readable presentation favored by the philosophes. Neither does Ralph have much to say about cultural history. In the most critical areas, however, Ralph belongs with the philosophes. He explained and generalized about the course of events, and he explored far more sources than any other student of his period. And Ralph's was a civil history. He devoted relatively little space to military campaigns; he did not stoop to entertain readers with colorful tales of court intrigue, and though he certainly had his favorites, he was not interested in eulogizing great men. Ralph also looked beyond politics to the economic innovations of the financial revolution. We may dispute his judgments, but Ralph conveyed a sense of the social and political repercussions of the "new system" that took root after the Glorious Revolution. Above all, we see in Ralph's *History* a secular analysis, which formed the essence of the "new history." Religious themes and allusions play almost no part in his works. His philosophical roots came from Sydney, Locke, Hobbes, and Bolingbroke, secularists all. It is probably no coincidence that Ralph's two distinguished friends, Benjamin Franklin and Dodington, were freethinkers, as was his political ally Bolingbroke. A professional journalist unconnected with the Church, Ralph's experience was very different from that of clerical historians like Kennett, Echard, and Carte. And his anti-party, Country interpretation projected a tone of cynicism and skepticism that is strikingly different from the Whig/Tory histories of the eighteenth century - or, for that matter, from the cocksure Whiggery of Lord Macaulay in the nineteenth century.

Notes

[1]Unless otherwise noted, biographical information on Ralph is drawn from Robert W. Kenny, "James Ralph: An Eighteenth Century Philadelphian in Grub Street," *The Pennsylvania Magazine of History and Biography* (1940) LXIV, 218-242; John Burke Shipley, "James Ralph: Pretender to Genius" (Ph.D. dissertation, Columbia University, 1963).

[2]Quoted in Kenny, 219.

[3]Ralph wrote plaintive letters to associates in the late 1720s and 1730s bemoaning his fate. He wrote to Thomas Birch pleading for money. Ralph to Birch, B.L. Add. MS. 4317. f. 99; see also f. 8; Ralph to S. Gough, May 7, 1728, B.L. Add. MS. 4291. f. 210.

[4]See Shipley, 295-308.

[5]*Ibid.*, 376.

[7]See Kenny, 230; Shipley, 403-405.

[8]See T. W. Perry, *Public Opinion, Propaganda, and Politics in Eighteenth Century England: a Study of the Jew Bill of 1753* (Cambridge, Mass., 1962), 106-109.

[9]Quoted in Shipley, 507.

[10]Guthrie described himself in a letter in 1767 as "the oldest author by profession in England." See Robert Chambers, *A Biographical Dictionary of Eminent Scotsmen* (London, 1875), 188.

[11]See Kenny, 232-241.

[12]James Ralph, *The Case of the Authors by Profession or Trade stated* (London, 1758), 47.

[13]*Ibid.*, 4-5.

[14]James Ralph, *The Other Side of the Question* (London, 1742), 206-207.

[15]James Ralph, *Of the Use and Abuse of Parliaments* 2 vols. (London, 1744), I, 80.

[16]*Ibid.*, 146.

[17]*Ibid.*, II, 679.

[18]*Ibid.*, 718.

[19]Ralph's *History* was also praised by the eighteenth-century republican historian Catherine Macaulay. However, Ralph was also referred to as a Tory historian. It was perhaps natural that Court Whigs like Thomas Birch and Philip Yorke would lump all opposition writers together as Tories. Succeeding defenders of the Whig government perpetuated this misconception. William Coxe, for example, labeled Ralph a "violent Tory writer," and the *Edinburgh Review* in 1831 noted that the *History* had a Tory bias; see Kenny, 232, and Shipley, 430; Catherine Macaulay, *The History of England from the Accession of James I to the elevation of the House of Hanover* 5 vols. (London, 1763-83), II, 330; William Coxe,

Memoirs of the Duke of Marlborough 3 vols., orig. pub. 1818-19 (London, 1847) I, iii; *Edinburgh Review* (March 1831) LIII, 13.

[20]Philip Yorke told Thomas Birch in August 1743 that Thomas Waller - Ralph's publisher - wanted to be released from his contract with Ralph and Guthrie. And by 1746 Waller's co-publisher, Francis Cogan, found himself in debt to Ralph to the tune of one hundred pounds. Yorke to Birch, Aug. 20, 1743, B.L. Add. MS. 35396. f. 134; Shipley, 452.

[21]Averyl Edwards, *Frederick Louis: Prince of Wales* (London, 1957), 160.

[22]James Ralph, *The History of England during the reigns of King William, Queen Anne, and King George I, with an introductory Review of the Royal Brothers, Charles and James* 2 vols. (London, 1744-46) I, 477.

[23]*Ibid.*, II, 1024.

[24]*Ibid.*, 141.

[25]*Ibid.*, 141, 1004.

[26]*Ibid.*, 686.

[27]*Ibid.*, 485; in the *Continuation of Rapin*, Birch had extolled Charles Montagu in glowing terms for overseeing the financial revolution in William's reign. Ralph's verdict was far more critical: "If he was not the father of corruption, he fostered it, as if all his hopes were built upon it." *Ibid.*, 785-786.

[28]*Ibid.*, I, 424.

[29]*Ibid.*, 61-62.

[30]*Ibid.*, 765.

[31]*Ibid.*, 1.

[32]*Ibid.*, 863; Ralph is quick to find fault with both Kennett and Echard, as for example refuting the assertion by both men that a highly dangerous republican plot in the North was only just foiled in 1663. Correspondence

between the Duke of Ormonde and Secretary Bennett, he pointed out, cast doubt on the authenticity of this supposed plot. *Ibid.*, 97-98.

[33]*Ibid.*, 1-25.

[34]*Ibid.*, II, 227; for other criticisms of Burnet, see I, 856; II, 183, 188, 929.

[35]Ralph was a most careful and meticulous chronicler in terms of getting his facts straight. No one, he remarked, was so negligent with dates as Burnet. Ralph's meticulousness is indicated by his comment on the convening of the Scottish Parliament in 1685. "Oldmixon erroneously says it was opened March the 28th, whereas that was only the date of the King's letter. And Bishop Burnet, yet more erroneously, places this meeting after the execution of the Earl of Argyle." *Ibid.*, I, 856.

[36]At many places in his history, Tindal transcribed Burnet's profile of King William "virtually word for word." Commenting on "the stupid and servile reflections made by our pretended historians" on the First Partition Treaty, Ralph observed that Abel Boyer, Kennett and Tindal used almost precisely the same wording in praising the treaty and that Oldmixon said much the same thing in paraphrased form. Ralph pointed out that Burnet's account of the Succession Bill was copied from a tract called *A Plain Proof that all Tories are Jacobites*. *Ibid.*, II, 439, 612, 626, 804, 921.

[37]*Ibid.*, I, 538, 807.

[38]*Ibid.*, 980.

[39]*Ibid.*, 926.

[40]*Ibid.*, 936.

[41]*Ibid.*, 997.

[42]Ralph also made use of the as yet unpublished Parliamentary journals, which would go to make up the *Parliamentary or Constitutional History of England* (1751-62) and A. Grey's *Debates of the House of Commons* (1763). He examined the diary and letters of Henry Sidney and even Treasury records and the Privy Council Registers.

[43]Among the newly published books that Ralph studied were Roger North's *Examen* (1740) and the *Lives* of his brothers (1742-44); John Campbell's *Lives of the Admirals* (1742-44), the *Letters* of d'Estrades (1743) and, most importantly, the several collections of Parliamentary proceedings that appeared in the early and mid-1740s. Older authorities of particular value to Ralph included Abel Boyer's *Life of King William*, Carte's *Ormonde*, Reresby's *Memoirs*, C. Cole's *Memoirs of Affairs of State*, and the published letters of William Temple, Leoline Jenkins and the Earl of Danby. Like Macaulay after him, Ralph relied upon Burnet more than any other single source. He was more critical of Burnet than was Macaulay, to whom the Whig Bishop was a kindred spirit.

[44]Shipley, 428-430, 599.

[45]Ralph, *History*, I, 1032.

[46]*Ibid.*, 562.

[47]Suddenly the bishops were all for "new laws to secure civil liberty." But in reality "civil liberty was so far from being any concern of theirs that the grievous shock it had received was owing principally to them." The "bishops had for so long placed the sum of all public virtue in implicit obedience that they were at some loss for a plausible pretence to eat their words." For this and other attacks on the Church, see *ibid.*, I, 983-984; II, 978.

Chapter IX

William Guthrie

Until very recently, William Guthrie's *A General History of England* was among the most obscure of eighteenth-century histories. It may not have been quite the total commercial failure that Ralph's history was, but it went almost unnoticed in the contemporary press and was certainly not successful. It was ignored by nearly all succeeding historians. Not until Duncan Forbes took Guthrie's *History* out of mothballs in the mid-1970s to compare it with Hume's *History of England* was the work subject to any substantive examination. In his five-page discussion of Guthrie, Forbes aimed to show how he foreshadowed Hume in his relatively impartial approach to history and politics, even though he did not produce the kind of "philosophical" history of civilization that was Hume's great achievement.[1]

The discussion that follows shifts the focus; Guthrie's history, even more than Ralph's, should be classified as a specimen of the emerging Enlightenment school. Guthrie's conception of history, like Ralph's, owed much to Bolingbroke. Guthrie, however, was Scottish, and parallels can be drawn between his work and the historical productions of the Scottish Enlightenment. Guthrie presented a secular, mundane interpretation of English history. He fashioned a well-written explanatory narrative based on critical methods of documentary analysis and did not indulge in the rancorous partisanship that had undermined English historical writing. He at least observed the importance of cultural history. Above all he placed great weight on the socioeconomic changes that underlay the growth of liberty and civilization in England.

Of all the histories to precede Hume's, Guthrie's was closest in its themes and overall interpretation. But although Guthrie's *General History* never won the popular and critical recognition bestowed upon Hume, it was, in fact, a more original and scholarly work. Guthrie made far more extensive and judicious use of original sources than Hume did, without sacrificing clarity of expression. Since Guthrie's *History* was a work of considerable importance, he deserves to be profiled in some depth. Unfortunately, Guthrie - historian, political writer, drama and literary critic, novelist - is an even more obscure figure than his colleague Ralph.[2] One obvious parallel with Hume was Guthrie's nationality. He was born in Brechin, Scotland, in 1708. His father was a nonjuring episcopal minister and reportedly a Jacobite. Having graduated from the University of Aberdeen, Guthrie labored for a time in Edinburgh as a preceptor in various gentlemen's houses. An indiscreet love affair, combined with Guthrie's rumored Jacobite views, purportedly made it difficult for him to continue working in Edinburgh. Hence, Guthrie moved to London in the early 1730s and resolved to establish himself as an "author by profession." It was in the metropolis that Guthrie made his mark; he does not appear to have known any of the Scottish philosophes.[3] Guthrie's fellow Scot, John Ramsay of Octertyre, described him as "one of the first of his countrymen who endeavored to make bread by his pen."[4] Francis Palgrave, writing in 1844, called Guthrie "the earliest professional author known to have been paid by the sheet."[5]

The first literary undertaking that we know Guthrie embarked upon after coming to London was as a Parliamentary reporter for Edward Cave on the *Gentleman's Magazine* from about 1735 to 1740. Guthrie would attend the debates and then write them up in the *Gentleman's Magazine*, sometimes making up the speeches when his memory or notes failed him. In about 1738 he was joined in this enterprise by young Samuel Johnson, who revised the debates from Guthrie's transcript and subsequently took over the job completely. Johnson remembered Guthrie as a "man of parts" who had acquired a considerable stock of learning over the years. In fact he thought highly enough of Guthrie to suggest that someone should write his life.[6]

Unlike Ralph, Guthrie did not have to endure long years of travail before finding his niche as a political journalist. By the late 1730s he was a ranking propagandist for the Country opposition circle around Prince Frederick, which included the Duke of Argyle and the Earls of Chesterfield, Lyttleton, Marchmont, and Dodington.[7] He became the chief writer for the opposition's two leading papers, *Common Sense* and *Old England*. He conducted the former from approximately 1738 to 1743. Under the pseudonym of Jeffrey Broadbottom, Guthrie launched *Old England: or the Constitutional Journal* in 1743.[8]

These newspapers carried on the Country, Old Whig tradition inherited from Bolingbroke's *Craftsman*. Moreover, at least three of the politicians who sponsored and contributed to *Common Sense*, *Old England*, or the *Englishman's Evening Post* were close allies of Bolingbroke: Chesterfield was a long-time close friend and political ally, and probably no one was closer to Bolingbroke after William Wyndham's death than Marchmont and Lyttleton. For that matter, Bolingbroke himself may have been an occasional contributor to one or more of these journals. Years later, in 1768, Guthrie reminisced to James Boswell: "Ah, when Lord Bolingbroke and I wrote together, when the *Craftsman* came out, when *Old England* by Jeffrey Broadbottom came out."[9]

Guthrie was scheduled to be pensioned or given office once his political friends were admitted to the administration. When, however, leading opposition politicians were brought into the so-called Broad Bottom administration, 1744-45, Guthrie found himself left out in the cold, a circumstance that elicited this comment from his successor on *Old England*: "Jeffrey, going to compliment the junto on their places, modestly asked where was his: they answered with a broad laugh, you may drop your pen, the work is done."[10]

Meanwhile, in the early 1740s Guthrie had begun working on his *History* under the patronage of his Country Whig masters, Chesterfield and Dodington. The first numbers began appearing in early 1744, but the last volume was not completed until 1751, five years after he had been pensioned into silence by the Pelhams. Guthrie received a stipend of 200 pounds a year from the Treasury for the rest of his life. This sinecure by the court all but ended his career as a polemicist. The government was content to keep him, like his confederate Ralph, quiet and out of the way.[11] When the Old Corps were turned out of office after the accession of George III, Guthrie deftly switched allegiances and retained his pension. Just as Ralph returned briefly to political propagandizing at this juncture, so too did Guthrie, now for the government.[12] From the late 1750s until his death in 1770, he also reviewed books anonymously for the *Critical Review*, the only rival to the prestigious *Monthly Review*.

By all accounts Guthrie was overbearing and vainglorious. In his *Autobiography*, Alexander Carlyle recalled encountering Guthrie in a coffeehouse in 1746:

> Guthrie arrived, dressed in laced clothes and talking loud to everybody, and soon fell to a wrangling with a gentleman about tragedy and the unities, etc., and laid down the law of the drama

in a peremptory manner, supporting his arguments with cursing and swearing.

Carlyle was "disgusted with his vapouring manner."[13]   The fancy dress observed by Carlyle also struck Boswell when he first met Guthrie at a coffeehouse in 1768:   "He was an old gentleman about sixty, had on a white coat and a crimson satin waist-coat with broad gold lace and a bag-wig." Boswell liked him but concluded that "it was curious to sit with the very person whom in a little while I should look upon as an awful reviewer."[14]   Ramsay of Octertyre described Guthrie as "a dissipated man."[15]   It may be that Guthrie's taste for showy clothes was one manifestation of a propensity to spend beyond his means. At any rate he seems to have run into recurrent financial difficulties, despite his pension and his income from books and criticism.[16]

Although Guthrie wrote on a wide range of subjects, he was first and foremost a historian. Besides the English history, he produced at the same time a much inferior *General History of Scotland* in ten octavo volumes. He collaborated on another second-rate work, the *General History of the World from the Creation to the Present Time* (1762), a vast compilation. Next to the *History of England*, Guthrie's most ambitious and illustrious work was *The Complete History of the English Peerage* (1762). Dedicated to George III, this handsome, two-volume work presented the lives of twelve peers, in addition to members of the royal family.

Guthrie's *General History of England* began largely as an extension of his political journalism for the opposition in the late 1730s and early 1740s. In order to appreciate fully the ideological underpinnings of Guthrie's *General History*, we should consider the historical aspect of his newspaper essays. The one essayist that can definitely be identified as Guthrie is Jeffrey Broadbottom of *Old England*. The pseudonymous Broadbottom, more than the writers of *Common Sense*, drove home his attacks on the ministry with many references to English history. The essays convey the same Old Whig views propounded by Bolingbroke in the *Craftsman*. One issue of *Old England*, from 1745, was devoted to a long, quasi-Harringtonian sketch of English history and outlined many of the themes subsequently elaborated upon in Guthrie's *General History*.[17] Guthrie took the position that prior to the Tudor epoch the king, nobility, and Church possessed two thirds of the land. Henry VII favored the people over the nobility, and although his successor was an arbitrary king, the dissolution of the monasteries diffused land to the commonalty. After an unsuccessful aristocratic reaction in the reigns of Edward VI and Mary, Elizabeth recognized the new economic reality and "sought to form her government upon its natural basis, the affections of the people." James I and Charles I tried and failed to turn the clock back and revive "aristocratical government." Nevertheless the stillbirth of triennial parliaments meant that the people were fairly represented; the constitution remains unpurified.

The *General History of England* was published serially through subscriptions between 1744 and 1751 and was ultimately bound in four weight folio volumes.[18] The *General History* extends to more than 3,000 folio pages of detailed narrative. Guthrie's central theme is clearly discernable. His exposition describes how the growth of English commerce and the statecraft of Tudor monarchs swelled the wealth and property of "the people" represented in the House of Commons; simultaneously, king, lords, and Church lost ground. Liberty and civilization gradually rose in the course of the sixteenth and seventeenth centuries, largely as a result of the economic changes.

Hume's interpretation of English history resembled Guthrie's. Both writers delineated the diffusion of property and power to the people and commons. They also charted the growth of liberty and civilization. The principal differences were two-fold. First, Hume did not attach quite the same degree of importance to economic change, the balance of property, as did Guthrie. Secondly, Guthrie, true to his Country Whig background, was an ancient constitutionalist, albeit of a more subtle, less doctrinaire variety than his fellow Country publicists or most of the traditional Whig historical writers. Hume, on the other hand, made it one of his prime objectives to dispel that imaginary kingdom of Anglo-Saxon freedom and immemorial law that historians continued to conjure up.

Guthrie would not dispute Hume's description of Anglo-Saxon England as "one of the freest nations of which there remains any account in the records of history."[19] Unlike Guthrie, however, Hume held that true liberty was actually nullified from the start by the "barbarism" and anarchy of the age. Both agree, however, that by the time of the Norman Conquest Anglo-Saxon government had become elitist and tyrannical, a view not shared by classical ancient constitutionalists like Edward Coke or James Tyrrel. Guthrie's view of the Norman Conquest is that of the

traditional Whig - William conquered Harold but not the English people.[20]
As for the Magna Charta, Guthrie actually says little about the specific
guarantees of the charter but maintains that it confirmed the liberties of
"the nobility and nation as a people, and is founded upon the Saxon
constitutions, together with the grants of the Norman Kings."[21]   The
charter's chief importance was that it legitimized the right of resistance.

Guthrie presented an idealized version of the Anglo-Saxon
constitution that does not bear close scrutiny.   Although Guthrie
occasionally refers to the Parliamentarians striving for Anglo-Saxon
principles of government, the thrust of his discussion is that a "new system
of liberty" developed during the course of the Tudor epoch. When liberty
began to revive in the sixteenth century, it was not spearheaded by ancient
constitutionalists; it evolved as part of a profound intellectual, scientific,
political, and, above all, socioeconomic transformation.   Here is how
Guthrie begins volume II of his *General History*.   The year is 1485; Henry
VII has just been made king:[22]

> At the period we now intend to treat of, the people began to see
> that no constitution, in and of itself is of divine right; but that public
> consent, universal agreement, or original acts, stamp the marks of
> divinity and of liberty upon every constitution in every country, be
> the succession of its government hereditary or elective; be the force
> of its government visited in the princes, or the people, or the nobles
> . . . . We shall see the interest of the people of England partaking
> the nature of its government. We shall see a system of order arising
> from the confusion, and strength, wealth, and liberty at last emerging
> from the presence of corruption, oppression, and prerogative. We
> shall see the fair creation of English glory breaking from chaos till
> the whole at last is resolved into a system, which we hope will be as
> permanent as natural order and moral obligation.

Guthrie viewed Tudor-Stuart England as the great divide in English
history, an epoch that saw the emergence of a modern and enlightened
civilization.   He also makes the point, though not so emphatically as
Hume, that the great changes underway were European in scope.   In
England they took a distinctive form that was particularly favorable to
liberty.

In the *Proposals* and the preface to this *General History*, Guthrie made the commonplace observation that political partisanship had ruined historical writing in England.[23] He made the equally predictable claim that he would rectify the situation by producing a truly impartial history. The difference was that Guthrie came closer than any of his predecessors, including Rapin, to keeping his promise: *A General History of England* is far more notable for its scholarship and incisive narration than for its Whiggish slant. Guthrie echoed the familiar Country refrain that genuine political parties no longer existed; only a few "non-essentials" separated the factions. What was needed, therefore, was "a body of English history which might reconcile the most prejudiced of all denominations to one another." Like Ralph, Guthrie pronounced harsh verdicts against nearly all his predecessors, whatever their political persuasion: history had been a plaything of faction ever since the Reformation; before that it had been subject to Church dogma. Originally, Guthrie believed:

> that the business of an historian was merely to state matters of fact in order of time, without any intermixture of conjectures, colourings, reflections, or inferences of his own. But when I took a nearer survey of the period before me, and found it so much misrepresented by others that I was forced to confute and relate together. Kennett, Echard, Oldmixon, North, had each his followers and advisors: something was to be gleaned from every one of them, and much was to be rejected.

Rapin-Thoyras did not escape Guthrie's barbs:

> Rapin's *History* appeared at a time when the principles which he wrote were useful to a party, who therefore powerfully recommended it from the press of which they were then masters. To this, and to the ridiculous prepossession that a foreigner was best fitted to write the English history, was owing the reception it met with from the public.

Important new sources, he pointed out, had appeared since Rapin wrote, including Sydney's *Letters*, Reresby's *Memoirs*, and North's *Examen*. The only historian upon whom Guthrie bestowed praise (albeit qualified) was Clarendon.

Guthrie resolved to produce a new kind of history, one that would go beyond a mere political chronicle of events: "Particular care will be taken to interweave it with an account of the rise, progress, improvement, or decay of trade, manufacturing, learning, arts, sciences of the English nation, upon a more extensive and useful plan than has hitherto been attempted." He coupled this lofty aim with the implicitly Whiggish vow "to give a general view of our fundamental liberties and constitutions, and to describe the great scenes of action, with the characters of its chief performers in as warm and animating a way as possible" He specifically forswore glorifying great men or titillating readers with a sensationalistic narrative.

Not only the substance of Guthrie's *History* set it apart from earlier works. Guthrie's style was all his own and was, arguably, superior to that of all his Augustan rivals, not excluding Hume. His prose did not conform to the kind of simple, unadorned style that had become fashionable and which Hume affected. Guthrie's writing was often ornamental, even florid.

Of Guthrie's four volumes, the last three are devoted exclusively to the Tudor-Stuart period. This imbalance reflects Guthrie's belief that a "new system"[24] - the modern system - of liberty, civilization, and economic transformation began to emerge at the end of the fifteenth century, grew during the sixteenth century, and was unsuccessfully challenged by the Stuarts in the seventeenth. Guthrie concluded his history with the Restoration.

It was the "chief glory" of Henry VII to help elevate "the industrious commons, who, not living in an abject, despicable dependence on the great, availed themselves of the rising arts and flowing commerce which began now to distinguish England."[25] Knowing that trade and manufacturing sprang chiefly "from the middling order of commons," Henry VII resolved to sunder the feudal bonds that shackled them. No eighteenth- or nineteenth-century British historian has so much to say about social class or class conflict as Guthrie. As we have seen, others before him had exhibited a pronounced socioeconomic, quasi-Harringtonian orientation; Guthrie's was by far the most coherent and thoroughgoing.

Henry VII, Guthrie continues:

> perceived that there was a strong tendency in the great landholders of England to envy and oppress the wealthy merchant and the ingenious mechanic; he wanted to draw the necks of the people out of the yokes of feudal tenures . . . . It is now time for us to proceed in our review of Henry's commencement toward a new system of polity in England.

Thus, despite the economic interpretation, Guthrie still points to the epoch-making leadership of a single individual. Henry did not create the "new system of polity in England" out of whole cloth. He took his initiatives at a time when profound societal changes had laid the foundation for the rise of the commons.[26] The Wars of the Roses and the conspicuous consumption of the aristocracy had already weakened the feudal barons. Sustained economic growth worked against the English nobility: "The vast increase of commerce had enabled the commons to make a much greater figure in life than they had done before: and this put the noblemen, barons, and chief gentlemen of the kingdom to a vast expense in trying to out-shine them."[27] The Henrecian Reformation initiated a massive transferal of property from the Church to the commons.[28] Henry's inclinations were despotic, but his reliance on the House of Commons to implement the break with Rome and the dispersal of Church property to the commons served to fortify the strength of Parliament.

Guthrie describes the reigns of Edward VI and Mary as years of thwarted feudal reaction.[29] Mary Tudor led the forces of reaction: "She greatly affected the character of being the restorer of the rights and grandeur of the ancient nobility," granting many licenses to nobles for the maintenance of retainers. Guthrie equates Mary's Catholicizing and pro-Spanish posture with feudal reaction. The prospect of Spanish domination was particularly repugnant: "The English commons, who had emancipated themselves from the slavery of feudal tenures and were daily more and more warmed by the spirit of reviving arts and improving commerce, at once envied, hated, and despised a race who had fallen from those noble characters." Only Mary's timely death prevented the reimposition of "the feudal constitution."

Guthrie took the Bolingbrokian position that the reign of Elizabeth was blessed with a "happy poise" between the House of Commons and House of Lords, the commonalty and peerage.[30] As the reign progressed, Elizabeth actually came to resent the mounting power of the commons. The main task in the first part of her tenure was to blunt the feudal counter-revolution that had gotten underway in Mary's reign. Elizabeth reversed her predecessor's policy and enforced legal restrictions on the number of aristocratic retainers. By promoting commerce and the propertied strength of the commons, Elizabeth, paradoxically and unintentionally, augmented English liberty.

Guthrie devotes his fourth volume, around 750 pages, exclusively to the Early Stuart and Cromwellian era. This compares to about 900 pages for the entire Tudor epoch. In his preface Guthrie singled out the Early Stuart era as that period of English history most in need of clarification by an impartial historian.

James I was no friend of liberty, and his reign marked the last time that the old nobility could conceivably have wrested back their pre-Tudor powers.[31] After James got through ruining the aristocracy, however, all hope was lost. Guthrie captures the intellectual, pedantic character of the first Stuart, observing that "his merits would have been great had a college instead of a kingdom been his province of government." James lacked Elizabeth's tact and her public relations flair in dealing with Parliament. Further, he faced a far more intractable House of Commons than the Tudors had to put up with.

> James did not sufficiently reflect on the vast difference between his and their situation. The ignorance and, consequently, the tameness of the English was now vanished. They were resolved to defend with courage what they had acquired by industry. The whole system of property amongst them was now altered. Their minds were enlightened with reading and reflection. Their principles of government rested upon liberty and moderation.

Elizabeth had bequeathed a large debt to James, run up in her Irish wars. Part of the way James strove to overcome his financial troubles was to put titles and honors up for sale. This had the effect of further depreciating the value and dignity of the "great nobility." A much weakened and divided nobility doomed Charles I in his drive to bring back "some of the feudal principles" that Henry VII had relinquished.[32]   Guthrie does not mince words in characterizing Charles as an arbitrary and maladroit ruler. On the whole, however, his discussion of Charles I's reign and the English Revolution was the most judicious and balanced to appear in any eighteenth-century general history.

The Civil War, as Guthrie sees it, was brought on by the combination of royal intransigence and Parliamentary aggression. It was far from inevitable.   From the moment Charles became king in 1625, the House of Commons refused to grant him the customary subsidies he asked for. Charles, in his turn, governed arbitrarily.   The Petition of Right justly denied the king's right to levy forced loans or imprison citizens without trial.   Guthrie was the first Whiggish historian to declare that the English people were lightly taxed in comparison with other Europeans and that they enjoyed relative peace and prosperity during the "Eleven Years Tyranny."

Guthrie argues that the tables turned against Charles with the controversy over Ship Money in 1637, a controversy that posed a threat to all men's property.   The issue of Ship Money prompts Guthrie to give a learned analysis and brief history of the various feudal dues, which were now seen as obsolete and onerous.[33]   When the Long Parliament met in 1640, its grievances came in three areas: ecclesiastical; political - the threat to liberty; and economic, by which is meant the crown's encroachment on property rights.   Probably Guthrie's best sustained piece of historical analysis is to be found in his detailed narrative of events at Westminster and of the City generally as the nation slid into civil war. He charts the rush of events, the ebb and flow of support for the king, the shifting political and social alignments in the City, and the fortuitous circumstances that plunged the country into war.

When Guthrie describes the breakdown of the two sides in the Civil War, he describes a socioeconomic clash of interests revolving around the attempt by Charles to repeal the powers that the commons had assumed over the past century.[34]   The "peerage," determined "to retain all the reverence that was due to nobility" fought for Charles, as did their dependents.   So too did "many gentlemen" who were big landowners:

Very different were the principles of that part of the nation which opposed Charles.   Property, arising by commerce, would not brook the insults of the landed interest. The idolatry that had been paid to nobility was daily wearing off in those parts that were supported by trade; which soon taught sensible men that in a regulated government power ought to follow property. Charles, who never would descend to any contemplation of the inferior spheres of mankind, thought all power acquired by property and not communicated by the crown to be unlawful.

Especially impressive is Guthrie's analysis of the social composition of the City.[35]   He distinguishes three classes of men, all of whom supported Parliament. First there was the wealthy financial and mercantile oligarchy, which, he correctly points out, backed the king until almost the last moment. Pressure from the Parliamentarian populace in the City and its geographical remoteness from the Royalist strongholds finally swung the City plutocrats against the crown. Second, a rung down on the social ladder from these eminences were the middling merchants and craftsmen. This stratum was thoroughly estranged from the court: the merchant or trader was determined "to guard his own property, and to be, or appear to be, extremely zealous for religion." Third, and connected to this class, were the apprentices. They and their mercantile masters led the shock troops of the Revolution in London, "the journeymen, the day-labourers, and the lower rank of people, even to the women and children."

No historian had heretofore drawn the kind of sociological profile of the City Roundheads that Guthrie produced. It is all the more impressive because its general outlines have been upheld by modern scholarship. Guthrie's account of the Civil War concentrates much more on political developments than on the battlefield. His narrative is distinguished by the care and disinterest with which he scrutinizes the various negotiations and intrigues involving the king, the Presbyterians and Independents, and the Scots.

The dissolution of the government in the early 1640s followed by the execution of the king made property relations in the state chaotic:[36] "The landmarks of the constitution being now removed, no man knew how his property stood."[37] Parliament's confiscation of Royalist estates and Church property contributed to the unsettled condition of land ownership. The disruption in the structure of property enabled a man of modest means like Oliver Cromwell to rise to the top: "For though under a regular government power follows property, yet when a state is distempered and disordered, the maxim is reversed, and property must sink under power."[38]

Guthrie's profile of Cromwell was characteristically fair-minded and perceptive, the most thoughtful assessment of the man yet to appear.[39] He grasped Cromwell's pragmatic, opportunistic nature. Cromwell was no ideologue. As Guthrie makes clear, Cromwell was, in fact, a social conservative who suppressed the reformist and radical sects - the Levellers, Diggers, and Fifth Monarchists. Guthrie's remarks on the Levellers are disappointingly brief and uninformative. But true to his fascination with the balance of property, he was the first historian to discuss in some depth and without condescension those primitive communists, the Diggers.[40] He describes their beliefs and quotes a substantial passage from George Winstanley's account of their settlement on St. George's Hill.

Guthrie describes the relative frugality and probity of the Protectorate. Particularly striking is his portrayal of daily life during the Interregnum.[41] He completely rejects the stereotype, perpetuated to this day in some history books, that Cromwell and his fellow "saints" were killjoys and philistines. During the Protectorate, wealth was flaunted and Cromwell himself was "no foe of magnificence." A benefactor of learning, Cromwell befriended and patronized Bishop Usher and the Cambridge Platonist, Richard Cudworth.

Having pinpointed the irreconcilable split between Parliament and the army as the underlying sticking point that brought down the Cromwellian Republic, Guthrie abruptly closes his narrative.[42] This may well have been because he had already written many more pages than he had intended, even though his original goal was to conclude the *History* at the Glorious Revolution. "The prejudices of parties," Guthrie notes in his final remarks, had so misconstrued his country's history that extensive revision proved necessary; he apologized for not carrying the work through to 1688-89.[43]

It is easy today to find fault with Guthrie's economic interpretation, but he must be credited with being the first author to present an extensive and cogent materialist, structural analysis of English political history. Little has been said about religion or the Church for the simple reason that Guthrie himself did not treat these subjects in any depth. He shared that "philosophical" lack of interest in Church history that permeated

Enlightenment historical writing. Ecclesiastical and doctrinal issues did not attract his attention, though he did discuss to some extent the political function of the Church as a bulwark of the state.[44] A strong anti-clerical tone marks *A General History of England*. Guthrie says practically nothing about the religious issues involved in the Reformation: property and power were what Henry VIII was interested in.[45] Guthrie has few, if any, kind words for bishops. Their worldliness sapped public support for the Church and, consequently, for the state. Perhaps the most succinct expression of Guthrie's view on the role played by religion in history comes when he considers the religious causes of the English Civil War:[46]

> The historian who writes or the reader who believes that religion itself, abstracted from civil and secular interests and principles, had any influence upon the might movements of this time, are wretchedly deceived . . . . The reader is not to expect that with former historians I am to examine the phantasms of Presbery or the fopperies of Popery, or that I am to justify the purity of the English Church. These are not part of an historian's province. He is to endeavor to pluck the mask from all parties.

Guthrie puts little stock in the historical veracity of clerical authorities and Church historians. In connection with the Reformation, for example, he remarks that "I should be as tender of admitting the testimony of Protestants as of popish priests in matters wherein either their principles or their craft are attacked."[47]

Guthrie presented a secular analysis of historical causation. He did not actually deny that there was any divine plan for human history - as Hume did; he just ignored the subject. Guthrie saw no value in clothing his narrative in the rhetorical garb of providence and criticized Gilbert Burnet for so doing: "Even the right reverend historian of the Reformation has recourse to the stale apologies of providential dispensation in accounting for the whole"[48]

"Cultural history," writes Peter Gay, "in its modern sense is an invention of the Enlightenment."[49] He wisely adds the qualification that the philosophes' "intentions were better than their performance." Guthrie falls into this category. He vowed to write a history of civilization, of the "learning, arts, and sciences of the English nation upon a more useful and extensive plan than has hitherto been attempted."[50] Up to a point he succeeded. *A General History of England* does, indeed, contain more about literature and the arts than any previous English history. However, the amount of discussion actually devoted to cultural affairs was small.

What was most significant about Guthrie's treatment of the arts and learning was the attitude he took toward them. Guthrie incorporated culture with politics and economics under the rubric of civilization: a precondition for the growth of political liberty and commerce in the sixteenth century was the revival of learning. No previous general historian had made this explicit connection, and it was reiterated by Hume. The final paragraph on Elizabeth's reign makes the point that not only did royal patronage stimulate the arts, but it promoted the greatness of England as well. The passage is arrayed in rich prose and speaks volumes for Guthrie's literary imagination:[51]

> Such were the springs of liberality that gave verdure to the laurels and formed the shade under which Spencer saw his divine visions, where Shakespeare drew his sacred inspiration, where satire and Johnson laughed at the follies of mankind, and where Beaumont and Fletcher formed themselves to all that was great and graceful in the drama. It was under Elizabeth that Bacon caught the first dawn of that noble philosophy which now enlightens the world. To her patronage we owe the strength of Jewel's reasoning, the inimitable style of Hooker, and the extent and variety of Raleigh's learning. It was under her that the injured Hobbes formed his first notions; and toward the latter end of her reign Cromwell drew his earliest breath, as if it had been the will of heaven that she should not leave the world without leaving to it a spirit equal to her own.

This passage breathes the ardent patriotism and faith in progress of the Whig historian. It is as gushing as anything Macaulay wrote. Probably no Elizabethan, other than the Queen herself, was so admired by Augustan historians as Walter Raleigh. He was the Renaissance man par excellence - champion of Protestantism, explorer, historian. Guthrie devotes no less than ten adulatory pages to his career and writings.

Guthrie's *History of England* was the first history based extensively on Parliamentary journals.[52] He grounded his research in the extant journals, both printed and (probably) in manuscript, because he had so little faith in the authoritativeness of the secondary sources: the journals "are in themselves, if I may be allowed the expression, facts, and such facts as history ought to be built upon." As for his fellow historians, John Oldmixon and the "other rebel or republican writers are as contemptible as those of the royal party."[53]

In terms of scholarship, Guthrie succeeded in doing what he set out to do. His was the finest general history that had yet been written. But in terms of popular success, he was merely one in a long line of failures.[54] The *History* provoked virtually no comment in the press and was not even mentioned in most later histories of England. Having recently engaged Guthrie in a propaganda skirmish, Horace Walpole referred to the obscurity of his *History* in a 1768 letter to Thomas Gray. Gray responded that he had never seen Guthrie's *History*, "nor do I know anyone who ever saw it."[55] There is one obvious explanation why Guthrie's *History* failed to catch the attention of the reading public. The *General History* was very long, consisting of four large folio volumes.

Before we dismiss the popular impact of Guthrie's historical writing, one final work should be considered. Guthrie's last book, published in 1770 shortly before his death, was *A New Geographical, Historical, and Commercial Grammar*. This ranks as one of the most popular books of any kind published in Britain in the late eighteenth century. It went through at least thirty editions. In his *Biographical Dictionary of Eminent Scotsmen* (1875), Robert Chambers commented that "Guthrie's *Grammar* is known to everyone from the schoolboy to the philosopher as a useful and well digested manual of information." In the words of one authority, it "set the fashion for the nineteenth century" in the early study of geography.[56] The *Grammar* was a standard text in American universities during the late eighteenth century, and its nineteenth-century replacement by Jedediah Morse was in considerable portions a plagiarization from Guthrie.[57] In *Vanity Fair*, when Thackeray's heroine attended Miss Pinkerton's academy for young ladies, Guthrie's *Grammar* was required reading.[58]

A New Geographical, Historical, and Commercial Grammar was a combination travel book and almanac-like compendium of information. Published in octavo size, about 200 of the book's more than 1,000 pages consisted of English history - an abbreviated, popularized version of Guthrie's *General History*. The basic points from the earlier work are reiterated: the ancient constitutionalism, the belief that the sixteenth century was a turning point in English history in which the growth of trade and "monied property" in the hands of the commons extinguished "baronial powers"; and the belief that the Stuarts:

> made no allowances for the glories of Elizabeth, which, as I have observed, disguised her most arbitrary acts, and none for the free, liberal sentiments which the improvement of knowledge and learning had diffused through England. It is needless, perhaps, to point out the vast increase of property through trade and navigation, which enabled the English at the same time to defend their liberties.

Despite his greatness, Cromwell was "secretly thwarted by people of property all over England."[59]

Guthrie's historical writing bears the hallmarks of Enlightenment historiography. He detailed the growth of liberty and civilization, rooted in economic change. No historian before Hume had so perceptively delineated how the development of the English polity reflected the distribution of economic power in society. Guthrie possessed a panoramic conception of the interrelationship between property and politics. Cognizant of the way party politics had distorted history, Guthrie grounded his interpretation in a critical and wide-ranging analysis of the sources. Finally, Guthrie's tone was anti-clerical, his historical method secular.

Guthrie's intellectual pedigree can be traced back to the Country political philosophy and historical analysis of Lord Bolingbroke. Both as historian and journalist, Guthrie echoed Bolingbroke's ancient constitutionalism and his economic, balance-of-property interpretation of English history. Most of Bolingbroke' historical essays were propaganda broadsides against Robert Walpole's ministry. Guthrie too was an anti-ministerial propagandist when he began *A General History of England*, but the *General History* deviates at points from Bolingbroke's classic, "Old Whig" views: Guthrie did not idealize Elizabeth or vilify James I, nor did he share Bolingbroke's zeal to expose "corruption" and "faction" in English history. The *General History* was far less partisan than Bolingbroke's historical writing.

Guthrie's *General History* differed qualitatively from the kind of special pleading practiced by his predecessors. At a time when party strife had ceased to have much meaning, Guthrie's vaguely Whiggish, establishment history could potentially have found favor with the unified governing class. It patriotically celebrated England's constitution and the rise of liberty. It justified resistance to tyranny, if not actual revolution. And it illuminated the growth of commerce. It was the less scholarly, but shorter and more readable, establishment history of David Hume, however, that struck a chord with the book-buying public. Nevertheless, it would be wrong to assume that Guthrie's historical writing vanished without a trace. In the rather vulgarized form of the *Grammar*, his interpretation of English history must have reached a wide audience, helping, impalpably, to shape the historical consciousness of the British public.

Notes

[1]See Duncan Forbes, *Hume's Philosophical Politics* (Cambridge, 1975), 253-258.

[2]Unless otherwise indicated, biographical information on Guthrie is drawn from Forbes; John Burke Shipley, "James Ralph: Pretender to Genius" (Ph.D. dissertation, Columbia University, 1963), 370-378, 405, 679; and the article on Guthrie in Robert Chambers, *A Biographical Dictionary of Eminent Scotsmen* 3 vols. (Glasgow, 1875) and the *Dictionary of National Biography* article on Guthrie by Alexander Gordon.

[3]Forbes, 253.

[4]James Ramsay of Octertyre, *Scotland and Scotsmen in the Eighteenth Century*, ed. Alexander Allordyce, 2 vols. (Edinburgh, 1888) II, 54.

[5][Francis Palgrave], "Hume and his Influence on History," *Quarterly Review*, vol. 73 (March 1844), 542.

[6]James Boswell, *The Life of Samuel Johnson* 6 vols., ed. George Birbeck Hill (London, 1887) I, 117-118; IV, 52.

[7]This account of Guthrie's work for the Prince's faction is drawn from Shipley, 374-377; Laurence Hanson, *Government and the Press, 1695-1763* (London, 1936), 119; Morfio *pseud.*, *An Historical View of the Principles, Characters, Persons, etc. of the Political Writers of Great Britain* (London,

1740); memorial on Guthrie by his brother Hary in Yale Univ. Library, Boswell Papers, MS. C1411.

[8]Guthrie also collaborated with the Earl of Marchmont on the *Englishman's Evening Post*, circa 1740-43. And according to one observer, he was the principal writer for yet another opposition paper in the early 1740s, the *Westminster Journal*. See Alexander Carlyle, *The Autobiography of Dr. Alexander Carlyle of Inveresk, 1722-1805*, ed. John Hill Burton (London, 1910), 200.

[9]Quoted in Frank Brady and Frederick A. Pottle, eds., *Boswell in Search of a Wife, 1766-69* (London, 1957), 155.

[10]For a brief period, Guthrie continued to flail the new administration. The government even reportedly tried to have him arrested, this for a second time - a warrant had already been issued for his arrest in March 1743. See Hanson, 119.

[11]After Newcastle renewed Guthrie's pension in 1754, Guthrie wrote to an old Edinburgh acquaintance that he "never did the government a shilling's worth of service, nor was ever required to do it." The few extant letters to government ministers, however, indicate that Guthrie did proffer intelligence and occasional advice on political matters. See Forbes, 254; Guthrie to Bedford, Aug. 16, 1749, BL. Add. MS. 37894. f. 242; Guthrie to Newcastle, Jan. 13, 1762, BL. Add. MS. 32933. ff. 276-278; Guthrie to Liverpool, Dec. 22, 1763, BL. Add. MS. 38201. f. 358.

[12]George Grenville, the king's first minister in 1763, called upon Guthrie to defend the dismissal of General Henry Seymour Conway in *An Address to the Public in the Late Dismissal of a General Officer*. Horace Walpole responded to this broadside with *A Counter Address*, prompting Guthrie to rejoin with *A Reply to the Counter Address*. Guthrie also apparently contributed to the pro-government *Gazetteer* in the early 1760s and recommended that a new government paper be set up. See Guthrie to Liverpool, Dec. 22, 1763, BL. Add. MS. 38201 f. 358.

[13]Carlyle, 201.

[14]Brady and Pottle, 154-155.

[15]Ramsay, II, 548.

[16]Guthrie wrote to one of Newcastle's underlings in 1757 complaining that illness and indebtedness induced him to request a higher pension. Guthrie's amanuensis, a Mr. George, told Ramsay that Guthrie died poor, even though his earnings over the years were considerable. See Guthrie to H. V. Jones, Sept. 20, 1757, BL. Add. MS. 32874. f. 228; Ramsay, II, 548-549.

[17]*Old England* (March 2, 1745) no. 99.

[18]Since Guthrie's *History* has been so overlooked, opinions about the work are hard to come by. Philip Yorke, no friend of Guthrie's, confided to Birch that the work was superior to its predecessors, since Guthrie had access to new sources. The republican historian Catherine Macaulay, writing in the 1760s, cited Guthrie frequently as a source, calling him "a very judicious historian" though "of monarchical principles." C. H. Firth, on the other hand, dismissed him as "another industrious compiler," notable for being the first to employ the journals of the two Houses of Parliament. See Yorke to Birch (Nov. 2, 1749), BL. Add. MS. 35397. f. 234; Catherine Macaulay, *History of England* 5 vols. (London, 1763-83) II, 330; V, 97; C. H. Firth, "The Development of the Study of Seventeenth Century History," *Transactions of the Royal Historical Society* (1913) VII, 37.

[19]Quoted in Forbes, 300.

[20]See Guthrie, III, 1384-87; David Hume, *The History of England* 6 vols. (Phil., 1871) I, 429-435.

[21]On Magna Charta see Guthrie, I, 664; Forbes, 302-303.

[22]Guthrie, II, 771.

[23]Guthrie's remarks on the nature of English historical writing are found in his *Proposals for printing by weekly subscription at six-pence each number of a new general history of England* (London, 1743), 1, 4; *A General History of England, from the Invasion of the Romans under Julius Caesar to the late Rebellion in 1688* 3 vols. printed as 4 (London, 1744-51) I, i, ii, lv.

[24]Guthrie, *History* II, 789.

[25]On Henry VII see *ibid.*, II, 789, 795-809, 834, 849; IV, 1393-1440.

[26]Guthrie placed the "new system" in a European context, commenting that in the late fifteenth century Europe "teemed with men of enterprising means in arts, arms, and sciences. The spirit of invention and discovery moved upon the face of the mighty chaos, and began to clear the darkness which had so long brooded over the human understanding." He proceeded to discuss the invention of printing and firearms and the flowering of the arts. See *ibid.*, II, 802, 808-809.

[27]*Ibid.*, II, 834.

[28]"Like grain that passes from one sieve into another, the immense estates of the Church passed from the King into the hands of his open-handed courtiers, till they settled with the commons." *Ibid.*, IV, 1394.

[29]On Edward and Mary, see *ibid.*, III, 100-101, 127, 165; IV, 1394-1395.

[30]For Guthrie's discussion of Elizabeth's reign, see especially III, 365, 378, 381, 485, 525, 528.

[31]For Guthrie's discussion of James I, see especially IV, 631, 635, 819, 822.

[32]The discussion of Charles I's reign prior to the meeting of the Long Parliament is drawn from IV, 834, 884, 896, 906-907, 939 1395.

[33]*Ibid.*, 926-927, 939.

[34]*Ibid.*, 1064-1065.

[35]*Ibid.*, 1071.

[36]Guthrie's view of the king's execution was unusually clear-eyed and unsentimental: "The putting to death of a king naturally, indeed, strikes us with horror." But "if the demerits of a king can reduce him to a private station, justice ought not to stop her pursuit there." From the point of view of Cromwell and the Independent army chiefs, the king's death was a harsh necessity. See *ibid.*, IV, 1161.

[37]*Ibid.*, 1127-1128.

[38]*Ibid.*, 1226.

[39]*Ibid.*, 1196. The discussion of Cromwell is drawn from Guthrie, IV, 1196, 1271, 1278, 1309, 1342.

[40]*Ibid.*, 1237-1238.

[41]*Ibid.*, 1278, 1342.

[42]*Ibid.*, 1318, 1324, 1370.

[43]An appendix to his narrative returns to the balance of property theme and explains why the Protectorate could not be institutionalized. The Parliament felt its property threatened by army rule and so cooperated in the Restoration of Charles II. For all his failings, Charles did not challenge the balance of property like his father and grandfather, and he drew more upon the new men in the House of Commons for his advisors and bureaucrats. The House of Commons, for its part, did not beggar Charles II as it did the first two Stuarts. Had it done so, another revolution would have taken place.

[44]Guthrie had very little to say about Puritanism, and the only detailed discussion of the Church is to be found in his treatment of Laud and Laudianism in the reign of Charles I. Guthrie undertakes a lucid examination of Laud's doctrinal and ceremonial innovations, the suppression of Puritan lecturers and the manner in which the Laudian Church served as a pillar of the Stuart regime. See Guthrie, *ibid.*, I, 349; II, 591-596; III, 32; IV, 643, 888-889. Moreover, Guthrie was forever doubting the sincerity of religious belief. Cromwell, for example, "neither knew nor cared about religion"; he masqueraded as God's Englishman to advance his own ambitions. Guthrie's rationalist attitude toward religion led him to make the remarkably liberal assertion that the Roman Catholics at the time of the Spanish Armada were loyal and patriotic Englishmen. See *ibid.*, IV, 1216, 1296; III, 473.

[45]For Guthrie's discussion of the Church, see I, 349; II, 591-596; III, 32, 473; IV, 643, 888-889, 1216, 1296.

[46]*Ibid.*, IV, 1026-1027.

[47]*Ibid.*, III, 115, 136.

[48]On providence see II, 1031; III, 5, 147.

[49]Peter Gay, *The Enlightenment: An Interpretation* 2 vols. (New York, 1969) II, 393.

[50]Guthrie, *History* I, i.

[51]*Ibid.*, III, 580.

[52]Unfortunately, Guthrie failed to name the vast majority of his sources or else merely contented himself with vague references like "Parliamentary journal." It is clear that he studied the Parliamentary journals of Simond D'Ewes and Edward Husband's printed collection of Parliamentary debates, which offered erratic coverage of the Interregnum. Guthrie's detailed and thorough reportage of Parliamentary history in the early Stuart period suggests that he probably obtained access to the debates that went to make up the *Parliamentary of Constitutional History of England* (1751-62). Guthrie used Cotton Library sources, and he and Ralph were the first historians to make extensive use of Privy Council and Exchequer records. He also gained access to the State Paper Office. Guthrie tapped recently published collections - the Thurloe Papers (1742), Burleigh Papers (1740-59) and the correspondence of Reginald Pole (1739). And he made extensive use of the standard collections, annals and lives of Speed, Stowe, Bacon, Collier, Herbert, Strype, Jewel, Spotswoods, Rymer, Nalson, Clarendon, and Rushworth.

[53]See *ibid.*, IV, 1225-1226.

[54]There are indications that Guthrie's *History* did meet with some ephemeral early success. No subscription lists survive, but Thomas Birch noted that the work was "tolerably well supported." In his memoirs Ramsay of Octertyre commented that Guthrie had written "a voluminous history which was much admired for a season on account of the beauty and energy of its style. But it has been much neglected ever since the new fashion of writing history was introduced by Voltaire, Hume, and their

imitators." Ramsay's next sentence indicates another reason why people may not have been eager to subscribe to the *General History*: "It did not acquire additional popularity from the personal character of the author, who was a dissipated man, ready to write for anybody that would pay him." See Birch to Yorke, Sept. 22, 1744, BL. Add. MS. 35396. f. 257; Ramsay, II, 548.

[55]Cited in Forbes, 253.

[56]J. N. L. Baker, *The History of Geography* (Oxford, 1963), 28.

[57]J. K. Wright, "Some British Grandfathers of American Geography," in *Geographical Essays in memory of Alan G. Ogilvie*, ed. R. Miller and J. W. Watson (London, 1959), 151-154.

[58]Cited by William Warntz, *Geography Now and Then* (New York, 1964), 135.

[59]William Guthrie, *A New Geographical, Historical, and Commercial Grammar* (London, 1770); see especially 149-151, 232, 235, 239, 245.

Chapter X

David Hume

Since the publication of David Hume's *History of England* in 1754-62, critical assessments of the work have changed. During Hume's lifetime it was, on the whole, favorably received. It is true the first volume, treating the Early Stuarts, met initially with a cold reception. The London booksellers, resentful of the *History*'s Scottish publishers, waged a successful campaign to stifle its commercial success.[1] The sympathetic portrait that Hume drew of the Stuarts, especially Charles I, provoked a round of rebuttals against this "Tory" historian. Nevertheless, Hume's succeeding volumes met with a far kinder fate, and the complete history, ten years after the Stuart volume appeared, had already established itself as by far the most popular history of England ever written. Even from Hume's detractors there was widespread praise for his literary grace and narrative clarity. Also, the response from the Continent was enthusiastic. Voltaire's rapturous assessment echoed the views of many: "Nothing can be added to the fame of this history, perhaps the best ever written in any language . . . . Mr. Hume, in his *History*, is neither Parliamentarian nor Royalist, nor Anglican nor Presbyterian - he is simply judicial."[2]

Hume's *History* continued to sell well long after Macaulay's *History of England* and finally eclipsed it in popularity and prestige. Macaulay accused Hume of being more an advocate than an historian, and in the nineteenth-century Whig epoch of Macaulay, Froude, Green and Gardiner, Hume's *History of England* was generally denigrated as an old-fashioned Tory history, based upon a superficial and tendentious reading of the sources.

As the Whig interpretation of history came under fire in the early twentieth century, Hume's reputation was gradually and partially rehabilitated. But it was not until the 1960s and '70s that the *History of England* was again widely praised as a groundbreaking contribution to British historiography.[3] In 1965 the intellectual historian Richard Popkin classified Hume as a philosophical historian par excellence, a skeptical mind who stood above the clerical and partisan passions of the age. Constant Nobel Stockton in the 1970s praised Hume for exploding Whig myths of the ancient constitution and for integrating a science of man into the traditional political chronicle; among other things the *History of England* was a pioneering work of economic history. Victor Wexler pictured Hume as an embattled philosophe who brandished his pen against the accumulated falsehood of party historiography.

The most thorough and influential examination of Hume's historical writing has come from Duncan Forbes, first in a long introduction to the Penguin edition of Hume's Early Stuart volume (1970), then in a book on Hume's political philosophy (1975).[4] Forbes sees Hume's historical writing, especially his narrative English history, as the key to his "philosophical politics." According to Forbes, Hume wanted to discredit the conventional party histories and supersede them with a work of political moderation that would help harmonize the pointless political and ideological divisions that continued to bedevil the state. Above all this meant weaning the Whigs away from their archaic and potentially subversive adherence to the shibboleths of social contract and resistance. Hume wanted to "provide the Establishment (that is the Revolution Settlement, the Union of 1707, the Hanoverian Succession) with a respectable, modern, post-revolutionary intellectual basis."[5] Forbes calls Hume's political philosophy "skeptical" or "scientific" Whiggism, as opposed to the prevailing "vulgar" Whiggism, the Whiggism of ancient constitutionalism, contract and resistance pieties, crude and superannuated Tory baiting.[6]

Recent Hume scholarship, particularly the work of Forbes and Wexler, has portrayed the *History of England* as an important and innovative Enlightenment history. Commentators have long noted the "philosophical" themes in his historical writing - the scornful contempt for the Middle Ages as an epoch of ignorance and barbarism, the religious skepticism and anti-clericalism, the attempt to combine political narrative with cultural history, the concise and elegant style, and the supposedly uniformitarian view of human nature.

Forbes emphasizes Hume's relationship to the Scottish Enlightenment. Hume shared the cosmopolitanism of the Enlightenment, holding to the view that civilization had advanced throughout Europe. The *History of England* detailed the progress of society and stages of civilization for one particular country:[7]

> For Hume, civilization is essentially a political concept, meaning law and order or liberty; and the history of civilization is the history of

"liberty" and the conditions which make liberty possible: especially economic progress and the rise of the "middling rank of men."

Among the tasks Hume set for himself in his English history was that of disclosing how Parliamentary government and political liberty took root. Liberty owed nothing to the mythical ancient constitution. It emerged from social and economic change, the rise of the "middling rank," and the fanatical commitment to liberty by the Puritan faction in Parliament.[8]

The Enlightenment meant, in part, the popularization of knowledge. Hume's *History* was a highly readable synthesis that did much to rework and disseminate the ideas of earlier historians, most notably the medievalist Robert Brady.[9] Hume repeated Brady's views that the House of Commons could not be traced back to the Anglo-Saxon period and that the Norman Conquest imposed feudal despotism on England. Magna Charta began the shift from royal despotism to baronial despotism. Hume recognized, however (which Brady did not), that Magna Charta "became a kind of epoch in the constitution" by prescribing legal limits on royal power, to which the nation as a whole could subsequently appeal. Hume adopted Brady's position that the House of Commons emerged only in the late thirteenth century.

Hume's Tudor volume relied primarily on the histories of Polydore Virgil, John Camden, and John Strype, the documentary collections in Rymer's *Foedera*, and the published Parliamentary statutes. The Tudors, according to Hume, checked the nobility and erected an absolutist regime. They were able to do so not only because of skillful statecraft but also because of underlying social and economic change. The economic center of gravity gradually shifted from the nobility to the commons. During Henry VII's reign "the enlargement of commerce and navigation increased industry and the arts everywhere: the nobles dissipated their fortunes in expensive pleasures. Men of an inferior rank both acquired a share in the landed property, and created to themselves a considerable property of a new kind."[10] Tudor rule fell during an epoch when the economic strength and political power of the nobility had eroded, but the middle rank in society, represented in the House of Commons, was still too weak to offset the crown. Parliament was therefore never more servile than under Henry VIII. Elizabeth bedazzled her subjects, ruling like a "Turkish divan."[11]

The roots of liberty and limited government in England could be traced back to the rise of commerce and learning that began in the late fifteenth century, which, however, did not bear fruit until the Early Stuart period. By James I's reign "after the power of alienations, as well as the increase of commerce had thrown the balance of property into the hands of the commons, the situation of affairs and the disposition of men had become susceptible of a more regular form of liberty."[12] The first two Stuarts, especially James I, acted rashly and aggressively at times, but fundamentally it was the Commons that attacked the crown. It was Parliament's aggression in turn that provoked the sometimes heavy-handed actions of the king. Infused with Puritan zeal, M.P.s strove deliberately to establish a limited, Parliamentary government in England.[13]

Hume did not cite William Guthrie among his sources, but there are striking parallels between the two in their interpretations of the Tudor-Stuart epoch. To both Henry VII's reign coincided with a revival of learning and trade. Property shifted from the aristocracy to the gentry and merchants. The Tudors governed arbitrarily, but as property was dispersed to the commons, liberty gradually took hold. James I had to face a more intractable House of Commons than Elizabeth ever put up with. For all the political turmoil, Charles I's reign, the two historians agree, was a time of relative peace and prosperity. But the nouveaux riches resented the privileges of the old nobility. "Many families," Hume wrote, "which had lately been ennobled by commerce, saw with indignation that they could not raise themselves to a level with the ancient gentry."[14] Guthrie had made a similar point, observing that "property, arising by commerce, could not brook the insults of the landed interest."[15] Hume and Guthrie concur in the view that James and Charles were less able but no more fundamentally aggressive than their much idealized predecessor. The two historians' views of the Long Parliament in 1640-42 are also, up to a point, similar. Neither approves of the uncompromising stance taken by Pym, Hampden and the aggressive party, once the structure of Tudor-Stuart despotism had been dismantled. Neither attaches much importance to religious grievances. Hume, however, clearly leans to the "Tory" side of the political spectrum whereas Guthrie does not. Hume champions Strafford wholeheartedly, condemning the impeachment proceedings against him. Guthrie supports the impeachment, but not the execution. Hume finds nothing wrong with the Five Members episode; Guthrie describes it as illegal and disastrous to the king's position.[16]

Hume had more to say about Puritanism than Guthrie, but his remarks were neither subtle nor balanced.[17]   He concedes that the Puritans carried a spark of liberty; but the clear message, broadcast over and over, is that the Puritans were raving fanatics, stupefied with religious delusions - "rapturous flights, ecstasies, visions, superstitions." Hume's censure of the Puritans reflected the scorn felt by an anti-clerical skeptic toward the religious zealot.   No doubt this was one reason why the *History* was much admired by the philosophes.

The Puritan-Parliamentarian rebellion, Hume believed, lacked any constitutional justification. The "illegal violence" led, almost inevitably, to Cromwellian despotism.[18]   Nevertheless, the Revolution and Civil War altered the political landscape. Henceforth, monarchy, to be successful, would have to be limited.   Unfortunately this was a lesson lost on the Later Stuarts, especially James II.[19]   The Restoration monarchy was bereft of its "ancient demesnes" and thus dependent on parliamentary taxation. Parliament, however, haunted by the memory of arbitrary kingship, refused to grant Charles II the revenues he needed to govern effectively. Parliament's fears were exaggerated but not entirely without foundation since Charles did at one time conspire with Louis XIV to subvert Church and state. The constitution and liberty were not secured until the Revolution of 1688. Hume adapted the argument of the Court Whigs that liberty was essentially a modern practice, ushered in and safeguarded by the deposition of James II and the Revolution Settlement.[20]

On one level Hume's *History of England* can be seen as part of his attempt to fashion a moderate, essentially nonpartisan defence of the eighteenth-century constitution.   The *History* was cold comfort for Tories seeking justifications of divine right rule or Jacobitism, but it certainly did not endorse resistance or appeals to the ancient constitution. The Stuart volumes describe a century-long conflict between authority and liberty, crown and Parliament, Court and Country.   Stability and liberty gradually developed in the crucible of war and revolution.

Duncan Forbes regards Hume's controversial first volume, covering the Early Stuarts, as "the vital sector on the historiographical front in Hume's campaign to educate the Whigs in political realities," because it provided a unifying, establishmentarian political ideology.[21]   When Hume began work on his *History*, however, he had other concerns in mind besides political philosophy. Hume, as Victor Wexler points out, had an axe to grind. The *History* was, in part, a "vehicle" for attacking the Whigs because Hume resented the Whig monopoly of place, position, and literary taste.[22] He wrote with an intense desire to discredit the Whig interpretation of history as popularized by Rapin. The Whig hegemony, Hume commented, "has proved destructive to the truth of history and has established many gross falsehoods." He judged Rapin to be too critical of the Stuarts and "totally despicable."[23]

Running parallel to Hume's philosophical reflections about the growth of civilization was this zeal to repudiate the Whig view of seventeenth-century history. Indeed Hume's interpretation of the Revolution and Civil War harked back to Clarendon's *History of the Rebellion*, a work that Hume much admired. The Royalist nobility and gentry, he maintained, "breathed the spirit of liberty" and wanted to preserve "limited government."[24] His heroes are Royalists. The able but autocratic Strafford is transfigured into "one of the most eminent personages that has appeared in England."[25] Hume's description of Lord Falkland paraphrases Clarendon's idealized character portrait.[26] Hume's characterizations of Parliamentarian leaders - John Hampden, Henry Ireton, Thomas Fairfax - are, on the contrary, decidedly negative.[27]

Like Clarendon before him, Hume submitted that Charles I lacked the vigor and dexterity needed to overcome "the encroachments of a popular assembly." However, Hume eulogized the king as a man whose "virtues predominated extremely above his vices, or more properly speaking his imperfections; for scarce any of his faults rose to that pitch as to merit the appellation vices."[28] Hume's Charles I is free of duplicity. His concessions to the opposition sprang from a genuine willingness to limit his prerogatives and curtail the powers of the Church. Charles I was not the stupid tyrant of Whig legend, but his "bottomless duplicity" and "perverse ineptitude" are well known to modern historians, as they were to many commentators in the seventeenth and eighteenth centuries.[29] Hume simply ignored the mountain of evidence against Charles.

Hume's strictures against the Puritans clearly conformed to the philosophical distaste for religious enthusiasm. They also echoed a long tradition of Royalist-Tory hostility to Puritanism. His denunciations of Puritan fanaticism, ambition, and hypocrisy call to mind the fulminations of Thomas Salmon and Thomas Carte. The Puritans and Parliamentarians are depicted as self-conscious revolutionists, hypocritically paying lip service to the ancient constitution. Hume ignored the fidelity, however mistaken, that the Parliamentary opposition felt toward medieval precedents.[30] Hume was also critical of the Whig opposition to Charles II and James II. He faulted the House of Commons for not granting Charles the revenues he needed to govern effectively; and although he regarded the Glorious Revolution as necessary for securing liberty in England, he, paradoxically, condemned the opposition to James II.

The *History of England* has been rightly praised for its literary value. Hume produced an elegantly readable synthesis. His critical methods, however, did not match his literary finesse. His account of the Revolution and Civil War drew uncritically upon the work of pro-Royalist writers. The debt to Clarendon has already been noted. Hume's descriptions of Strafford's impeachment, Cromwell's relationship to the Agitator movement in the army, and the passage of the Self-Denying Ordinance were all paraphrasings of Clarendon with much of his phraseology repeated almost verbatim.[31] Clement Walker's Royalist *History of Independency* was another pro-Royalist work that Hume followed closely for the Civil War years.[32]

Hume's approach to his sources can be illustrated by the following example. Here is how he describes reaction to the execution of Charles I:[33]

Never monarch, in the full triumph of success and victory, was more dear to his people, than his misfortunes and magnanimity, his patience and piety, had rendered this unhappy prince. In proportion to their former delusions, which had animated them against him, was the violence of their return to duty and affection; while each reproached himself, either with active disloyalty towards him, or with too indolent defence of his oppressed cause. On weaker minds, the effect of those complicated passions was prodigious. Women are said to have cast forth the untimely fruit of their womb; others fell into convulsions, or sunk into such of themselves, as though they could not or would not survive their beloved prince, it is reported, suddenly fell down dead. The very pulpits were bedewed with unsuborned tears; those pulpits which had formerly thundered out the most violent imprecations and anathemas against him.

The image of women miscarrying and men falling down dead all over England because of a king's death is not what we expect to see evoked by a skeptical philosophe. In Richard Perrenchief's *The Royal Martyr, or the Life and Death of King Charles I,* we find the following passage:[34]

> Never any king, not only of the English, but of whatsoever throne, had his death lamented with greater sorrows, nor left the world with a higher regret of the people. When the news or his death was divulged, women with child for grief cast forth the untimely fruit of their womb, like her that fell on travail when the glory was departed from Israel. Others, both men and women, fell into convulsions and swounding fits, and contracted so deep a melancholy, as attended them to the grave. Some, unmindful of themselves, as though they could not or would not live when their own beloved prince was slaughtered (it is reported) suddenly fell down dead. The pulpits were likewise bedewed with unsuborned tears; and some of those for whom the living king was for episcopacies' sake less acceptable, yet now bewailed the loss of him when dead.

Perrenchief was an arch-Royalist of the most extreme sort. Hume paraphrased him at several points in his narrative. Yet neither Perrenchief nor anyone else was cited for this passage.

Hume reiterated the arguments of Tory historians and his interpretation of the Civil War exhibited a pro-Royalist bias. This is not to say, however, that Hume was a Royalist/Tory historian in the mold of Clarendon, Echard, Salmon, and Carte. Hume was never a party man nor a Tory. He strove in his political writings to replace the anachronistic Whig/Tory dichotomy with an up-to-date establishment political philosophy. Even though Hume wrote with an anti-Whig animus, it is, paradoxically, correct to regard the *History* as an establishment work that implicitly endorsed the ruling oligarchy. The Glorious Revolution, Hume argued, brought a century of conflict to a close and established a stable government that balanced liberty and authority. Although Hume did not hesitate to attack particular Whig administrations and policies, he believed that the Hanoverian constitution preserved what was most important to him - order and property. The greatest threat to the post-revolutionary state came from the Whig's timeworn allegiance to the dogmas of social contract and resistance. Hume's objections, however, were directed primarily at the

Old Corps Whigs, not at the structure of politics in Georgian England or the governing class as a whole.

Hume's rather idiosyncratic *History* reflected the decline of party strife in mid-eighteenth-century England. And the *History of England*, in conjunction with Hume's political essays, contributed to the formation of a new establishment conservatism. This conservative, neo-Tory ideology took shape after the accession of George III, partly in response to the American Revolution and the popular reform movements that emerged in the 1760s and '70s. It came to mean a generalized opposition to political and religious reform and a belief in "the divine right of properly constituted authority."[35] As political debate spread beyond the confines of the ruling class to the middling and lower class, the central ideological division became not Whig versus Tory or Court versus Country but conservative versus radical.

While Hume became the favorite establishment historian, his principal rival, the republican historian Catherine Macaulay, was the darling of reformers and radicals. Macaulay agreed that Whig and Tory partisanship had impeded English historical writing, even as her *History of England from the Accession of James I to the Revolution* (1763-83) vindicated the champions of liberty, especially the Independents, against Hume's aspersions.[36] Macaulay was a serious scholar. She conducted meticulous research among the records and manuscripts in the British Museum and State Paper Office. Her fluent narrative covered not only political affairs but cultural and economic developments: her neo-Harringtonian analysis of the Civil War emphasized economic issues and class conflict. Macaulay was a Dissenter, and allusions to providence occasionally crept into her narrative. However, she disliked "religious enthusiasm" and decried the fact that "the engine religion had been used with never-failing success to enslave the many to the few.[37] Much admired by the French philosophes, Macaulay, like her antagonist Hume, should be regarded as an Enlightenment historian.

Hume's secularism, his occasional praise for the Parliamentary opposition to James I and Charles I, and his unfavorable portraits of the later Stuarts in the succeeding volumes of his *History* distinguished his work from that of the Tory historians who preceded him. In his zeal to repudiate Whig historiography, Hume restated some classic Tory positions, but his approach to English history was closer to the work of William

Guthrie, though there is no evidence that he used him as a source. Both traced the rise of liberty and the power of Parliament through the matrix of social and economic change. Both spurned party and providential history as well as the chronicles and compilations that passed for history in the Augustan era. Guthrie was more scholarly and less tendentious than Hume, but Hume fashioned a relatively concise synthesis and came closer to the Enlightenment ideal of a history of civilization, describing the transition from feudalism and "barbarism" to modernity and occasionally linking political change to alterations in the "manners of the age," cultural and artistic, as well as economic.

Notes

[1] See Ernest Campbell Mossner, *The Life of David Hume* 2nd edition (Oxford, 1980), 312-313.

[2] Quoted in Mossner, 318.

[3] For this reevaluation see Richard H. Popkin and David Fate Norton, eds., *David Hume: Philosophical Historian* (Indianapolis, 1965); Constant Noble Stockton, "David Hume: Historian of the English Constitution," *Eighteenth Century Studies*, IV, no. 3 (spring 1971), 274-294; Stockton, "Economics and the Mechanism of Historical Progress in Hume's History," in *Hume: A Reevaluation*, eds. Donald W. Livingston and James T. Kind (New York, 1976), 296-320; Victor G. Wexler, "David Hume's Discovery of a New Science of Historical Thought," *Eighteenth Century Studies*, X, no. 2 (winter 1976-77), 185-203; Wexler, *David Hume and the History of England* (Philadelphia, 1979); John J. Burke, Jr., "Hume's History of England: Waking the English from a Dogmatic Slumber," in *Studies in Eighteenth Century Culture*, ed. Roseann Runte (Madison, Wisconsin, 1978), 235-251.

[4] Duncan Forbes, "Introduction" to *David Hume, History of Great Britain: The Reigns of James I and Charles I* (London, 1970); Forbes, *Hume's Philosophical Politics* (Cambridge, 1975). Forbes' interpretation is ensconced in J. W. Burrow's *A Liberal Dissent: Victorian Historians and the English Past* (Cambridge, 1981), 26-27; and H. T. Dickinson, *Liberty and Property: Political Ideology in Eighteenth Century Britain* (New York, 1977), 132-139.

[5]Forbes, "Introduction," 10-11.

[6]*Ibid., Hume's Philosophical Politics*, 125-192.

[7]*Ibid.*, 276.

[8]*Ibid.*

[9]On Hume's use of Brady, see Wexler, *David Hume and the "History of England"* (Philadelphia, 1979), 75-80, 101-103.

[10]David Hume, *The History of England* 6 vols. (Philadelphia, 1871, new edition) III, 75.

[11]On Henry VIII and Elizabeth, see *ibid.*, III, 78-319; IV, 1-343.

[12]*Ibid.*, IV, 414.

[13]See *ibid.*, V, 126-140.

[14]*Ibid.*, 227.

[15]Guthrie, *History*, IV, 1064.

[16]See Hume, V, 168, 210-211.

[17]For Hume's characterization of the Puritans, see *ibid.*, V, 145, 331, 358.

[18]On the rise of despotism, see particularly *ibid.*, 434-435.

[19]On the Restoration monarchy, see especially *ibid.*, VI, 32, 35, 36, 76-77, 85, 94-96, 116, 130.

[20]On James II and the Revolution, see *ibid.*, 353-371.

[21]Forbes, 10-11

[22]See Wexler, *David Hume and the History of England*, 8.

[23]Quoted in *ibid.*, 14.

[24]Hume, V, 235.

[25]*Ibid.*, 168.

[26]See *ibid.*, 257; Clarendon, *History of the Rebellion and Civil Wars in England* 6 vols. (Oxford, 1888, new edition) III, 187-188.

[27]See Hume, V, 247, 289, 299.

[28]*Ibid.*, 379.

[29]See Lawrence Stone, *The Causes of the English Revolution* (New York, 1972), 138; and J. P. Kenyon, *Stuart England* (London, 1978), 42.

[30]On the ancient constitutionalism of the Parliamentary opposition, see J. P. Kenyon, *The Stuart Constitution* (Cambridge, 1966), 7; and Stone, 105.

[31]On Strafford's impeachment see Hume, V, 130-131; Clarendon, I, 222-225. On the Agitator movement, see Clarendon, IV, 223; Hume, V, 335. On the Self-Denying Ordinance, see Clarendon, III, 451-460; Hume, V, 282-288.

[32]See especially Clement Walker, *The Complete History of Independency* (London, 1661), 8-9, 70; Hume, V, 338-353.

[33]Hume, V, 378.

[34]Richard Perrenchief, *The Royal Martyr, or the Life and Death of King Charles I*, 3rd ed. (London, 1684), 228-229.

[35]Paul Langford, "Old Whigs, Old Tories, and the American Revolution," in *The British Atlantic Empire before the American Revolution*, eds. P. Marshall and G. Williams (London, 1980), 124. See also Frank O'Gorman, *The Emergence of the British Two-Party System 1760-1832* (London, 1982), 45.

[36]On Catherine Macaulay see Bridget and Christopher Hill, "Catherine Macaulay and the Seventeenth Century," *Welsh Historical Review*, III (Dec. 1967), 381-402.

[37]See Hill, 391.

Conclusion

The Enlightenment has been characterized by Peter Gay as "aggressive secularism and its accompaniment - a commitment to the critical spirit."[1] In the province of historical writing the early eighteenth century witnessed a process of secularization. Theocentric, providential history, written primarily by clerics, gave way to the mundane, naturalistic approach favored by political writers and professional journalists. Accompanying the rise of secular history was the development of an economic interpretation, a greater emphasis on "civil" history rather than on military affairs, and at least an intention to treat culture and the arts. At the same time, historical writing gradually freed itself, slowly and partially, from the trammels of party politics. Stylistically, the "critical spirit" meant a more discriminating and judicious use of documents - many more of which came into print in the early eighteenth century - combined with a transition from the chronicle-compilation form to an explanatory, continuous narrative.

The new approach to history, like the Enlightenment itself, derived, ultimately, from the intellectual and philosophical repercussions of the seventeenth-century scientific revolution - and secondarily from the decline of clerical authority and the rise of the Erastian state.[2] The interfusion of inductive science and Lockean-liberal views of religious freedom gave rise to latitudinarianism in the Church. The intellectual revolution of the seventeenth century helped undermine the High Church ideology that was at the heart of Toryism: scriptural and Filmerite theories of divine right kingship could not be plausibly reconciled with Newtonian concepts of the universe. The Whigs were the beneficiaries of the Tory loss of faith. The ideological and intellectual perspectives conveyed in the histories we have examined do not lend support to the view of some recent scholars that Tory and High Church ideals flourished in Georgian England.[3]

Queen Anne's reign was the Indian summer of Toryism - particularly the last four years - and this was reflected in the historiography of the time. Augustan historical writing was shaped not only by the new intellectual currents but also by the changing face of British politics. Early eighteenth-century historical writing in England, unlike on the Continent, was bound up with the political parties. The old issues and battles of the seventeenth century were fought over again in the history books, the

209

Tories regarding themselves as the descendants of the Royalists, the Whigs of the Parliamentarians. Until the appearance of Rapin's *History of England* (1726-31), the Tory version of English history had the upper hand, mainly due to the publication of Clarendon's *The History of the Rebellion* (1702-04).

Even the Whig histories in the age of Anne were conservative and religious in tone. Historians have traditionally exaggerated the influence of liberal and Lockean ideas in the quarter century after the Glorious Revolution: Whig divines did not forsake Hooker's *Ecclesiastical Polity* for Locke's *Reasonableness of Christianity*. The Whig Burnet and the Tory Echard both wrote providential history in which the government was divinely sanctioned and the Church was a linchpin of the state. Neither made mention of the people's natural rights, and popular participation in politics was scorned. Even in this late Stuart period, however, strictly ecclesiastical matters, questions of Church discipline and practice, were glided over.

The decades between the Glorious Revolution and the publication of Rapin's *History* were significant insofar as we see the emergence of the general narrative history, extending from the Roman invasion (or before) to the seventeenth century. In most respects, however, historians continued to write within the parameters of traditional Tudor-Stuart humanist historiography. They wrote, ultimately, to reveal the working of providence and to illustrate how God punished vice and rewarded virtue, both for individual great men and for the nation as a whole. And the general histories of Echard and Kennett lacked a clear narrative voice: authors were partly compilers, weaving their own words indistinguishably with paraphrasings, plagiarisms, and transcriptions from other authorities.

In the 1720s and '30s this style changed markedly, especially, though not exclusively, in Rapin's *History of England* and in newspaper historical essays. Appeals to providence were fewer, and the Country-Court essays expounded a structural, economic interpretation, a la James Harrington. Simultaneously, we see in the historical writing of this period more explanation and generalization, less conflation of documentary extracts. These innovations reflected the diffusion of the new rationalist and secular ideas. More specifically, they reflected the ascendancy of a secular, liberal Whiggism and the eclipse of High Church Toryism.

Two men in particular were responsible for introducing the new style of historical writing in the age of Walpole: Paul de Rapin-Thoyras and Viscount Bolingbroke. A friend and client of the Whigs during his residence in England, Rapin was the first historian of English history to write from a rationalist and liberal political perspective, a mentality he probably acquired during his association with the freethinking circle around Jean Le Clerc and Le Clerc's *Bibliotheque ancienne et moderne*. Although Rapin did not abjure providence, he possessed a more secular orientation than his predecessors, he treated his authorities skeptically and critically, and he perceptively analyzed English politics and parties. He was the first writer to show that English history had been distorted by party prejudice.

Bolingbroke was an important figure in the history of eighteenth-century historical writing because he combined Rapin's insights with a neo-Harringtonian economic interpretation. Rapin had almost completely neglected the economic side of history. It is a measure of the change in British politics that the one-time head of the Tory party should find ammunition for his broadsides against the ministry in the most fashionable of Whig histories. Walpole's talented squadron of publicists retaliated with a variation on the opposition's Harringtonian analysis. Despite the transparently propagandistic intent of the Country-Court essays, they were a welcome antidote to the cumbersome general histories. They commented pithily and in completely secular terms about the shape of English history.

The Court and Country quasi-Harringtonian interpretations of English history during the age of Walpole sprang at least in part from differing reactions to the financial revolution. To many, the South Sea Bubble (1720) foretold economic disaster and political corruption. The attack on the monied men was inextricably connected with the attack on Walpole because the Robinocracy meant the institutionalization of monied wealth. Whereas Bolingbroke glorified landed property throughout English history, Walpole's journalists retorted that movable wealth derived from commerce or finance was equally valid and valuable.

Many of the Court political essays were straightforward popularizations of Locke. They invoked the state of nature, original contract, "the people's" right to liberty and property; they bore witness to the liberalization of Whiggery after the Hanoverian Succession. However, it was the establishment Locke that was accepted - the defender of property rather than the champion of liberty. A more anti-establishment liberalism colored the histories of John Oldmixon and Daniel Neal, two independent supporters of Walpole's administration. Oldmixon attacked the Church at every opportunity and wrote favorably of popular political agitation. Neal was even more disposed to celebrate "the people's" involvement in politics. Although he was a Dissenting minister and perceived the hand of God behind events, *The History of the Puritans* presented a secularized conception of Puritanism: it was the foundation of liberty in the state.

The histories of Oldmixon and Neal lacked the economic dimension that so distinguished the newspaper debate, and Tory historian Thomas Salmon was equally deficient in this respect. While we can see more of an attempt to elucidate distinctive themes in the general histories of the 1720s and '30s, the works were still marred by a careless approach to the sources and by a propensity to compile data rather than formulate a cogent narrative. With the exception of Rapin, the historians were all dogmatically partisan. No general history had yet appeared that displayed a thoroughly secular understanding of causation, gave a coherent treatment of economics and social class, and transcended the traditional Royalist-Parliamentarian, Tory-Whig party ideologies.

During the years of ministerial instability following the fall of Walpole, several political factions maneuvered for power. Four of the histories undertaken during these years were sponsored by three political groups. The histories were produced to lend historical justification for each party's political ideals and at the same time answer the call for a worthy English successor to - or for a continuator of - the Frenchman Rapin. Ministerial Whig politicians sponsored the establishment Whig *Continuation* of Rapin. The opposition Whigs Chesterfield and Dodington backed the histories of Ralph and Guthrie. And a host of prominent Jacobites supported Thomas Carte and his ambitious *History of England*.

Of these histories, only the Tindal-Birch *Continuation* was a compilation. Carte was well aware of the inadequacies of English historical writing, and he resolved to correct them. He wrote the most learned and well researched history yet to appear, one that demonstrated a keen awareness of socio-economic change and the class structure underlying political conflicts. Despite its scholarly trappings, Carte's *History* was self-evidently an apologia for the Pretender and the Jacobite cause. It projected an aura of reverence for the sanctity and godlike qualities of the Stuart race.

Ralph and Guthrie were two of the premier political writers in England during the late 1730s and early 1740s. They poured out a stream of Country Whig propaganda, continuing the anti-ministerial line broached by Bolingbroke in the *Craftsman*. Both writers had begun their histories as an extension of their political pamphleteering. Although Guthrie began his *History* as an opposition publicist and referred to Bolingbroke in later years as a journalistic ally, his *History* veered from the regular Country line. This may well have been because he was pensioned off by the Court long before his work was finished and consequently wrote free of party pressures. It was certainly not a Court Whig history, no elaboration upon the pro-administration essays of the '30s. Guthrie's ancient constitutionalism vouches for his Whig leanings, but on balance his was a singularly objective and innovative scholarly performance.

It was the essentially nonpartisan nature of Guthrie's *History* that elevated him above his colleague Ralph. Guthrie possessed what Ralph lacked, a panoramic conception of the interrelationship between property and power in history. No historian before Hume had so perceptively delineated how the development of the English polity reflected the distribution of economic power. In a more circumscribed way, and from his Country perspective, Ralph analyzed the interaction of economics and politics when he discussed the financial revolution. Both Guthrie and Ralph recognized how the rage of party had twisted historical writing. They excoriated their Whig and Tory forebears, grounding their strictures in a critical and wide-ranging examination of the sources.

Although Guthrie's work diverged from the Country interpretation of history, his method of approach, like Ralph's, owed much to Bolingbroke. The quasi-Harringtonian perspective, the skeptical attitude toward previous authorities, the secular view of causation, and, of course, the ancient constitutionalism - all bespeak the two historians' earlier career as publicists of Bolingbroke's Country ideology. What is notable about Guthrie's history, politically, is not its vaguely Whiggish slant but the fact that it was an establishment history. As such it reflected the decline of party strife within the English ruling class and foreshadowed the establishmentarianism of Hume's *History of England*. Guthrie wanted to repudiate the party histories and replace Rapin with a truly impartial work.

Guthrie's history succeeded as scholarship but failed commercially. In all likelihood his massive folios, detailed narrative, and ornate, sometimes longwinded diction made the work too formidable for most readers. David Hume, on the contrary, was determined to produce a popular history that would win him the acclaim and wealth that his philosophical writings had not. His octavo volumes were not so long as previous general histories, and his crisp, fast-moving style was more readable. Unlike Guthrie's history, however, it was not based upon much scholarly research. Whereas Guthrie tilted slightly toward the Whigs, Hume wrote with a marked anti-Whig spirit. Besides his desire for wealth and fame, Hume wanted to repudiate the prevailing Whig interpretation of history as set forth by Rapin. This stemmed in part from the resentment he felt about the Whig administration's monopoly on pensions and places and its indifference to literary outsiders like himself. In writing against the Whig conventional wisdom, Hume did not hesitate to draw heavily upon often unreliable Royalist-Tory authorities, treating them uncritically.

Nevertheless, Hume should be regarded, like Guthrie, as an establishmentarian and philosophical historian. He did diverge from the Tory interpretation on many points, and his secular, skeptical outlook was antithetical to traditional Toryism. Hume's achievement, politically, was to reformulate Tory arguments in order to overturn the Whig interpretation of history and the Whig shibboleths of social contract and resistance. He regarded these as potentially dangerous anachronisms for mid-eighteenth-century England with its stable, homogeneous ruling class. The Whig mythology contained democratic implications that could only redound to the benefit of anti-establishment radicals. Hume's *History of England* was neither Whig nor Tory; it was a conservative, establishment history. In the end, Hume's imaginative, philosophical conception of history transcended his pro-Stuart, anti-Puritan sympathies. His flowing narrative explained the rise of civilization in England, linking the growth of liberty with the arts. He did not place the same emphasis on class conflict as Guthrie did but clearly connected the progress of society with the decline of feudalism, with commercialization, and the rise of the middling rank.

Hume's *History of England* was among the first historical productions of the Scottish Enlightenment. It was followed by William Robertson's *History of Scotland during the Reigns of Queen Mary and King James VI*

(1759) and his *Charles V* (1769) and *History of America* (1777). Adam Ferguson's *Essay on the History of Civil Society* appeared in 1767. John Millar's *Origin of the Distinction of Ranks* and *Historical View of the English Government* were published in 1771 and 1787 respectively. Less well known was the Edinburgh historian Robert Henry. In his six-volume *History of Great Britain on a New Plan* (1771-93), Henry addressed economic, social, and cultural affairs in much detail. He criticized narrative history and arranged his chapters topically rather than chronologically.[4]

Tobias Smollett was a London-based Scotsman whose popular *Complete History of England* (1757-58) has usually been dismissed as a superficial Tory compilation. However, the Tory label fits Smollett even less comfortably than it does Hume. Donald Greene has noted Smollett's "dry, sometimes almost cynical skepticism about politicians and political activities in general."[5] In fact Smollett's independent-minded, anti-ministerial perspective was virtually identical with Ralph's Country ideology. And like Ralph, Smollett was sharply critical of the Church and offered a secular, nonprovidential analysis of English history. Moreover, the *Complete History* was a well-written synthesis, not a compilation.

Smollett's *Complete History* enjoyed great commercial success, but no eighteenth-century history matched the success of Hume's *History*. Gradually over the course of the nineteenth century Hume was superseded by a series of mainly Whig-Liberal historians: George Brodie (1822), Henry Hallam (1827), Lord Macaulay (1848-61), Francois Guizot (1827-58), J. A. Froude (1870), J. R. Green (1874), Samuel Gardiner (1875-96). By the time Gardiner and Leopold von Ranke came to write their histories in the late nineteenth century, historical writing had become professionalized, academic, "scientific." Manuscript collections had finally been catalogued, state papers were being calendared, the Historical Manuscripts Commission was established, and historical societies sprang up. Nevertheless, the prevailing nineteenth-century view of English history perpetuated the moderate Whiggery of the eighteenth century, exemplified by Rapin-Thoyras: that is, the ancient constitutionalism (in attenuated form), the image of Tudor England as turning point in which authoritarian but constitutional monarchs neutralized the baronage, the identification of Protestantism with liberty and the Puritans as defenders of the constitution against despotism, the mixed portrait of Cromwell as a great leader tarnished by his tyrannical methods, the glorification of the Glorious

Revolution as the work of trimmers, moderate men from both parties, but in which Whig statesmen took the lead and Whig principles triumphed.[6]

The early eighteenth century was a watershed in the development of early eighteenth-century English historical writing. Historical compilations and collections were replaced by continuous narratives, based upon rationalistic and critical methods of scholarship. History was no longer confined to affairs of state, and historians demonstrated a much sharper awareness of historical change, registering such long-term developments as the growing power of Parliament and the rise of political parties, alterations in land distribution and class structure, and, to a lesser extent, the expansion of England overseas. Nineteenth-century historians wrote more picturesquely and had far more documents at their disposal, but the foundations of modern English historiography were established during the Augustan era.

Notes

[1]Peter Gay and R. K. Webb, *Modern Europe to 1815* (New York, 1973), 358.

[2]Reflecting upon the new science and learning at the close of the Stuart era, J. R. Jones describes succinctly the emerging spirit of the age:

> The interest in scientific inquiry and its achievements that gave late Stuart England its distinctive reputation is indicative of several characteristics of what we call the modern, that is our, world. First, it was secular. Although English scientists, unlike the philosophes of eighteenth century France, were confident that science would reinforce, not undermine revealed religion, it nevertheless diminished the place of theology in intellectual life. Secondly, it was self-consciously modern. The authoritative systems of knowledge being disproved were not only medieval in origin, but were derived from classical antiquity. Now, as Sprat claimed, modern man was daily passing the ancients, and there was no apparent limit ahead to the advance of knowledge.

[3]See especially Linda Colley, *In Defiance of Oligarchy: The Tory Party, 1714-60* (Cambridge, 1982) and J. C. D. Clark, *English Society, 1688-1832* (Cambridge, 1985). The two works differ markedly in their overall interpretation.

[4]J. P. Kenyon, *The History Men: the Historical Profession in England Since the Renaissance* (London, 1983).

[5]Donald Green, "Smollett the Historian: A Reappraisal" in *Bicentennial Essays Presented to Lewis M. Knapp* G. S. Rousseau and P. S. Bouce, eds. (New York, 1971), 45.

[6]On nineteenth-century historical writing, see J. W. Burrow, *A Liberal Dissent: Victorian Historians and the English Past* (Cambridge, 1981); A. Dwight Culler, *The Victorian Mirror of History* (New Haven, 1985); Rosemary Jann, *The Art and Science of Victorian History* (Columbus, 1985).

Bibliography

I. Primary Sources - Manuscripts

British Library	-	Hardwicke Papers
	-	Birch Papers
Bodleian Library	-	Carte Papers
Yale University Library	-	Boswell Papers

Newspapers

Applebee's Original Weekly Journal
Common Sense
The Craftsman
The Critical Review
The Daily Gazetteer
The Examiner
The Flying Post
Fog's Weekly Journal
The Free Briton
The Gentleman's Magazine
The Grub Street Journal
The Jacobite Journal
The London Evening Post
The London Journal
The Monthly Review
Old England: or the Constitutional Journal
The Westminster Journal

I. Primary Sources - Printed books*

Birch, Thomas. *An Enquiry into the share which King Charles I had in the Transactions of the Earl of Glamorgan.* A. Millar, 1747.

--------------, Bernard, John Peter, Lockman, John. *A General Dictionary, Historical and Critical.* 10 vols. James B. Bettenham, 1734-41.

Blennerhassett, William. *A New History of England from the time that the Phoenicians first landed in this island to the end of the Reign of King George I.* Newcastle upon Tyne: John Goodwin, 1751. 6 vols., octavo.

Bolingbroke, Lord. *Lord Bolingbroke: Historical Writings,* ed. Isaac Kramnick. Chicago: University of Chicago Press, 1972.

Boswell, James. *Life of Samuel Johnson,* ed. George Birbeck Hill. 6 vols. Oxford: Clarendon Press, 1934.

Boyer, Abel. *The History of Queen Anne.* T. Woodward, 1735. Orig. published 1722.

Burnet, Gilbert. *The History of His Own Time.* Henry G. Bohn, 1857.

Calamy, Edmund. *A Letter to Mr. Archdeacon Echard upon Occasion of his History of England.* John Clark, 1718.

--------------, *An Historical Account of My own Life, 1671-1731.* 2 vols. John Towill, eds. Henry Coburn and Richard Bentley, 1829.

Carlyle, Alexander. *The Autobiography of Dr. Alexander Carlyle of Inveresk, 1722-1804,* ed. John Hill Burton. T. N. Foulis, J. Coote and others, 1910.

[Carte, Thomas.] *A Collection of Seveal Papers published by Mr. Carte in relation to his History of England.* M. Cooper, 1744.

* All works published in London unless otherwise noted.

A Collection of Original Letters and Papers, concerning the affairs of England from the year 1641 to 1660. Found among the Duke of Ormonde's Papers. Society for the Encouragement of Learning, 1739.

----------------, *A Full and Clear Vindication of the Full Answer to the Letter from a Bystander.* J. Robinson, 1743.

----------------, *A Full Answer to the Letter from a Bystander.* J. Robinson, 1742.

----------------, *A General History of England.* 4 vols. J. Hodges, W. Russel, 1747-55.

Clarendon, Lord. *The History of the Rebellion.* 7 vols. Oxford: Oxford University Press, 1849.

[Duncombe, William]. *Remarks on Mr. Tindal's translation of Rapin de Thoyras' History of England.* J. Roberts, 1728.

Durand, David. *Histoire d'Angleterre de Monsieur de Rapin Thoyras, continuee jusqu' a L'Avenement de George I.* 3 vols. Jean Van Duren, 1735.

Echard, Laurence. *Appendix to the three volumes of Mr. Archdeacon Echard's History of England.* Jacob Tonson, 1720.

----------------, *The Gazetteer or Newsman's Interpreter.* John Knapton, F. Robinson, S. Ballard, 1732 edition.

----------------, *The History of England from the First Entrance of Julius Caesar and the Romans to the conclusion of the Reign of King James II and the Establishment of King William and Queen Mary upon the Throne in the year 1688.* 3 vols. Second edition. Jacob Tonson, 1718.

----------------, *The History of the Revolution and the establishment of England in the year 1688.* Tonson, 1725.

----------------, *The Roman History from the Settlement of the Empire by Augustus Caesar to the Removal of the Imperial seat by Constantine the great.* 5 vols. Fourth edition. R. Bowicke, W. Freeman and others, 1706.

Gibbon, Edward, *Memoirs of the Life of Edward Gibbon.* ed. George Birbeck Hill. Methuen, 1900.

Grey, Zachary. *A Defence of our Ancient and Modern Historians against the frivolous cavils of a late pretender to Critical History.* C. Rivington, 1725.

--------------, *A Vindication of the Great Doctrine and Worship of the Church of England during the reign of Queen Elizabeth.* New edition. C. Davis, 1740.

--------------, *An Impartial Examination of the Fourth Volume of Mr. Daniel Neal's History of the Puritans.* A. Bellesworth, 1739.

--------------, *An Impartial Examination of the Second Volume of Mr. Daniel Neal's History of the Puritans.* R. Gosling, 1736.

Guthrie, William. *A General History of England from the invasion of the Romans under Julius Caesar to the late Rebellion in 1688.* 3 vols., folio, bound as 4. Daniel Brown for T. Waller, 1744-51.

--------------, *A General History of Scotland from the earliest accounts to the present time.* 10 vols., octavo. A. Hamilton, 1747-48.

--------------, *A New Geographical, Historical, and Commercial Grammar.* J. Knox, 1770.

--------------, *An Essay upon Tragedy.* T. Waller, 1735.

--------------, *Proposals for printing by weekly subscription at six-pence each number a general history of England.* T. Waller, 1743.

--------------, *Proposals for printing the third and last volume of Mr. Guthrie's History of England.* T. Waller, 1747.

--------------, *The Complete History of the English Peerage.* 2 vols., folio. Printed by Dryden Leach for J. Newbury, S. Crowder, J. Coote, J. Gretton and others, 1762.

[Hampton, James.] *Reflections on Ancient and Modern History.* Oxford: J. Rivington and R. Dodsley, 1746.

Hearne, Thomas. *Remarks and Collections.* 11 vols. ed. C. L. Noble. Oxford: Clarendon Press, 1885-1921.

--------------, *The Remains of Thomas Hearne.* 3 vols. ed. John Russel Smith. J. R. Smith, 1869.

Hume, David. *The History of England.* 6 vols. Philadelphia: Lippincott, 1871.

[Kennett, White.] *A Complete History of England.* vol. III, folio. Second edition. R. N. Bonwicke and others, 1719.

[Kimber, Isaac.] *The History of England.* 4 vols., octavo. E. Bell, J. Darby, 1722.

[Lockman, John.] *A New History of England by Question and Answer, extracted from the most celebrated English historians, particularly Rapin de Thoyras, for the entertainment of our youth of both sexes.* Twenty-fifth edition. C. & J. Rivington, 1811.

MaCarte, Duncan (pseud.). *A Letter to John Trotplaid, esq. author of the Jacobite Journal, concerning Mr. Carte's General History of England.* M. Cooper, 1748.

Macaulay, Catherine. *The History of England from the Accession of James I to the elevation of the House of Hanover.* 5 vols. E. Edwards and Charles Dilly, 1763-83.

Morforio (pseud.). *An Historical View of the Principles, Characters, Persons etc. of the political writers in Great Britain.* W. Webb, 1740.

[Morris, Corbyn.] *A Letter from a By-stander to a Member of Parliament.* J. Robinson, 1743.

---------------, *A Letter to the Rev. Mr. Thomas Carte, author of the Full Answer to the Letter from a Bystander.* Jacob Robinson, 1743.

Neal, Daniel. *A Letter from a Dissenter to the Author of the Craftsman.* J. Peele, 1733.

---------------, *The History of the Puritans or Protestant Non-conformists from the Reformation under King Henry VIII to the Act of Toleration under King William and Queen Mary.* 2 vols., folio. William Boyne, 1822. First edition, 1732-38.

Nichols, John. *Illustrations of the Literary History of the Eighteenth Century.* 8 vols. Nichols, Son and Bentley, 1817-58.

---------------, *Literary Anecdotes of the Eighteenth Century.* 9 vols. Nichols, Son and Bentley, 1812-16.

North, Roger. *The Examen, or an Enquiry into the Credit and Veracity of a pretended Complete History.* Fletcher Gyles, 1740.

Oldmixon, John. *A Review of Dr. Zachary Grey's Defence of our Modern and Ancient Historians.* J. Roberts, 1725.

---------------, *Clarendon and Whitlock compared.* J. Pemberton, 1727.

---------------, *Memoirs of the Press.* T. Cox, 1742.

---------------, *The Critical History of England, Ecclesiastical and Civil.* J. Pemberton, 1724.

---------------, *The History of England during the Reigns of Henry VIII, Edward VI, Queen Mary, Queen Elizabeth, including the History of the Reformation of the Churches of England and Scotland.* folio. T. Cox, 1739.

---------------, *The History of England during the Reigns of the Royal House of Stuart.* folio. T. Cox, 1729.

D'Orleans, Father. *History of the Revolutions in England under the family of Stuarts, 1603-1690.* E. Curll and R. Gosling. 2nd ed., 1722.

Perrenchief, Richard. *The Royal Martyr, or the Life and Death of King Charles I.* Richard Chiswell. 3rd ed., 1684.

Pointer, John. *A Chronological History of England.* L. Lichfield, 1714.

Ralph, James. *Of the Use and Abuse of Parliaments.* 2 vols. F. Freeman, 1744.

--------------, *The Case of the Authors by Profession or Trade stated.* R. Griffiths, 1758.

--------------, *The Other Side of the Question.* T. Cooper, 1742.

--------------, *The History of England during the reigns of King William, Queen Anne, and George I, with an introductory Review of the royal brothers, Charles and James.* 2 vols., folio. Daniel Browne for F. Cogan and T. Waller, 1744-46.

Ramsay, John of Octertyre. *Scotland and Scotsmen in the Eighteenth Century.* 2 vols. ed. Alexander Allordyce. Edinburgh: William Blackwood and Sons, 1888.

Rapin-Thoyras, Paul de. *Dissertation on the Rise, Progress, Views, Strengths, Interests, and Characters of the Two Parties of the Whigs and Tories.* trans. by Nicholas Tindal. John and Paul Knapton, 1733 ed.

--------------, *The History of England as well Ecclesiastical as Civil, done into England from the French, with large and useful notes (and a summary of the whole) . . . by N. Tindal.* 2 vols., folio. John and Paul Knapton. 2nd ed., 1732.

Remarks upon the Reverend Mr. Archdeacon Echard's History of England. James Roberts, 1724.

Salmon, Thomas. *A New Geographical and Historical Grammar.* William Johnston, 1749.

--------------, *A Review of the History of England as far as it relates to the Titles and Pretensions of our several kings.* 2 vols. Charles Rivington, 1722-24.

--------------, *An Impartial Examination of Bishop Burnet's History of His Own Time.* 2 vols. C. Rivington, 1724.

--------------, *The Chronological Historian.* R. Ware, T. Longman, T. Shewell and others. 3rd ed., 1747.

--------------, *The Modern Gazetteer or a Short View of the Several Nations of the World.* S. and E. Ballard, D. Browne, A. Millar and others, 1759.

--------------, *The Modern History, or the Present State of All Nations.* 31 vols., octavo. Thomas Wooton, J. Shuckburgh, T. Osborne, and James Crockatt, 1724-38.

[Squire, Samuel.] *Remarks on Mr. Carte's Specimen of His General History of England.* J. Robinson, 1748.

Stockdale, Percival. *The Memoirs of the Life and Writings of Percival Stockdale.* 2 vols. Longman, Hurst, Rees, and Orme, 1809.

Tindal, Nicholas. *The History of England by Rapin de Thoyras. Continued from the Revolution to the accession of George II.* 13 vols., octavo. J. and P. Knapton, 1744-47.

Walpole, Horace. *The Correspondence of Horace Walpole*, 42 vols. eds. W. S. Lewis, George L. Lam. C. H. Bennett. New Haven: Yale University Press, 1937-80.

Whalley, P. *An Essay on the manner of writing history.* M. Cooper, 1746.

II.   Secondary Sources - Printed Books

Aiken, William. *The Conduct of the Earl of Nottingham.* New Haven: Yale University Press, 1941.

d'Albissin, Nelly Girard. *Un Precurseur de Montesquieu: Rapin-Thoyras.* Paris: no publisher listed, 1969.

Allibone's Dictionary of English Literature and British and American Authors. 2 vols.   Philadelphia: J. B. Lippincott, 1887.

Bennett, Gareth V. *White Kennett, Bishop of Peterborough.* London: S.P.C.K., 1957.

Bloom, Edward A. *Samuel Johnson in Grub Street.* Providence, Rhode Island: Brown University Press, 1957.

Bongie, Laurence L. *David Hume: Prophet of the Counter-Revolution.* Oxford: Oxford University Press, 1965.

Brady, Frank and Pottle, Frederick. *Boswell in Search of a Wife, 1766-69.* London: William Heineman, 1957.

Brodie, George. *A History of the British Empire.* 4 vols. Edinburgh: Bell & Bradfute, 1822.

Browning, Reed. *Political and Constitutional Ideas of the Court Whigs.* Baton Rouge: Louisiana State University Press, 1982.

Brumfitt, J. B. *Voltaire, Historian.* London: Oxford University Press, 1970 ed.

Burrow, J. W. *A Liberal Dissent: Victorian Historians and the English Past.* Cambridge: Cambridge University Press, 1981.

Burton, John Hill. *The History of the Reign of Queen Anne.* 2 vols. London and Edinburgh: W. Blackwood & Sons, 1882.

Butterfield, Herbert. *The Englishman and His History.* Cambridge: Cambridge University Press, 1944.

--------------, *The Whig Interpretation of History*. London: G. Bell and Sons, 1931.

Cannon, John, ed. *The Whig Ascendancy*. London: Edward Arnold, 1981.

Carswell, John. *The Old Cause: Three Biographical Studies in Whiggism*. London: The Crescent Press, 1954.

Cazenove, Raoul de. *Rapin-Thoyras, sa familie, sa vie, et ses Oeuvres*. Paris: A. Aubry, 1866.

Chambers, Robert. *A Biographical Dictionary of Eminent Scotsmen*. 3 vols. Glasgow: Blackie, 1875.

Clark, J. C. D. *English Society, 1688-1832*. Cambridge: Cambridge University Press, 1985.

Cochrane, Erich, *Historians and Historiography in the Italian Renaissance*. Chicago: University of Chicago Press, 1981.

Colley, Linda. *In Defiance of Oligarchy, the Tory Party, 1740-60*. Cambridge: Cambridge University Press, 1982.

Coltman, Irene. *Private Men and Public Causes: Philosophy and Politics in the English Civil War*. London: Faber and Faber, 1962.

Coxe, William. *Memoirs of the Duke of Marlborough*. 3 vols. London: Henry G. Bohn, 1847.

--------------, *Memoirs of the Life and Administration of Sir Robert Walpole, Earl of Oxford*. 4 vols. London: T. Cadell and W. Davies, 1798.

Cruickshanks, Eveline. *Political Untouchables: The Tories and the '45*. London: Duckworth, 1979.

Delany, Paul. *British Autobiography in the Seventeenth Century*. London: Routledge and Kegan Paul, 1969.

Dickinson, Harry T. *Bolingbroke*. London: Constable, 1970.

--------------, *Liberty and Property: Political Ideology in Eighteenth Century Britain.* New York: Holmes and Meier, 1977.

Dobree, Bonamy. *English Literature in the early Eighteenth Century, 1700-1740.* Oxford: Clarendon Press, 1959.

Douglas, David C. *English Scholars, 1660-1730.* London: Eyre and Spottiswade, 1951.

Firth, Charles H. *A Commentary on Macaulay's History of England.* London: Macmillan, 1938.

Forbes, Duncan. *Hume's Philosophical Politics.* Cambridge: Cambridge University Press, 1975.

Froude, J. A. *The History of England from the Fall of Wolsey to the death of Elizabeth.* 12 vols. New York: Scribner, Armstrong & Co., 1877-1878.

Gay, Peter. *The Enlightenment: An Interpretation.* 2 vols. New York: Yale University Press, 1969.

Gooch, G. P. *History and Historians in the Nineteenth Century.* London: Longmans, 1952 ed.

Goulding, Richard W. *Laurence Echard. M.A., F.S.A., Author and Archdeacon.* No publisher listed, 1926.

Green, J. R. *A Short History of the English People.* 4 vols. New York: Bigelow, Brown & Co., 1893.

Haig, Robert L. *The Gazetteer, 1735-1797.* Carbondale, Ill.: University of Illinois Press, 1953.

Hallam, Henry. *The Constitutional History of England.* 3 vols. London: Thomas Y. Crowell, 1880.

Hamburger, Joseph. *Macaulay and the Whig Tradition.* Chicago: University of Chicago Press, 1976.

Hanson, Laurence. *Government and the Press, 1695-1763.* London: Oxford University Press, 1936.

Harris, George. *The Life of Lord Chancellor Hardwicke.* London: Edward Moxon, 1847.

Holt, J. C. *Magna Charta.* Cambridge: Cambridge University Press, 1965.

Holmes, Geoffrey. *British Politics in the Age of Anne.* New York: Macmillan, 1967.

Jacob, Margaret. *The Newtonians and the English Revolution.* Ithaca: Cornell University Press, 1976.

--------------, *The Radical Enlightenment: Pantheists, Freemasons, and Republicans.* London: Allen & Unwin, 1981.

Johnson, James William. *The Formation of English Neo-Classical Thought.* Princeton: Princeton University Press, 1967.

Kenyon, J. P. *Revolution Principles.* Cambridge: Cambridge University Press, 1977.

--------------, *The History Men: The Historical Profession in England Since the Renaissance.* London: Weidenfeld and Nicolson, 1983.

--------------, *The Stuart Constitution.* Cambridge: Cambridge University Press, 1966.

Kramnick, Isaac. *Bolingbroke and His Circle: The Politics of Nostalgia in the Age of Walpole.* Cambridge, Mass.: Harvard University Press, 1965.

Livingston, Donald W. and James T. King, eds. *Hume: a Reevaluation.* New York: Fordham University Press, 1976.

Macaulay, Lord. *The History of England from the Accession of James II.* 4 vols. London: J. M. Dent & Sons, 1934.

Macgillivray, Royce. *Restoration Historians and the English Civil War.* The Hague: Martinus Nijhoff, 1974.

McKendrick, Neil, John Brewer, J. H. Plumb, eds. *The Birth of a Consumer Society: The Commercialization of Eighteenth Century England.* Bloomington: Indiana University Press, 1982.

Mossner, Ernest Campbell. *The Life of David Hume.* Second edition. Oxford: Oxford University Press, 1980.

Ollard, Richard. *The Image of the King.* London: Hodder and Stoughton, 1979.

Owen, J. B. *The Rise of the Pelhams.* London: Methuen, 1956.

Peardon, Thomas Preston. *The Transition in English Historical Writing, 1760-1830.* New York: Columbia University Press, 1933.

Plumb, J. H. *England in the Eighteenth Century.* London: Penguin, 1950.

---------------, *The Death of the Past.* Boston: Houghton and Mifflin, 1970.

Pocock, John G. A. *Politics, Language, and Time: Essays on Political Thought and History.* New York: Atheneum, 1971.

---------------, *The Ancient Constitution and the Feudal Law.* Cambridge: Cambridge University Press, 1957.

---------------, *The Machiavellian Moment: Florentine Political Thought and the Atlantic Republic Tradition.* Princeton: Princeton University Press, 1975.

---------------, *Virtue, Commerce, and History.* Cambridge: Cambridge University Press, 1985.

Popkin, Richard and David Fate Norton, eds. *David Hume: Philosophical Historian.* Indianapolis: Bobbs-Merrill, 1965.

Porter, Roy. *Gibbon.* New York: St. Martin's Press, 1988.

232   *Augustan Historical Writing*

Porter, Roy and Mikulas Teich, eds. *The Enlightenment in National Context.* Cambridge: Cambridge University Press, 1981.

Richardson, R. C. *The Debate on the English Revolution.* London: Methuen & Co., 1977.

Robinson, F. J. G. and Wallis, P. J. *Book Subscription Lists: a Revised Guide.* Newcastle-upon-Tyne: H. Hill, 1975.

Rogers, Pat. *Grub Street: Studies in a Subculture.* London: Methuen, 1972.

--------------, *The Augustan Vision.* New York: Barnes & Noble, 1974.

--------------, ed. *The Eighteenth Century.* London: Methuen, 1978.

Redwood, John. *Reason, Ridicule, and Religion in the Age of Enlightenment in England.* London: Thames and Hudson, 1976.

Smyth, William. *Lectures on Modern History.* 2 vols. Cambridge: William Pickering, J. and J. J. Deighton, 1848.

Speck, W. A. *Stability and Strife: England, 1714-1760.* Cambridge, Mass.: Harvard University Press, 1977.

Stevens, David Harrison. *Party Politics and English Journalism, 1702-42.* Menasha, Wisconsin: George Banta, 1916.

Sykes, Norman. *William Wake, Archbishop of Canterbury, 1657-1732.* 2 vols. Cambridge: Cambridge University Press, 1957.

Thompson, E. P. *Whigs and Hunters: The Origins of the Black Act.* London: Allen Lane, 1975.

Thomson, M. A. *Some Developments in English Historiography during the Eighteenth Century.* London: H. K. Lewis, 1957.

Trevelyan, G. M. *The History of England.* 3 vols. New York: Doubleday, 1952; orig. published 1926.

Trevor-Roper, H. R. *Men and Events.* New York: Octagon Books, 1976.

Wade, Ira. *The Intellectual Development of Voltaire.* Princeton: Princeton University Press, 1970.

Ward, A. W. and Waller, A. R. *The Cambridge History of English Literature: The Age of Johnson.* Cambridge: Cambridge University Press, 1913.

Warntz, William. *Geography Now and Then.* New York: American Geographical Society, 1964.

Weinbrot, Howard D. *Augustus Caesar in Augustan England.* Philadelphia: American Philosophical Society, 1978.

Wexler, Victor G. *David Hume and the History of England.* Philadelphia: American Philosophical Society, 1979.

Wiles, R. M. *Serial Publication in England before 1750.* Cambridge: University Press, 1957.

234 Augustan Historical Writing

Secondary Sources - Articles

Atto, Clayton. "The Society for the Encouragement of Learning." *The Library*, XIX, 1939, 236-81.

Clifford, James L. "Roger North and Biography" in *Restoration and Eighteenth Century Literature: Essays in Honour of Alan Dugald McKillop*. Lois G. Schwoerer, ed., 275-85. Chicago: University of Chicago Press, 1963.

Davies, Godfrey. "Doctor Johnson on History." *Huntington Library Quarterly*, XII, 1948-49, 1-21.

Davis, Herbert. "The Augustan Conception of History" in *Reason and the Imagination: Studies in the History of Ideas, 1600-1800*. J. A. Mazzeo, ed., 213-29. New York: Columbia University Press, 1962.

Edinburgh Review. March 1831, LIII, 1-43; January 1847, LXXXV, 1-72.

Firth, C. H. "The Development of the Study of Seventeenth Century History." *Transactions of the Royal Historical Society*, VII, 1913, 25-40.

Forbes, Duncan. "Introduction" in David Hume, *History of Great Britain: the Reigns of James I and Charles I*. London: Penguin, 1970.

--------------, Review of Guiseppe Giarrizzo's David Hume, *Politico e Storizo*. *Historical Journal*, VI, 2, 1963, 280-312.

George, C. H. "Puritanism as History and Historiography." *Past and Present*, No. 41, December 1968, 77-104.

Kelton-Cremer. "Roger North." *Essays and Studies, 1959*. The English Association, 1959, 73-86.

Kenny, Robert W. "James Ralph: An Eighteenth Century Philadelphian in Grub Street." *The Pennsylvania Magazine of History and Biography*, LXIV, 1940, 218-42.

Korshin, Paul J. "Types of Eighteenth Century Patronage." *Eighteenth Century Studies*, VII, No. 4, summer 1974, 453-74.

Kramnick, Isaac. "Augustan Politics and English Historiography, The Debate on the English Past, 1730-35." *History and Theory*, VI (1967), 33-56.

[Mill, John Stuart.] *Westminster Review*, II, 1824, 346-402.

Osborn, J. M. "Thomas Birch and the General Dictionary." *Modern Philology*, XXXVI, 1938, 25-46.

[Palgrave, Francis.] "Hume and his Influence upon History." *Quarterly Review*, CXLIII, March 1844, 536-92.

Pocock, John G. A. "Post-Puritan England and the Problem of the Enlightenment" in *Culture and Politics from Puritanism to the Enlightenment*. Perez Zagorin, ed., 91-111. Berkeley: University of California Press, 1980.

Rogers, Pat. "Book Subscriptions among the Augustans." *Times Literary Supplement*. Dec. 15, 1972, 1539-40.

--------------, "John Oldmixon in Bridgewater (1716-30)." *Somerset Archaeology and Natural History*, CXIII, 1969, 86-98.

Schwoerer, Lois G. "The Chronology of Roger North's Major Works." *History of Ideas Newsletter*, III, October 1957, 73-8.

Snyder, Henry L. "David Jones, Augustan Historian and Pioneer English Annalist." *Huntington Library Quarterly*, XLIV, 1, 1980, 11-26.

Stockton, Constant Noble. "Hume: Historian of the English Constitution." *Eighteenth Century Studies*, IV, 3, 1971, 277-294.

Wexler, David. "David Hume's Discovery of a New Science of Historical Thought." *Eighteenth Century Studies*, X, 2, 1976/77, 185-203.

Secondary Sources - Unpublished Works

Rogers, Pat. "The Whig Controversialist as Dunce: A Study of the Literary Fortunes and Misfortunes of John Oldmixon." Cambridge University Ph.D. thesis, 1972.

Shipley, John Burke. "James Ralph: Pretender to Genius." Columbia University Ph.D. thesis, 1963.